Sport in the Global Society

General Editor: J.A. Mangan

DISCIPLINING BODIES IN THE GYMNASIUM

T0386600

SPORT IN THE GLOBAL SOCIETY
General Editor: J.A. Mangan

The interest in sports studies around the world is growing and will continue to do so. This unique series combines aspects of the expanding study of *sport in the global society*, providing comprehensiveness and comparison under one editorial umbrella. It is particularly timely, with studies in the political, cultural, anthropological, ethnographic, social, economic, geographical and aesthetic elements of sport proliferating in institutions of higher education.

Eric Hobsbawm once called sport one of the most significant practices of the late nineteenth century. Its significance was even more marked in the late twentieth century and will continue to grow in importance into the new millennium as the world develops into a 'global village' sharing the English language, technology and sport.

Other Titles in the Series

DISCIPLINING BODIES IN THE GYMNASIUM

Memory, Monument, Modernism

Editors
PATRICIA VERTINSKY
SHERRY McKAY

University of British Columbia

Routledge
Taylor & Francis Group

LONDON AND NEW YORK

First published 2004
by Routledge
2 Park Square, Milton Park, Abingdon, Oxon OX14 4RN

Simultaneously published in the USA and Canada
by Routledge
711 Third Avenue, New York, NY 10017

Routledge is an imprint of the Taylor & Francis Group, an informa business

British Library Cataloguing in Publication Data
A catalogue record of this book is available from the British Library

ISBN 0-7146-55104 (cloth)
ISBN 0-7146-84090 (paper)
ISSN 1368-9789

Library of Congress Cataloging-in-Publication Data
A catalog record of this book is available from the Library of Congress

Typeset in 10.75 on 13pt Times New Roman by FiSH Books London

Contents

List of Illustrations

Series Editor's Foreword

> Human knowledge doesn't accumulate like a brickwall which grows regularly, according to the work of the mason. Its development, but also its stagnation or retreat, depends on the social, cultural and political framework.[1]

No neater description of this absorbing book can be found than in this succinct introductory statement by its editors: 'it portrays the changing landscape, sportsscape and memoryscape of the [University of British Columbia] War Memorial Gymnasium, examines the meanings ascribed to its changing spaces, and explorer the shifting patterns of relationships between the body and its academic and physical environment in higher education'.[2]

Dull stuff? Empirically not.

Fewer statements, for one thing, on the history of the body in education are more astute than this one from the very opening paragraph: 'At the heart of the matter is a much larger – and longer – social debate about the relative positioning of mind over body in educational circles, especially in higher education. And within this debate is the compelling and complicating issue of gender, for just as the Cartesian imperative has traditionally placed mind over body, so has the hegemony of masculinity been enshrined in the training and celebration of the athletic body.'[3]

The pre-eminent virtue of *Disciplining Bodies in the Gymnasium* is its crystalline complexity: at one and the same time – stimulating, penetrating, thought-provoking.

The embodied practices of athletes and dancers, it has been observed, 'afford not merely pleasure and entertainment but powerful means for celebrating existing social arrangements and cultural ideals and for imagining and advocating ones'.[4] This is equally true of physical educationalists, games players and gymnastics in gymnasiums. These practices have spawned multi-dimensional identities 'frivolous yet serious; categorical yet personal; ephemeral yet abiding... supposedly on the margins of everyday life yet the focus of burgeoning economic [and academic] industries and formidable political interests'.[5] And if a 'more nuanced and comprehensive view of sport and dancing would identify them as ingenious and compelling means for reflecting, commenting and acting on existing social, political and moral arrangements', this is equally true of physical educationalists, games players and gymnasts in gymnasiums. Marcel Mauss,[6] the distinguished early twentieth-century anthropologist, noting sensibly that the body was as much a social as psychological and biological phenomenon, once asserted with good reason that education is the dominant element in the 'art of using the human body'.[7] 'What takes place is a prestigious imitation - the child, the adult, imitates actions which have succeeded ... The action is imposed from without, from above ... involving his body.'[8]

The War Memorial Gym at the University of British Columbia has been a place of changing spaces infused in *Disciplining Bodies in the Gymnasium* with human intention,[9] and within its now ageing walls 'working spaces have been reapportioned, administrative structures changed, social relations configured and areas of activity transformed'[10] as a consequence of ideological fashion, reconstructed memory and adapted perspectives.

In short, changing beliefs have been encapsulated in a changing building. Even more to the point, change has been brought about by the definition of knowledge as 'those beliefs and practices that are successful in helping official groups *do what they want to do*' (emphasis added).[11] With the result that the gymnasium first proposed as a place of celebration and a celebration of the sacrificial dead, has become, in the view of the editors, 'a machine for competition and measured success, for therapy and muscle-mending, and in the academic arena, a repository for sophisticated equipment and reductionism experiments rather than the enlightened education of bodies'.[12]

Yet, perhaps now paradoxically, each Remembrance Day its hall is re-established as a monument to memory as the war dead are remembered. Thus the contemporary conceptualization of the War Memorial Gymnasium provides, among other things, a modern commentary on the present confrontational relationship 'between the body and architecture, between memory and monument'.[13] As the editors finally remark: 'the power of memory does not rest in the gymnasium; rather power and memory are in need of political upkeep'. Hence their admirable ambition in *Disciplining Bodies in the Gymnasium* 'has been not merely to document the history of the War Memorial Gymnasium but [the] politicizing of this history'.[14] This they have achieved. We are all beneficiaries.

J. A. MANGAN Director,
International Research Centre for
Sport, Socialization and Society,
De Montfort University (Bedford)
November 2003

Preface

This book is the circumstance of a happy meeting place of a group of scholars who have embraced the pursuit of interdisciplinarity at the University of British Columbia (UBC). We all know the basic map of the disciplines and the enduring social structure of academic labour, but within the microstructure of our own disciplines and departments we have joined together as a larger interactional field where we have learned from, and with, each other in ways that you can see in the various chapters of this book.

We realize that disciplines legitimate our necessarily partial knowledge, so throughout our interdisciplinary conversations we have sought to move beyond that partiality. Of course, there's nothing new about inter-disciplinarity or about approaching 'themes' or 'problems' from multiple perspectives, but we have tried to share our knowledge and ideas rather than compete for control over such metaphorical 'texts' as the body, the building, and the landscape of higher education. In creating our own knowledge exchange space to analyse the spaces of the gymnasium and the authors of its fortunes, as well as the architectural and human movement disciplines it shaped, we have tried to exemplify the best aspects of cross-boundary work and talking back to the centre. And we have tried to do that while some of the actors of our story are still able to narrate their stories and record their memories – though many are not. We are also aware that historians make histories which are influenced by their own perspectives and experiences, whether or not they realize it at the time. So it is clear that the memories of the War Memorial Gymnasium that we have chosen to record, and the activities which took place within it, resonate with some of our own experiences and have thus been imprinted upon our writing bodies too.

Acknowledgements

We would like to thank UBC's Hampton Research Fund for financial assistance, and Fred Hume, dedicated historian of UBC athletics and its Hall of Fame, for his early inspiration and resources. The university archivists in special collections at UBC have been extremely helpful to each of us. Special thanks are also due to those whom we have interviewed and who so willingly and enthusiastically contributed their own memories of their experiences in and around the War Memorial Gymnasium. In addition, a number of valued colleagues have read our early drafts and contributed substantially to our insights. We are grateful for the assistance of Mabel Yee, who provided exemplary assistance in the typing and organization of the manuscript.

Introduction

PATRICIA VERTINSKY

In the history of physical education there are few more long-standing, impassioned and yet inconclusive debates than those around the fate and fortunes of the discipline and the profession. Within academic circles, as departments and faculties of physical education have been reoriented,[1] renamed,[2] and even closed down in recent decades, the rationale has been put forward that physical education lacks a unifying paradigm which precludes it from being and behaving like a proper discipline. Within the school system, where the central role of physical educators has been to help students learn motor skills and enjoy games and health-promoting exercise, the subject has both a perceived decline in relevance and has been increasingly pushed out of the curriculum in favour of more pressing social and academic needs. As David Kirk points out, 'in light of the historical positioning of physical education as a site in which the modern body has been made and remade, its continuing educational viability and social relevance are clearly in question if popular physical culture is moving on and young people are moving with it'.[3] In higher education, debates increasingly swirl around the pressures to focus upon the scientific development of knowledge about human movement rather than its professional application, as well as the manner in which the demands of athletic competition have often triumphed over the needs of physical education instruction for students and facilities for recreational sport and exercise. At the heart of the matter is a much larger – and longer – social debate about the relative positioning of mind over body in educational circles, especially in higher education. And within this debate is the compelling and complicating issue of gender, for just as the Cartesian imperative has traditionally placed mind over body, so has the hegemony of masculinity been enshrined in the training and celebration of the athletic body.

In *Disciplining Bodies in the Gymnasium: Memory, Monument, Modernism* we approach important aspects of this debate from a new and more interdisciplinary direction than that usually taken in commentaries about the discipline and profession of physical education in higher education. Our focus is upon the disciplining of the body in educational and architectural space. We want to understand how knowledge about the body's physical education and training is culturally embedded, constituted at the 'local' level in a particular historical era and geographical place, yet influenced by the broader Enlightenment project of technological rationality and ordered progress. A central challenge for anyone reflecting on the life sciences these days is to understand in what ways knowledge claims around the body are permeated by cultural values and yet are also empirically reliable. One approach is to accept that knowledge development and the trajectory of disciplinary paradigms 'are fully part of their historical era, bearing the cultural fingerprints of those eras and the subsequent ones that practice and maintain them in their cognitive core'.[4]

In the years following World War II, physical education in North American higher education was already dividing in its various professional and scientific missions, but there was a common desire to shape and order the biological and social body as part of the modernist project. It was a time of growing optimism that physical education could provide the knowledge and professional dedication to promote healthier and more responsible citizens through sport and exercise. Where the generation of new knowledge about human movement was underway in university departments it was largely based on the positivist paradigm and its dominant model of orthodox science.[5] These positivist scientific models 'were a clear reflection of the modernist world view that a singular, universal, unchanging reality existed independent of socio-historical context and individual perspective'.[6]

In retrospect, and from postmodern and poststructural perspectives, we can see how the framework and contexts, the 'lived realities' within which human movement studies and physical education training historically occurred, have not been substantially addressed by researchers in the sport and exercise sciences. This has limited our understanding of the means through which cultural values and situational influences affect the training of the body in context. As Brustad points out, without reference to culture we cannot understand how individuals differing in gender, age and race actually experience sport, play and exercise, nor can we understand the purpose and meaning of movement practices without closer examination of the immediate social situation or context.[7] Given Shilling's prescient observation that social location and 'habitus' play an important role in the ways in which bodies (and their techniques) are socially constructed and constituted, then it is clear that carefully contextualized studies of embodiment in a range of settings are needed to provide useful perspectives on practices around the disciplining of the body.[8] As Kirk comments, 'They may also throw some light on the nature of transitions currently taking place from modernity to the postmodern era [and beyond] across a number of social sites.'[9]

In response to such a challenge this book draws upon recent concepts in the history of science and technology, cultural geography, social history and anthropology, architecture, literary criticism and cultural studies to map and explore the disciplining of bodies in a historically and geographically specific educational space and place – a university gymnasium that was built to serve as a war memorial as well as a vehicle for the production of the physically educated person. Just as we learned more about rugby and its role in educating leaders of imperial England from Tom Brown's exploits on the school's playing fields, and have glimpsed the heartbeat of communities from studies of much loved city baseball stadiums, we may get a fresh and more compelling view of the development and vicissitudes of physical education and the human movement sciences in higher education by looking closely, not only at the role of a gymnasium within a developing modern university, but at the orchestration and building of the gymnasium itself. We must also look at its design and use, and examine the players who were central to the control, management and utilization of the spaces of the disciplinary and professional machine, as well as those who were excluded.

We have chosen for our focus, not a well-documented gymnasium, such as one of those in the Ivy League colleges on the Eastern seaboard where physical education, in the embrace of the medical profession, had its birth and heyday more than a century ago, but a gymnasium in one of Canada's largest research universities where the whole panoply of issues critical to the complex story of the development of physical education and movement sciences in North America over the last half century have been played out in unique, and yet familiar, ways. Local gyms and sporting sites, unlike Olympic sites and monumental city stadiums, have tended to be neglected as a site of study, yet they reflect particular notions of the training and education of the body while their orderings of space embody complex constructions of race, place, gender and identity.

In discussing the historical enclosure of the body within the gymnasium, Eichberg points out how the physical culture of the industrial revolution not only produced exercises of the body but it also necessitated the establishment of a separate environment for them. Physical culture and building acted upon each other.[10] Early gymnasia in Germany, for example, were outdoor places, open to the public gaze in the woods and fields, with playgrounds attached. The indoor gymnasium by contrast was structurally related to and arose simultaneously with the prison, the asylum and the schoolhouse in the context of a spatial disciplining and functionalization of social life.[11]

If we look back at the earliest years of the physical education profession in North America, the college gymnasium was an essential facility for early gymnastic and calisthenic programmes designed to remediate the health and strength of students in higher education. Given the anxieties surrounding the rise of unregulated outdoor sports of a competitive nature, gymnasia were seen as a useful tool for securing discipline among the students and promoting the virtues of regularity, efficiency, respect and obedience as well as engendering health. The colleges could not ignore the spontaneous activities of a new generation of students, but they could attempt its domestication by defining the proper time, place and manner of exercise.

'Thus the gymnasium was a vigorous experiment in the shaping of new spaces within the polity of knowledge and in the sanctioning of new styles of behaviour proper in that context.'[12] The motto on Amherst College's Barrett Gymnasium in the 1860s told students (in considering their own body within a specific place of exercise) to 'strive to realize the conditions of the possession of this wondrous structure. Think about what it may become – the Temple of the Holy Spirit.'[13] Interestingly, within this early college gymnasium, the only non-gymnastic facilities available were the bowling alleys, heavily used for recreational purposes.[14] When a new gymnasium was donated by a wealthy Amherst alumnus, Charles Pratt, 'it was more amply furnished, with appropriate appliances as to give every man a chance for some physical exercise'.[15] Dudley Allen Sargent, Director of Physical Training at Harvard and one of the most influential founders of the North American physical education profession, said of his own facility, the Hemenway Gymnasium, 'the great aim of the gymnasium is to improve the physical condition of the mass of our students, and to give them as much health, strength and stamina as possible, to enable them to perform the duties that await them after leaving college'.[16] It was 'built of brick with sandstone trimmings in the colonial style, with the Harvard coat of arms carved over the main window as if to assure the community that the activity within it was proper and authorized'.[17] And to accomplish his goals, Sargent installed 80 development machines in the gym as well as boxing, rowing and fencing rooms, a baseball cage, bowling alleys, a running track and heavy apparatus for formal gymnastics. Gymnasiums designed in this way, he suggested, would fulfil America's need for the appropriate training of the student's body in higher education. Later, at the Sanatory Gymnasium, built not far from the Hemenway as home to the famous Sargent Summer School for Physical Education, we learn that it was

> the largest, and most completely equipped Normal School gymnasium in the world ... The building is about eighty feet long by fifty feet wide and five stories high with a total floor space of about twenty thousand square feet. It contains a swimming tank in the basement, together with adequate lockers and bathing facilities, two gymnasiums, with complete and separate equipment, one above the other, a running track, baseball courts, lecture rooms, library, laboratory, assembly hall and a sun parlour on the roof.[18]

On the other side of the continent, another wealthy patron wrote to the Board of Regents of the University of California, 'I could do for the young men at the University that which would be of much profit and pleasure to them ... if I would construct on the university grounds a building to be used as a gymnasium.'[19] Once built, the Harmon gymnasium became a prominent building on campus, much loved by exercising students and demonstrating, as the fourth President of the University pointed out, that the importance of physical education was already recognized by some of the best colleges in the country.[20]

In her study of the Harmon gymnasium, Roberta Park suggests that 'everyone knows, or thinks they know what a gymnasium is, what kinds of programs are conducted within them and for what purposes'.[21] They have been such integral parts of North American college campuses that it is easy to assume a kind of linear progress from Amherst's small 1860s gymnasium to the more elaborate and grandiose gymnasia of Sargent at Harvard, to today's vast complexes of exercise rooms, basketball pavilions, squash and racquetball courts, athletic facilities, and pubs and snack bars, such as Harvard Business School's recently built Shad Hall.[22] But when questions are asked about such things as their centrality or marginality (geographically or philosophically) on a campus – their architectural design, their specific functions, programmes, spatial divisions and allocations, their financing and management – then it becomes evident that the realities are far more complex and nuanced. 'Here conceptions that coalesce in, construct and reinforce such cultural values as power, weakness, masculinity and femininity are, quite literally, acted out … such that complex – and often paradoxical – matters, which are infused with ever present Cartesian dualisms, merit far greater attention than they have received to date.'[23]

In the various chapters of this book, therefore, we have tried to 'read' the gymnasium as an exemplary site for developing and elaborating social theories of the body, discipline and memory. We agree with Smith and Katz that 'with the reassertion of space in social and cultural theory, an entire spatial language has emerged for comprehending the contours of social reality'.[24] Examining the design and production of space in the place where physical education knowledge was constructed and purveyed, citizenship values embodied, sporting identities formed and relationships developed can thus be a more evocative and revealing approach to the social history and comparative study of physical education and sport than written records alone. Spatial readings can illustrate what Raphael Samuel in *Theatres of Memory* calls 'memory's shadows' – those sleeping images, which spring to life unbidden and serve as ghostly sentinels of our thoughts.[25] Spatial concepts can illustrate how a monument – a memorial gymnasium – became a partner in a dialogue with the bodies of students and bodies of memory. They can infuse our everyday understandings of what fits where – how the academic landscape is articulated for teaching and learning – whose knowledge is seen to be legitimate and how the boundaries of disciplines are formed and defended.[26] We are able to ask under what circumstances the gymnasium evolved into an arena of contested spaces and functions around gendered, racial and sexualized bodies, as well as bodies of knowledge and the shape of disciplines. What were the circumstances of the students, faculty and staff who worked, played and struggled in the gymnasium as administrations and students came and went and the changing face of knowledge, economics and the world of competitive sport demanded new accommodations, shifting spatial arrangements and acquiescence or resistance to past memories of how young students and athletes should be educated for tomorrow? Spatial inquiry thus permits both broadly focused studies of the evolution of educational spaces during particular time periods, as well as micro-historical studies – 'history on the ground' you might call a study of particular spaces at particular moments.

In some ways this collection of stories is unique by virtue of the fact that our gymnasium was built and dedicated as a war memorial – not uncommon in the years after World War II – but consequential in its effects on attitudes toward the training of the body in higher education. Projects concerning what we want our built environment to be are very much projects about who we want to become. Winston Churchill understood this very well. Determined to rebuild the House of Commons after the German blitz in a design that he thought particularly conducive to parliamentary debate, he insisted that 'we shape our buildings and afterwards our buildings shape us'.[27] No doubt with such an aim, the War Memorial Gymnasium was dedicated by students and friends of the University of British Columbia in 1951 'to the men and women of our university and province who gave their lives for freedom'. Though sports training and recreational facilities are not uncommon as war memorials, our interest here lies in how the university constructed its own myths of origin through a commemorative symbol such as the memorial gymnasium, and what the design, construction and shifting functions and spatial configurations of the building revealed about the values and aspirations of this pedagogical institution in the post-war years.

The gymnasium was also the first building of modern style on the campus and it was seized upon as the standard bearer of modernism's aims and axioms. Space was celebrated as ideally unencumbered and visually dynamic while functionally apportioned and technologically mastered. Structure was deemed best when stripped of superfluous material to become a spare transcription of engineering science into architectural form. And, through the gym's tightly scripted corridors of movement and closely programmed rooms, modernist architecture aspired to produce the spirit and bodies of the modern citizen of the new world.

In relation to the important role of architecture, Elizabeth Grosz argues that there is a complex feedback relation between bodies and environment in which each produces the other.[28] Certainly, one of the critical contexts for the perpetuation and reproduction of social inequalities is the built environment, for most buildings can be understood in terms of power or authority – as efforts to assume, extend, resist or accommodate it. Since it has been observed that all architecture functions as a potential stimulus for movement, real or imagined, we can usefully explore how the architecture of the War Memorial Gymnasium became an incitement to action and a particular setting for movement and interaction.[29] Furthermore, architectural conceptions of the body, although assumed to be neutral, transparent, universal and normal, have tended to be infused with (male) gender, class and the embodiment of wealth and normality.[30] Architecture and design have thus been used as a means to exert control over bodies across lines of class, gender and race in a myriad of ways – restricting or allowing access to certain spaces and facilities, imposing physical or psychological barriers, and making possible particular activities for specific groups of students.[31] Our intention, then, is to link up the materiality of the building with the social and power relations among university administrators, architects and planners, faculty, staff and students, and discuss how the material culture and structure of the gymnasium affected and responded to changing ideologies of competition, discipline, profession, gender, race and health. The fact that the gymnasium also occupied First Nations land of the Musqueam (as did the university as a whole) carried with it the metaphorical and material politics of contestation, conquest, displacement and colonization. Far from being a neutral memorial and gymnasium for everyday athletics, the War Memorial Gymnasium regulated body, memory and movement within its modernist structures. Built form has politics, and culture – sporting culture – is politics by another name.

This book attempts to address these and other questions as it portrays the changing landscape, sportscape and memoryscape of the War Memorial Gymnasium, examines the meanings ascribed to its changing spaces, and explores the shifting patterns of relationships between the body and its academic and physical environment in higher education.

The first chapter focuses on war memorials as a site of contested and competing meanings, and examines how memory, in modernity, has become a key to personal and collective identities. Questions are posed about the motives of memory in the construction of monuments and how living memorials became idealized as didactic objects to instruct those who used them in the values and sacrifices of war, while simultaneously affirming the community's desire to ensure that those values are passed on in appropriate ways. We ask why a gymnasium was selected as a war memorial in an institution of higher education and look back at the historical connection between soldier and athlete within the university, and the constant interplay between the requirements of military training and student determination to foster their own sports arrangements and athletic facilities.

In the second chapter we look at the unique modernist design of Canada's largest and most modern gymnasium in the aftermath of World War II, and at the events and decision-making which would lead to the exclusion of the women's physical education programme from its spaces. We examine by whom and for whom the gymnasium was designed and dedicated as a memorial, what its design revealed about the community's views of the fallen young men and about the way those left living should be trained and educated within its walls. Architects and planners of the gym became, in a sense, partners in a dialogue with the body, and their views on design and society came to reflect an acute sense of how the body should be looked at and what it could and should become through appropriate discipline and education. In many respects, a modernist, rectangular gymnasium designed to promote organized movement and team sports was an inspired choice for a war memorial celebrating the virility and power of the young student/athlete/soldier who had gone to battle for Canada. Modernist design and its accompanying logic, particularly the inspiration of French architect Le Corbusier – whose work stood most immediately behind the design of this gymnasium, thus became an important disciplinary arena of power by which modern 'sporting' bodies were to be produced. Modernism reified a passion for large geometric spaces and perspectives, for uniformity and the power of the straight line that in some respects magnified the oppressive dimensions of the post-war belief in linear progress, absolute truth and technical rationality which informed attitudes toward educating the body.

The ability to influence the production of space is an important means to augment social power. Hence the story of the exclusion of women physical educators is taken up in Chapter 3 using Doreen Massey's notion of 'power geometries' to focus upon the shape and structure of the spaces in which lives are given meaning in particular locations over time. Feminist scholars complain how built landscapes have been remarkable in their desire to confine, control and exclude women, and just as Eichberg has drawn conclusions about the patterns and dynamics of physical culture from historically specific changes in sport architecture, so we can meaningfully trace the 'power geometries' – the effects of multiple configurations of space and social relations within and around the War Memorial Gym.[32] From the beginning, the spaces of modern sports facilities such as gymnasia were sexed spaces involved in the construction of sexed bodies. Male and female physical educators were able to mark and patrol the borders between masculinity and femininity through sex-coded activities and at UBC it was ideological issues around girls' basketball rules and competitive sport which affected most immediately the displacement of women from the newly built War Memorial Gym.

Bowling, whether recreation or sport, has been generally overlooked by historians and sociologists. In Chapter 4, Stephen Petrina uses the bowling alleys in the War Memorial Gymnasium to explore the politics of buildings and spaces and how such politics wore into the very fabric of what it meant to be academic. His story of the fortunes and fate of the bowling alleys at the University of British Columbia neatly captures how culture and power circulated in the machinations of university governance and student life during the 1950s and 1960s. At that time, bowling was Canada's most popular organized recreational activity – with more players than curling, golf and tennis combined. One out of eight Canadians bowled regularly and students were eager for bowling opportunities on college campuses. Petrina shows how bowling represented a convenient, but not altogether unique, site in which administrative and student politics – mundane interests concerning class, gender, labour, money and technology – could circulate. He goes on to argue that memories and politics built into facilities such as bowling alleys and recreation rooms inside campus gymnasiums and student unions are part of the larger processes of the commodification and embodiment of leisure time and recreation since World War II.

In Chapter 5, Becki Ross and Erin Bentley return to the central issues of gender and sexuality in the male domain of sport, and discuss the post-war university as a site of nation-building which occupied real and imagined spaces upon which processes of national identity formation were constituted. From rich archival sources they examine the material and discursive conditions under which female athletes strove for access to institutional resources and acknowledgement of their competitive efforts after World War II. Largely exiled from the modernist, masculinist War Memorial Gymnasium, and from the sports pages of the student newspaper, *The Ubyssey*, sporting women faced myriad barriers to funds, facilities and credibility. The same discourses which lampooned women's sporting prowess functioned both to justify the chronic underfunding of women's athletics at UBC and to buttress conformist notions that women's 'true place' was on the sidelines at men's sporting events, cheering the soldier/athlete on to victory. Social scripts that idealized and installed male sporting (and soldiering) heroes as 'natural' leaders and model citizens were hinged to scripts that idealized female co-eds as ladylike, unmistakably hetero-feminine and imminently marriageable helpmates. In effect, female students' pursuit of athletics, especially sports that demanded speed, physical strength, aggression and stamina, intensified moral panics around nationhood and the reproduction of 'healthy' white, Anglo-Canadian bodies. That some female student-athletes attained successes and gratification through participation in spite of ridicule, surveillance and structural disregard attests to the power of individual and collective resolve. That intercollegiate (and professional) women athletes still navigate gender, racial and sexual inequalities today, a half-century later, attests to the stubborn traces of regulatory discourses and practices rooted in age-old myths about the 'eternally wounded woman' and the infinitely superior man.

In Chapter 6, Sherry McKay explores the interrelationship between the ambition of architects and the aspirations of physical education. As much as the new gymnasium was concerned with the training of the body it was also concerned with the embodiment of modern architecture. The building of the War Memorial Gymnasium not only provoked and made urgent arguments about gender, professional status and physical development within the arena of sport, it also brought these issues into the ambit of modern architectural consideration. However, the two salient functions of the project, memorial and gymnasium, were not equally conducive to modernism's aims. Memorials, monuments and historical recall were problematic to modern architectural sensibilities that wished to escape the 'tyranny of the past'. The gymnasium, however, offered a more suitable and familiar venue for architectural thinking for it provided a practical precedent for the exchange between the discipline of architecture and that of physical education. It also served as theoretical support, for, as Sigfried Giedion proposed in the late 1920s and Beatriz Colomina retraced in the late 1990s, modern architecture found a useful paradigm in the gymnasium and its optimized spaces for honing the body.

Chapter 7 focuses on the gymnasium's plan, its occupation and occlusions. It takes up Robin Evans' insight that 'if anything is described by an architectural plan, it is the nature of human relationships'. Here, McKay analyses the prosaic elements of walls and windows, doors and stairs, and their more poetic transformations as a memorial window or architectural promenade, for what they reveal about modernism's concern with both the physiology of the body and the aesthetic energies of the psyche. The plan delineated an athletic ascending and descending, traversing and turning via bridges and stairs, corridors and shifted axes. It also complemented this visceral engagement of the building with a purely visual one, determined by unimpeded lines of sight across an expanse of play or the visual delight of hovering planes and cantilevered forms. This physical and aesthetic structure, however, calls forth the notion of certain modern bodies. It draws our attention from the occlusions and omissions suggested by the plans or claimed by their occupation. The landscape of war that existed on the UBC campus was effaced by locating the gymnasium elsewhere. Labouring bodies that manually transformed recalcitrant matter into architectural form are not users of the gym, their presence recorded inadvertently in construction photos and effaced in building costs. One female designer, Catherine Wisnicki, was also effaced from initial celebrations of the architectural modernism of the gym. The celebration of the male athlete in the sporting world had its influence, not only in the spaces of the gymnasium but also in the space of architecture.

In our conclusion we show that while the memorial hall continues to resonate with memories, the activities, functions and inhabitants of the larger gymnasium have changed considerably around it, although as McKay points out, it is the architect who haunts the abstract space of the memorial hall and who is illuminated by its harsh north light. We ask what evocations of memory now reverberate within the spaces of the gym as we move forwards in the new millennium, looking backwards at the ways in which formative spaces were used to facilitate behaviours, discipline bodies and focus the spectator's gaze, while reflecting upon the views we have articulated about educating the Canadian body. We examine the emergence of sport science and its technological emphasis upon the 'virtual' body, and wonder if there are any 'modern' bodies left to educate in the War Memorial gym or whether the sensory deprivation which some critics have suggested curses modernist buildings has dulled the quest for the study and celebration of the moving body. Finally, we confront the question of how memory, monument and modernity are constructed in war and note that the War Memorial Gymnasium, by its very existence, animated a particular body or image of war. Neither timeless nor frozen in time, the gymnasium continues to stir memories in the private and public body. After all, a good memorial doesn't clean up history, it leaves part of the mess, part of the argument.

Memory and Monument:
The Gymnasium as War Memorial

PATRICIA VERTINSKY

'Lest We Forget'

When trumpeter Rob Morson played 'The Last Post' on the eleventh hour of the eleventh day of the eleventh month of the last memorial service of the millennium in the War Memorial Gymnasium at the University of British Columbia, elderly stewards pointed out that the service was exactly the same as it had always been since the first memorial service in 1951, the year the gymnasium was built. There were a few differences, however, in the nature of the ceremony. The procession of dignitaries was led by a woman, the first woman to become president of the university, whose American upbringing and tourist experience at Dieppe compelled her to speak of her remembrances of war and valour in a quite different manner from that of the former Canadian soldier/scholar, President Norman MacKenzie in 1951.

President Mackenzie's first words at his inauguration had been a moving, personal tribute to the university graduates and students who had died in the war. 'I hope that the sacrifices these young men and women have made, and are making, will inspire the rest of us to do great things and to provide fitting memorials to their memory.'[1] The most significant of these memorials was the War Memorial Gymnasium (see Figure 1.1).

The number of participants at the service in 1999 was higher than usual; a relief to seasoned organizers who had seen Memorial Day audiences dwindle drastically over the past two or three decades. They know well the familiar core of regulars who pay annual homage to fallen friends and comrades. They know that to the eyes of those who have dwelt on the past, there is no repair that time and nature can effect. Yet many of those most directly linked to the tragedies of the World Wars are no longer living, or have disabilities which make access to the annual memorial service in the gymnasium restrictive. It is the surge of nostalgia, and the powerful anxiety of erasure – what Charles Maier has called the 'surfeit of memory', in the years leading up to the new millennium that seem to have rekindled interest among the relatives of lost uncles and grandfathers, school children seeking materials for class history projects on family genealogy, nation-building

Figure 1.1   'Memorial Service', Memorial Hall, War Memorial
Gymnasium.

stories and Canadian heroes on television, and curious university students
heeding public notices in their dorms to view the spectacle and take
refreshments. Affluence and the wholesale marketing of memory have
encouraged people to build bridges between family history and history *tout
court*, and to seek to experience the uncanny landscape of traumatic memory
through war narratives of heroes and suffering.[2]

   In the glass-and-steel case below the memorial window, the Roll of
Service (a single illuminated manuscript of 56 lettered pages bound in red
Morocco) listing the names of those killed in the two World Wars was

opened as usual at the same page. It used to be that the glass case was unlocked and propped open on Memorial Day for friends and relatives to turn the pages, searching for familiar names. Today, the glass case is locked and the pages undisturbed, by virtue of the little-known fact that a careless window cleaner accidentally filled the case with water, leaving some pages water-marked and discoloured. Now on display is the photograph and stirring story of fallen hero Lieutenant Robert Hampton Gray, RCNVR, who was credited with sinking a Japanese warship in 1945 and became the first UBC student, as well as the last Canadian of the twentieth century, to receive the Victoria Cross for valour in the World Wars (see Figure 1.2).

International students from Asia, or of Asian heritage, including Japanese, now make up a rapidly growing percentage of students on the campus. Whether Canadian-born or domiciled, few of them at the memorial ceremony could imagine that in 1949 (four years after the end of the war), the President of the Alma Mater Society (AMS) had felt compelled to write to the University's retained architects to insist on the deletion of a clause

Figure 1.2   DEDICATION: Six days before the atomic bomb put an end to war in the Pacific, Lieut. R. Hampton Gray D.S.C. sacrificed his life, sank a Jap destroyer, and was awarded the Victoria Cross. (*Totem,* 1945.)

forbidding the hiring of persons of Asiatic or African descent to work on the construction of the War Memorial Gymnasium. 'We feel', he wrote, 'that this restriction would be particularly objectionable in connection with a building dedicated to the memory of British Columbia servicemen, many of whom were Canadians of Chinese descent.'[3]

First Nation's elders were not included among the dignitaries at this ceremony and it was not clear whether their presence had been invited, or whether First Nation's soldiers are mentioned in the memorial book. In the memorial foyer one can examine the inscriptions on the plaques and the names of some of those lost in both wars and speculate whose bodies were memorialized and whether they reflected the divisions of the living at the time. Memory, says Pierre Nora, is blind to all but the group it binds,[4] and the commemoration was dedicated, as President Mackenzie clearly pointed out in the original ceremony in 1951, 'for those who, bred in the tradition of our society and of this university, honoured this tradition in their defence of our society'.[5] Nor was there any mention of the First Nation's land of the Musqueam, upon which the gymnasium stands. At the time of the installation of the memorial hall, the clause in the Indian Act that declared a 'person' to be an individual other than an Indian had only just been deleted.[6]

Women, though mentioned on the memorial wall, were not explicitly memorialized either. A sensitivity to issues of gender has not been a particular hallmark of war memorials. When it comes to remembering war heroes, especially in sporting environments, the militarized white male body holding the standard of the universal ideal of the fallen soldier tends to take precedence.

Draughty and shabby, the memorial hall of the gymnasium seems, in many respects, timeless and unchanged, annually echoing both Canadian and British anthems, and evocative renderings of 'Lest We Forget' and 'In Flanders Field'. It stands as a didactic object, silently instructing those who pass through it in the meanings and memories of the war(s) and affirming the University community's desire to ensure that those values are passed on. It tells how the university's war dead gave their lives to teach their fellow students how to live, shoring up the conviction that Canada's multitudes of dead soldiers gave their lives in the service of nation, freedom and civilization. It silently speaks of how, through their sacrifice and accomplishments on the battlefield, Canada's citizen/soldiers launched and sustained Canada as a nation. That is part of the story embedded in 'in Flanders Fields', and repeated every year in the hope that 'if the sacrifices were fixed firmly enough in the public consciousness through commemoration, the [ennobling] myth of the war would become self-perpetuating'.[7]

But how to live and what kind of lessons were to be taught by future teachers and learned by tomorrow's students within the walls of the War Memorial Gymnasium? Along with the drive to inculcate the memory of the fight against the 'foes of freedom' among those still living, the story of 'In

Flanders Fields' served as an anodyne to historical memory – sometimes described as a lofty message to keep the nightmare at one remove, to obscure 'the oldest lie of all'.[8] 'Any commemorative act, especially concerning war', says Jager, 'is a form of history-making that attempts to promote and secure a particular interpretation of events while at the same time blocking or erasing potentially contestatory meanings.'[9] The dual purpose of the War Memorial Gymnasium was thus quite clear: as a gymnasium its function was to educate and reform the body; as a memorial its purpose was to bless that newly acquired education with a spirit of reverence and a correct and unanimous understanding of Canada's patriotic history.

This chapter, therefore, examines war memorials as a site of contested and competing meanings and looks at their role in constructing a 'usable' past with a progressive narrative of nation building. Ideally, memorials were intended to be a kind of didactic object that instructed those who used them in the values and sacrifices of war and affirmed the community's desire to pass on those values. The memory of war was to act as a primer for citizenship. This justified the promotion of memorials to educate the active living, such as gymnasiums, community centres and swimming pools. The chapter goes on to explore how UBC's memory of war came to be embodied in a gymnasium and documents the historical development of military training and student athletics during the inter-war years. As the demands for competitive sport and intercollegiate athletics grew, the need for appropriate facilities became increasingly pressing and students played a leading role in generating funding for these facilities and in requesting physical education instruction. With the end of hostilities after World War II the time seemed ripe to memorialize the past with a new, and much needed, modern gymnasium.

War Memorials and the Soldier as 'Canada'

'Typically war memorials affirm the values upon which the war in question was based ... this is a matter of presenting a persuasive, publicly acceptable face'.[10]

Recent studies of history and memory have set out to unpack the particular ways in which nations and localities have memorialized their past. One way of memorializing the past has been expressed in mortar and stone, in buildings dedicated to wars and tragic events and remembered through a complex mixture of fact, wishful thinking, half truths and even outright inventions. The past thus becomes an excuse for the present, setting out what should be remembered (and what should be forgotten), justifying the social and political order and acting as a bulwark for establishment values.[11]

Not surprisingly, war memorials involve aspects of gender, class, religion, ethnicity, locality and nation in the construction of a usable past. Through the politics of memory production, memorials tend to reflect those aspects of the past seen as most 'usable', a past yielding what its creators wish to find and one which may evade confrontation with the more disturbing features of national and local history.[12] Indeed, the monument or memorial has increasingly become the site of contested and competing meanings, more likely the site of cultural conflict than of shared institutional values and ideals.[13] In modernity, memory has become the key to personal and collective identities, and in some respects the further the events of the World Wars recede into time the more prominent (and contested) the memorials become.[14]

Memorials have often been construed as the most conspicuous sign that a nation's people understands and values its own history. Public monuments help celebrate and cement this progressive narrative of national history. Many Canadian war memorials can be considered patriotic memorials, whose inscriptions render a value judgement on the courage and sacrifice of the nation's young soldiers, discarding where possible unpalatable facts in favour of more appealing, heroic images. Hence the motives of memory in the construction of monuments are not necessarily pure and we are obliged to ask in whose interests are commemorative projects framed and memory narratives legitimated. Memorials to heroes and events such as wars are not meant to revive old struggles and debates, but rather to put them to rest, to be redemptive by showing how great men and their deeds have made the nation better and stronger.[15] The elite memory of the two World Wars as a nation-building experience is meant to drive underground the vernacular memory of war as wasteful and tragic, wrought in violence and stemming from the avarice of political and economic elites. Thus the memorial can serve to implant the story of ennobling events and retell the martyrdom of those who gave their lives for the nation. It can assume the idealized forms and meaning assigned to wars by the state, or by the donors of the memorial, and help to concretize particular historical interpretations.[16]

Some argue that this logic of commemoration has obscured a broader history, since women, immigrants, labourers and others are not seen as advancing the master narrative of progress – defined by a white male elite – and thus figure little in commemorative displays. In this respect, locking up the past in this kind of narrative of progress encourages public history to be written from the point of view of the conqueror. To the extent that this is true for national or local histories, then some histories can be read as the story of colonization and imperialism through war, reiterating a story of how a nation has come into being and the practices through which it has been secured, maintained and legitimated.[17] Such stories are indispensable to claims about memory and identity, and are, of course, necessarily gendered, since concepts of public history can be considered reflections of the public and private spheres traditionally conceived as masculine and feminine. While famous events have been recorded as impacting upon a wide spectrum of lives, they nevertheless are often recorded as having been carried out by individual men acting as agents of change. And, 'as the very notion of history is gendered, then so too is commemoration'.[18] Indeed, the centrality of the male soldier/citizen in Jonathan Vance's discussions about the First World War excludes much consideration of how women, especially those at home, experienced the war and its effects.

As the 'real' environments of memory recede, memory becomes crystallized in 'sites of memory', (what Pierre Nora calls *lieux de mémoire*).[19] When we stop experiencing memory spontaneously from within, we begin to 'design' memory, to create its external signs and traces, such as monuments and museums and historical buildings. At the core of these sites of memory are the fallen, rhapsodized in the first decades of the twentieth century by J.H. Maloney as 'those strong virile men of the North, the Nordic or Anglo-Saxon race ... whose sons died on Flanders field'.[20] Such a view, of course, ignores ex-soldiers of many other origins, including the sacrifices of many Native Canadians. There is a strong and natural desire to say that the soldiers have not died in vain, and to comfort surviving relatives, making necessary the invention of a certain view of the fallen soldiers' attributes and exploits, accompanied by an intense anxiety and desire to somehow recover and keep the past (and its good qualities) alive.[21]

In order to justify Canadian sacrifices in both World Wars, the body of the fallen soldier at mid-century became an obligating and functional symbol for survivors – the soldier as 'Canada' (which was idealized as a peace-loving nation where the young citizen/soldier, 'the happy warrior', went willingly to war from its towns and fields to protect the things he loved). Wordsworth's description of heroism and the noble deeds of the ideal soldier in *The Character of the Happy Warrior* (1807) was often repeated in memorial volumes designed to remember the fallen in the best possible light.[22]

Furthermore, since memories are personal as well as social, memorials were intended to express the particular feelings of local communities toward the war they commemorated and its local victims. Ideally, memorials were to be a kind of didactic object that at once instructed those who used them in the values of the war and its sacrifice, and more importantly affirmed the local community's desire to ensure that those values were passed on in appropriate ways.[23] Collective local memory could thus become a necessary force in orienting people in terms of what to do, for it is the act of groups of people who gather bits and pieces of the past and join them together for a local public that will express and consume the constructed memory.[24] Gillis says 'identities and memories are not so much things we think about, but rather things we think with'. The memory of war acts as a primer for citizenship, for the ideal educated person and correct training in bodily practices, providing a means of Canadianization unlike any other.[25] It drives a conception of citizenship in which 'a good citizen is someone who is loyal and obedient, and knows and believes in the patriotic symbols and ceremonies as well as the national myths'.[26] Such a conception, of course, can obscure the fact that full access to civil, political and, to some extent, social rights were quite unequally distributed across the nation and province, and that schooling, training of the body, and higher education in general were ideological instruments for cultural reproduction.

Envisaging a Gymnasium as War Memorial

'Social memories are produced as bounded sets of symbolizations (texts, images, buildings, monuments, and rituals) and associated emotions. Collectivities share these as ways of stabilizing and transmitting particular versions of past events and, in so doing, attempt to offer perspectives on present dilemmas and future aspirations.'[27]

How, then, did the University of British Columbia's memory of the war, 'the soldier as Canada', come to be embodied in a War Memorial Gymnasium, and how was the promise of the myths of unity, peace and citizenship embodied in that place which hoped to provide 'twentieth century recreation for twentieth century men and women'? Memory, after all, plays a much larger part in developing and designing the built environment than is usually acknowledged. Underscoring the historical connection between male soldier and athlete, 'happy warriors jousting on the battlefield just as they had on the playing field', it was – in many respects – no coincidence that a new gymnasium came to be selected as a war memorial in an institution of higher education such as UBC. Nor was it a new idea there, nor indeed elsewhere in Canada, to dedicate athletic facilities to the fallen soldier. After World War I, the football stadium at Queen's University was built as a memorial to a Winnipeg businessman's brother who was killed in action. Acadia University erected a gymnasium as their war memorial, and in Toronto a proposal to build a War Memorial Stadium on the waterfront was only thwarted by too high a price tag.[28] At UBC, in 1926, former Alma Mater Society President Sherwood Lett, high-profile military man and ardent ice-hockey player and football fan (and later chancellor of the university (see Figure 1.4)), dedicated two concrete memorial tennis courts on Memorial Road to the athletic well-being of the students (see Figures 1.3 and 1.4).

At the dedication, Lett noted that the memorial tennis courts would keep

Figure 1.3   The 1929 'Old' Gymnasium, with memorial tennis courts.

fresh, through many generations of undergraduates, the memory of those who had displayed on the battlefields of France, 'the same spirit of courage and endurance that they had shown on the playing fields of UBC'.[29] This emphasis on martial masculinity, the connection between sport and the battlefield, which reached a climax, perhaps, during World War I but was sustained well through the inter-war years, focused keenly on character-building and the notion that the future of modern nations such as Canada rested in the hands and loins of virile athletic men. Lett's dedication speech showed he was deeply moved by such sentiments:

> To some of us this gathering and the silence we have just observed recalls another silence. Our minds go back to that memorable day – the day of the first convocation of this university. Amid the splendour of the robes and the galaxy of hoods and applause, a name was called – Edward Berry! And back came the answer, 'Absent on Active Service'. There was a pause, a silence such as this, then came the Chancellor pronouncing the words: 'Admitto Te' – and thunderous applause. Name after name was called and back came the answer: 'Absent on Active Service'.
>   What did that answer mean? There are some here today who know its meaning to the full … they are that gallant company of men who here, in this university, laid aside their cap and gown and went forth in uniform to give their services to God, King and Canada.

Figure 1.4   'Portrait of Brigadier-General Sherwood Lett', when he became Chancellor of the University. (*Totem,* 1955)

Lett then went on to recount some of the bloody battles in which men from UBC were involved, mentioning some of those who lost their lives and describing each of them as 'old rugby men, hockey men and tennis men'.[30]
     Drawing upon the Victorian tendency to blur the lines between war and sport and promote the ethos of muscular Christianity which equated 'playing the game', 'fair play' and 'supporting the team' with carrying out one's duty, the transition from student athlete to soldier was seen to be a natural one.[31] Evolutionary notions of the survival of the fittest and struggle for existence connected the attainment of civilization with the ability to wage war and do battle.[32] 'Manhood', David Leverenz has written, 'begins as a battlefield code ... to transform fears of vulnerability into a desire for dominance'.[33] Ralph Connor believed this when he wrote about soldiers who learned to attack in battle. 'They were all sportsmen, and had all experienced the anxious nervous thrill of the moments preceding a big contest. Once the ball was off, their nervousness would go, and they would be cool and wary, playing the game for all they had in them.'[34] Thus, in World War I, supposedly the 'greatest game of all', British soldiers kicked footballs into battle at the Somme and were mown down by an opposition for whom the sporting hegemony of British rules had only a limited appeal.[35] 'Real' athletes, like soldiers, were expected to epitomize the dominant middle-class values of discipline,

loyalty, order, productivity, self-reliance, manliness and team work, and these values were reflected in attitudes toward military training on university campuses.[36]

Military Training and Student Athletics in the Inter-war Years

For the first four years of UBC's existence (1915–19) military training was mandatory for all male students, a view rationalized by the notion that the university, as a publicly funded institution, had a responsibility to provide its male students with the benefits of 'physical exercise, discipline, organization, and study of military science (as well as producing trained soldiers for the war effort)'.[37] For two hours a week male students worked to quality for an 'A' or 'B' certificate in the campus reserve contingent of the Canadian Officers Training Corps (COTC). In 1919 the COTC was suspended at the request of the students, to reappear in 1929 as a voluntary pursuit open only to male students who were bona fide 'British subjects'. At that time Sherwood Lett wielded considerable influence in his Senate Committee to reinstate the Corps (and again, 20 years later to establish a squadron of officer cadets at UBC).[38] Participation in the corps remained voluntary until August 1940 when the 'Senate and Board of Governors of the University passed a regulation making military training compulsory for all physically fit male students for the duration of the war'.[39]

During the inter-war years there were also glowing reports of athletic teamwork and sporting victories at UBC as a result of the soldier/athlete combination. When the rugby team 'received a strong infusion of returned soldier–players' their teamwork was said to result in an almost legendary defeat of Stanford University on Christmas Day, 1920. Rugby, soccer and basketball, and to a lesser extent rowing, hockey, swimming and boxing, all had clubs containing returning soldier/student/athletes, although there were limited facilities for any of these sports.

Nor was it unusual at this time for students to show leadership in initiating campus buildings and facilities for physical activity and sport. Quite the contrary. Lacking a gymnasium and playing fields, the student council had endeavoured to raise funds in 1923 through 'shoe-shining, hairdressing, manicuring, fortune-telling and begging – and a mammoth *ceilidh*'.[40] By the time the University moved onto its current Point Grey campus in 1925, two playing fields had been etched out of the landscape by working groups of students, and fundraising for the institution's first gymnasium had begun. The student council first looked to the premier of the province for funds for the gymnasium but the result of this effort was so negative that they sought out the help of the inimitable Sherwood Lett. It was at this moment that Lett, as the AMS's lawyer, devised his scheme to incorporate the Alma Mater Society under the Societies Act so that it could levy annual fees and raise money for projects. Out of this the students raised a bond issue of 60,000 dollars to build the gymnasium.[41] Harry Logan claims that this scheme marked a significant landmark in UBC history, setting a precedent for future giving by student societies to the University and laying the groundwork for the periodic funding (if not control) of future athletic and training facilities by and for the students. Issues of student funding and student control of athletic and social facilities would take on a critical importance during the next half century, and have a substantial effect upon the activities which would take place within the spaces of both the first gymnasium and, after the Second World War, the War Memorial Gymnasium.

By 1929, funding for a gymnasium was complete and the new building was opened at homecoming by the Lieutenant Governor of the province who turned a gold key in the door. The gymnasium was designed so that its exterior harmonized well with other buildings on campus.[42] It housed a 6,000 sq. ft. playing surface, tiers of benches for 1,400 people on three sides, dressing rooms, drying rooms, locker rooms and shower baths. One third of the space was set aside for women who made up 40 per cent of the student body.[43] There were also four rooms: one for the boxing and wrestling club, one for the chess club, one for the music society and the fourth for a kitchen. The gym itself was used for basketball and badminton, class exercises and games, but it also became home to the voluntary UBC contingent of the COTC (despite opposition among some of the student body who objected to this direct display of militarism on the campus). 'Even the building of a miniature rifle range in the basement of the Arts building was regarded with hostility by many of the students.'[44] Instead, students made a plea for the provision of gymnastic instructors and the incorporation of regular physical culture into the curriculum.

Once the gymnasium was built, male and female instructors were hired to provide a voluntary programme of intramural sports for the students and a programme for training school physical education teachers.[45] The calendar reported that 'the University aims, primarily, to prescribe, under competent supervision, the essential physical training for corrective and developmental purposes, and to stimulate interest in the greatest possible variety of athletics for both men and women'.[46] It also pointed out that the geographical location of the university precluded the possibility of extensive intercollegiate competition, making greater emphasis upon intramural athletics desirable.

This viewpoint did not go unchallenged, and in the years to come the demands of competitive sport and intercollegiate athletics intensified, along with the need for appropriate facilities. Football, in particular, suffered from the high cost of competing in the Western Intercollegiate League (as well as the costs of training and equipment), but it survived and went on to flourish with the enthusiastic support of Lieutenant-Colonel Gordon Shrum, an active member of the Science faculty (see Figure 1.5). Hired in 1925, Shrum greatly admired the way American football teams were coached, disciplined and financed and used his considerable influence to promote the sport on campus despite spirited opposition from the campus rugby fraternity.[47] Properly organized and financed college football, he believed, would bring out the best in UBC – in competition, unity, pride and publicity, and for four decades Shrum tirelessly advocated excellence in intercollegiate athletics, athletic scholarships and the recruitment of the best athletic coaches. His early efforts contributed to the somewhat schizophrenic development of athletics at UBC, for they clashed with the general view on campus that had existed since the inception of the university that student sport should be non-professional and participatory. The consequences of these competing

Figure 1.5   Lt. Col. Gordon Merritt Shrum. (*Totem*, 1941.)

streams of influence on the development of the physical education programme and the campus sports community would be profound, both at UBC where Shrum's athletic philosophy never garnered a total commitment and at nearby Simon Fraser University where it did. Retiring in 1961 from his faculty position at UBC, Gordon Shrum became Chairman of BC Hydro and founder of Simon Fraser University (SFU). There, as Chancellor and Chairman of the Board he promptly set up a system of athletic scholarships and promoted the athletic philosophy at SFU that exists to this day.

Despite the existence of divergent views, a broad and varied sports programme emerged, supervised by a committee appointed by the president of the university. It drew 172 men and 300 women in the first year the gym was open.[48] Gertrude Moore, the first female physical education instructor to be hired, successfully recruited women students by pressing them to make an effort to balance their sedentary studies with 'wholesome athletic activity'.[49] Through her efforts, women were offered archery, basketball (women's rules), folk dancing, badminton and gymnastics, although they were forbidden rifle shooting on the campus rifle range for fear of hurting themselves.[50] Men could participate in gymnastics, basketball, boxing, track and field, volleyball and cross-country running (to which were soon added badminton, fencing, golf, football and rugby).

Athletic facilities remained a continuing focus for student funding initiatives throughout the inter-war years and in these early days intramural sports were often at the hub of campus sporting activity. Varsity competition also thrived in spite of the devastating impact of the economic depression in the early 1930s and the drastic reduction of the University's operating budget. In 1937, the varsity athletic stadium was completed at the heart of the campus at a cost of 40,000 dollars. Rugby, football, soccer, track and later on baseball teams all found a popular new home there during the 'golden age of student clubs', while wrestling and boxing took place in rooms under the stands.[51] Once again it was the students who raised the funds to underwrite the drainage of the stadium site, and the construction of the track and grandstand. Playing out of the old gymnasium was the basketball team under the early leadership of the men's physical education director, Maury Van Vliet, who coached the highly successful men's teams in the late 1930s and early 1940s.

The War Years and the Growing Importance of Physical Education

Canada's entrance into World War II in 1939 again changed the face of the campus, as faculty and students joined the forces and military training for those on campus was reinstituted. There was a growing sentiment in favour of discontinuing varsity athletics altogether, and congested parade grounds contrasted sharply with the almost deserted playing fields. 'War conditions were reflected in the physical appearance of the campus. Gun emplacements were erected; part of the forest belt was cleared; traffic was diverted from Marine Drive to the Main Mall; the wireless station was transferred; and blackouts were instituted.'[52]

Students slowly came to realize the impact of the war upon their daily lives as the daily orders for the COTC were published prominently in *The Ubyssey*. The corps more than doubled in size and increased again when military training became compulsory. By September 1940, there was an unprecedented number of trainees for whom the parade grounds were graded and regulation uniforms and equipment obtained.[53] Saturday afternoons were used for military drill and the facilities of the gymnasium and playing fields were commandeered for the corps. Each cadet devoted six hours a week to military activities whilst other students attended three hours of drill. Lacking adequate space for training, the University used its accumulated corps fund to build an armoury where not only the COTC but Navy and Air Force units also received basic training. By the end of the war, 1,680 students had enlisted whilst only one student 'officially' left the University as a conscientious objector. (Despite such evidence the local media was strongly critical of undergraduate male students who did not enlist immediately.)

Not surprisingly, women students were excluded from the corps' training. For them, war work consisted of two hours a week in Red Cross activities, home nursing, sewing and knitting sessions, or emergency

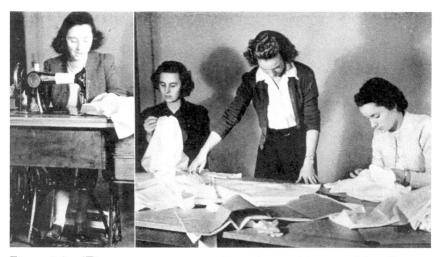

Figure 1.6   'The women too are serving... by machine... and hand'. (*Totem*, 1941.)

operations (see Figure 1.6).[54] During one of these hours, Gertrude Moore instructed the women students in keep fit classes.[55] They were further required to attend drill parades in the Armoury, though prejudice about women's capabilities continued to determine the kind of contributions they were allowed to make to the war effort. Carrying their knitting needles into class provoked strong irritation among some of the professors. And at blood donor clinics on campus women were not allowed to give blood (even though largely being in charge of taking it). 'Women are more difficult to bleed', the *Province* newspaper reported, 'their veins are not so prominent and they have a lesser amount of blood.'[56]

Women students were not, of course, the only group excluded from full participation in the war effort.[57] At the outbreak of the war, UBC had the highest number of Japanese Canadian students of any university in Canada, and, unlike most other Canadian universities, they were expected to join the COTC.[58] All this changed with the Pearl Harbour attack and when the Japanese Canadian students arrived back in school in 1942 after the Christmas break they were ordered by a Senate committee to turn in their uniforms. 'It's for their own protection as well as ours', said President Klinck. 'Japanese in uniform would be an unfortunate sight.'[59] The 70 Japanese Canadian students at UBC were thus abandoned, some finding other universities to attend, some being interned with their families in the BC interior or elsewhere in Canada. None of them were relieved from Federal government restrictions of movement until 1949.[60]

Formal physical education programmes developed rapidly during the war years as the Dominion government's National Fitness programme made expedient the establishment of a Department of Physical Education to train teachers and instructors. The student council of 1939 requested that physical education become compulsory in order to justify the demand for more athletic facilities, and when the Senate approved compulsory physical education for all first and second year students, the need for a Department of Physical Education and space for its activities was glaringly apparent. Supported by the Canadian Physical Education Association (CAPER), the AMS voted in favour of establishing such a department in 1943. Sherwood Lett was appointed chairman of the Senate committee to achieve that goal.[61] Two years later the Department was established under the leadership of former star UBC athlete and women's varsity basketball coach, Captain Robert (Bob) Osborne, who was recruited by the indefatigable Gordon Shrum from his job as an English teacher at a local high school. In 1946 a degree programme in physical education commenced.

Shortly thereafter, and in response to an increasing concern for population fitness as well as a growing lack of facilities for training and recreation, students and alumni joined to raise funds on campus for a larger, modern gymnasium. They claimed that a new gym was the most necessary and suitable building that could be erected as a memorial for British Columbia's veterans.[62] Space was certainly very limited for sport and physical training. The return of the veterans, proclaimed as the greatest single event in the history of university education at UBC,[63] brought over 5,000 students to the university by 1946, proportionately more than anywhere else in Canada. The result was a very 'tight pinch', said Bob Osborne, where 1,200 men squeezed in two hours a week of mandatory physical education classes in a gym now running on a 13-hour day basis. 'This schedule', he said, 'does not even include women [some small percentage of whom, of course were also veterans, though rarely acknowledged as such],[64] or the rest of UBC's 7,000 students who might be athletically inclined.'[65] Writing to her friend Miss Somers at the Margaret Eaton School in Toronto, one of the three women's physical education instructors, Jean Carmichael, commented on the pressing lack of space:

> Things are expanding on all sides at such a pace that buildings, grass, flowers and shrubs appear almost overnight. The campus is so filled with people between classes, it is practically invisible. We wonder where they all go when it rains – and they say it rains very frequently in the winter. Army huts are being converted into lecture rooms, labs, offices, snack bars, and residences. We teach in them, eat in them, and live in them and they are really quite nice and very necessary. There are more than 8,500 students in an institution filled to capacity by 2,000, so it is a bit difficult. We have about 800 women taking compulsory physical education and the first class of majors – a dozen girls – so our facilities are strained and the three of us are kept busy. We have classes in the gymnasium, in a hut and in the stadium as well as in a city swimming pool downtown. It will be grand when the new gymnasium is built.[66]

To alleviate the crush Bob Osborne provided plans to President McKenzie for a small extension to the old gymnasium, one which might be available for the several hundred women undergraduates. 'The Department would like to have a new modern gym', the President wrote in his list of building requests to the Premier John Hart in Victoria, 'but they have agreed to a less ambitious scheme of an extension to the existing gym.' 'Personally, I think this sum is too little', he said, 'but that is the amount given me by the Director of Physical Education.'[67] In fact, in McKenzie's list of needed buildings, ranked by relative importance, he placed the small extension to the gym number eight out of 11, before the Power Plant but after additions to Science, Arts, the Library, Residences, Applied Science, Home Economics and Agriculture.

The Soldier Returns to Sport: Memorials for the Living in the Aftermath of World War II

As the concept of memorials for the use of the living rather than to mourn the dead became increasingly popular in the immediate aftermath of the war, there was a growing sentiment favouring provision of specially dedicated playing fields, parks, swimming pools and glades of trees over the erection of monuments. 'The war is completely won', said the *Vancouver Sun* newspaper in 1945:

> ... and out of the mad delirium of joy should materialize the biggest sport boom ever seen in Canada. Athletes, from fighting fronts all over the world will be home again. The young man, who at age eighteen had to toss his athletics overboard to join the bigger fight will have a chance to develop. Together they will provide a brand of athletic endeavour not seen since the German hordes overran Poland ... soon the soldier will again find his place in sport.[68]

Thus the post-war decade's quest for monumentality as a form of cultural relevance focused particularly upon civic community facilities for leisure and sport. A national survey showed that approximately 90 per cent of Canadians favoured the building of recreational centres, gymnasiums, arenas and libraries as 'useful' memorials to those who had died during World War II and to help those survivors who were returning to civil life.[69] Not only were they perceived as immediately useful, there was a sentiment that servicemen who had become used to recreational facilities should not have 'a general let-down feeling' after the war.[70]

In 1944, the British Columbia Union of Municipalities at their annual meeting in Nelson asked that in place of hundreds of war memorials being built after the war, a series of universities be constructed along the international boundary line, 50 per cent to be in either country. 'War memorials', a spokesman said, 'have a sentimental value, but they increase no one's knowledge and mend no broken bones.'[71] In Vancouver, a proposal to build a memorial within a new main public library noted that:

> the indiscriminate erection of monumental memorials is no longer in tune with the times and the thoughts of the people ... a memorial should have a practical community utility, for the sacrifices our dead have made were inspired by the ideal of useful and effective service ... What could be better than a memorial dedicated to the service and re-establishment as citizens of the comrades ... who were spared to return to us.[72]

Other localities, such as Esquimalt, and Kitsilano in Vancouver, proposed large recreation centres, and war memorials were built for school activities at University School and Brentwood College in Victoria.[73] Citizens of Victoria proposed a civic arena and auditorium as a living, vital war arena,[74] and in North Vancouver the chairman of the school board begged for a memorial community centre with a much needed gymnasium and swimming pool.[75]

A special war memorial fund in honour of British Columbia Native Indians killed overseas fighting for Canada was announced in the *Daily Colonist* in November 1945. 'This war memorial will not be of stone or marble. It will take a practical form that will help to restore to the native Indian youth a pride in his race.' 'As remnants of a defeated race', the announcement continued condescendingly, 'Indians are losing their pride. Their culture has gone into the discard.' The proposed plan was to 'grant promising young Indians research scholarships in native arts and fine old handicrafts', as well as to collect handicrafts for demonstration and exhibition purposes.[76] It is not clear whether the fund ever came into being.

The student council at UBC first envisaged the construction of a war memorial as a permanent building on campus for the needs of students and returning soldiers on campus, and suggested a student union building, a student residence or a gymnasium as appropriate projects. 'Within any of these projects the special dedication of a room or section of the structure to the memory of Lt. R.H. "Hammy" Gray VC, DSC [was seen to] be essential', as was a sacred hall of heroes.[77] *The Vancouver News Herald* proposed that the names of former Thunderbird basketball greats – George Pringle, Pat Flynn, Art Willoughby and Doug Petlow – be placed, along with other UBC athletes who lost their lives during the war, in such a memorial hall.[78] Students and alumni, however, were insistent about the need for a new gymnasium and in January 1946 approved plans to construct a much needed gymnasium were unveiled by the Board of Governors.[79] The 'greatest campaign of the University's history' had begun.[80]

Designing the Million Dollar Gym: Modernism and Masculinity

PATRICIA VERTINSKY

The 'Million Dollar Gym' – 'A Palace of Sweat'

On the evening of 23 February 1951 it was reported that 'a useful and living memorial' came to life as the doors of the War Memorial Gym were first opened to a throng of several thousand students eager to attend the inaugural basketball game between UBC and Eastern Washington University. At the ensuing sock hop, the newly varnished floor was so springy that a folklore developed that layers of horse hair had been inserted beneath the wooden surface for flexibility. This was UBC's 'million dollar gym', the 'palace of sweat' – Canada's largest and most modern gymnasium, and recipient of the national Massey Silver Medal Design award (see Figure 2.1).[1] It was encouraging, said the jury, to see an established university strike into new paths.[2] Lauded for its simple dignity and imaginative quality, the UBC gym was voted the best of all recreational buildings erected in Canada since the end of the war.[3] The *Alumni Chronicle* claimed that it was 'probably the finest building the University has yet built on campus' and 'one of the finest college gyms on the continent'.[4]

The original design included four floors crammed with facilities for sport, recreation and training. In the sub-basement, a steam room, sun room, physiotherapy facilities, massage room, individual activities room and six bowling alleys were envisioned. On the next floor up, locker accommodation for 2,500 was planned, along with team rooms, a 42-seat snack bar, a small gymnasium for tumbling, wrestling and boxing, and a dance salon. On the main floor, space was allocated for the Physical Education Department, the Men's Athletic Directorate, the Memorial Lobby and the gymnasium proper. One floor above, a large common room was to be located overlooking the memorial hall. Vomitory corridors were to run the length of the building on both sides, with concession booths at each corner. The gymnasium itself was designed as a classic basketball gymnasium with roll-in glass backboards at each end – a brand new concept at the time. With a length of 160 ft and a width of 96 ft, it would have ample space for three full length basketball cross-courts or 12 badminton courts.

Figure 2.1   War Memorial Gymnasium, 'April 30, 1951'.

On three sides of the gym, permanent seating for spectators was designed to be accompanied later by sets of collapsible bleacher seats making possible a total seating of almost 7,000. With seats above, the players below, and an open space around the court, it was considered ideal for both the shooter and the spectator. The exterior of the building, resting on five slender white concrete columns, was to be painted green; blackish green at the base, set off by a lighter green from the base up to the glass walls. And, at the west end of the building an eight-lane swimming pool with seating accommodation for 700 was planned, with the Vancouver location of the British Empire Games of 1954 in mind. To ensure perfect lighting the entire west wall was to be made of glass.

The whole gymnasium project owed its inspiration to a motion at the student's council meeting on 26 November 1945 that a war memorial be considered in the form of a gymnasium and swimming pool with all the facilities to be included.[5] It was the same year that student hero Hammy Gray lost his life in a battle in the Pacific.[6] Chaired by Allan Ainsworth, President of the Alma Mater Society (AMS), student fundraising drives were begun, stimulated by provincial government pledges of $275,000 and the support of the Board of Governors. Students themselves pledged

$100,000, to be raised 'in the most concentrated appeal in the history of student canvassing'.[7] 'Let's build a better British Columbia, support the UBC's living war memorial', declared the student newspaper.[8] Using radio appeals, parades through the streets of Vancouver, golf tournaments, blind date dances, personal pledges and a variety of other campus fundraising activities, students raised a further $175,000. The required balance was taken care of by additions to students' AMS fees, a student council authorized loan of $150,000 and by local community sports organizations donating the proceeds of their games.[9] An ex-serviceman's club on campus known as the Jokers Club held a six-hour marathon roller-skating derby and proposed that co-eds at UBC sell kisses to swell the fund.[10] Junior Heather Blundell consented to be kissed by every man wishing to donate to the gymnasium fund.[11] The Jokers also sponsored an exhibition of goldfish swallowing, which received wide publicity.[12] Even the men's basketball team got into the act by staging a mock fire in the Varsity gymnasium.[13] President Al Westcott of UBC's branch of the Canadian Legion (No. 72) announced a 'buses to nowhere' project with proceeds going to the gym's fund-raising committee. The first trip in this project seems to have been a November trip when the bus unloaded its unsuspecting passengers in pastoral Bellingham for the evening night life.[14] Others found themselves dancing and dining at a local nightspot or driving up Grouse Mountain for an evening of square dancing at the Chalet.[15] *The Ubyssey* published a special issue with the appeal prominently displayed and distributed it downtown via a squad of fraternity men.[16]

On 11 November 1947, the Honourable E.C. Carson, provincial Minister of Public Works, turned the first sod during Remembrance Day ceremonies on the site selected by University authorities. The Minister was not the first choice of the War Memorial Gymnasium Committee, nor was the site.[17] In keeping with the theme of war memorial, their first inclination had been to send a letter to the American consul general in Washington to invite General Eisenhower to perform the laying of a corner stone. The Consul, however, left the AMS in little doubt that such a visit was neither desirable nor possible, given the fact that 'there are individuals who have spoken at the university whose political ideas are in my opinion contrary to yours and mine'.[18] Nor was the Governor-General persuaded to accept the committee's invitation to attend and promote the gym as a province-wide British Columbia war memorial.[19] In relation to the site, the first desire of the War Memorial Committee had been to locate the gym to the north-east of the original gym, forming a coherent unit with the old gym and the athletic stadium. The second site choice was finally settled at the corner of Wesbrook and University Boulevard, 'provided that the Board of Governors ensured that no building would ever be permitted to interrupt the view of the mountains from the memorial window'.[20]

The University-retained architects Sharp, Thompson, Berwick and Pratt were then asked to prepare drawings to include the desired facilities and organize tenders for construction. When tenders were called, however, the bad news emerged that because of increases in the cost of material and labour, the completed unit would be almost double the expected cost.[21] Despite efforts to raise more money and a further $200,000 contribution from the provincial government, the swimming pool, dance studio and a variety of other facilities were deleted from the contract before construction began. Indeed, there is abundant documentation in the University archives about the considerable sacrifices that had to be made to the original plans of the gym in the name of economy. Many of the facilities were never completed and the east wall of the gym was left as a temporary structure until such time as additions could be made (they never were). Accommodations around and beneath the gymnasium were substantially cut back. The promised extent and reverence of the memorial theme ultimately remained unfulfilled. The lawn and the cenotaph were never constructed, and instructions for a permanent view through the glass memorial wall to the inlet and mountains beyond were soon forgotten or eclipsed (what does happen to promises made in the dedication of funds for public buildings?). The plans for a cafeteria in the gym were eventually rescued by a donation from the Canadian Legion, who asked that any profits from the enterprise be channelled into a student scholarship fund, but even the cafeteria was to run into trouble and eventually be closed down by financial and staffing problems.[22]

In particular, the women's faculty and students fared badly. The trimming process prompted a lively competition between the male and female Directors of Physical Education at the time (who were both on the Gymnasium planning committee, as was the Head of the Department of Architecture, Frederic Lasserre). Writing from Toronto on 12 July 1947, female director Marian Henderson implored Dean Lasserre to 'guard my interests while I'm away. And also I think it would be well to remember that by 1950 one third of the students will be women. I want women's dressing room facilities now and no fooling.'[23]

On 3 August of the same year, Bob Osborne, forced to make dramatic cuts in the original design, instructed University architect Ned Pratt:

> I am writing to suggest certain courses of action that may be considered in view of the necessity of revising plans for the War Memorial Gym.
>
> The following personal opinions are coloured by my knowledge of the various developments of the Memorial committee since its inception and by my desire to see a building constructed as soon as possible which will be of greatest service to all parties concerned.

Although from a utilitarian point of view it would seem sensible to eliminate, or at least de-emphasize the Memorial Lobby, I feel that any serious deviation from the original plans would constitute a betrayal of trust. Therefore, against my personal wishes and the interests of the School of Physical Education I recommend (1) adherence in principle to the initial overall design, including the swimming pool, the Memorial Lobby and the first and second units of a gymnasium and (2) construction immediately of a modified building.

I further recommend, on the basis of numerous discussions with Miss Marian Henderson that accommodation for women be kept to an absolute minimum in the interests of economy and administrative efficiency. This presupposes that the women will have exclusive use of the present gymnasium.

He goes on to list a number of suggestions for consideration: '... according to plan B there would be no provision for women's offices. In plan C, eliminate women's dressing rooms and shower rooms. In Plan D eliminate the small gymnasium as well.'[24]

Two years later, Marian Henderson had little alternative but to capitulate, though she fought hard to nail down the promise that Bob Osborne would grant alternative facilities for the women in the old gymnasium. Writing to Pratt:

Like Bob I feel that the most important thing at this time is to get something, anything started. ... any economy that could be realized through Bob's suggestions I would support ... I know it is rank heresy but Bob's idea about a supplementary field house ... really appeals to me. The women have always been more interested in the functional end than in the spectator angle. Of course I realize that there is a War Memorial Committee and that it is their wish that must be fulfilled.[25]

Difficulties also arose during the construction phase, highlighting issues of race and ethnicity in relation to 'which' Canadian soldiers were to be memorialized and 'whose' body was to be educated in the spaces of the gym. Alerted to certain restrictive conditions on the hiring of workers, the President of the Alma Mater Society, J.J. Sutherland, felt compelled to write the following on 21 July 1949 to the architects – Sharp, Thompson, Berwick and Pratt – regularly retained by the University:

This is to confirm my recent telephone conversation with you regarding the deletion of the clause forbidding the hiring of persons of Asiatic or African descent on the construction of the War Memorial Gymnasium. We feel that this restriction would be particularly objectionable in connection with a building dedicated to the memory of British Columbia servicemen, many of whom were Canadians of Chinese descent. I trust that you have sent out the necessary addendum.[26]

A Courageous Stand for Modern Architecture

'It must always be remembered that the most forceful way in which the university can express its current spirit to the community and to future generations is by the construction of well laid out beautiful buildings, consistent with the highest principles of architecture.'[27]

What was particularly interesting about the campaign was the 'courageous stand for modern architecture in the new War Memorial Gym' taken by the student building committee and other influential groups and individuals on campus. Architecture functions as a potential stimulus for movement, real or imagined, hence the unique architectural and spatial arrangements of the gymnasium would become an incitement to action, a particular setting for movement and interaction.[28] In looking at what the building tells us about the place of bodies within and around, it is important to explore how the architects and planners of the gymnasium became, in a sense, 'partners in a dialogue with the body', and how their views on design and society came to reflect an acute sense of how the body should be looked at, and what it could and should become through appropriate discipline and education: '[Gym], body and mind are in continuous interaction, the physical structure, equipment, social conventions and mental images [of the gym] at once enabling, moulding, informing, and constraining the activities and ideas which unfold within its bounds.'[29]

The original architectural design, a collegiate gothic-style gymnasium to match other buildings on campus was challenged early on by critics who contended that twentieth-century recreation for twentieth-century men and women was unrelated in function and spirit to a fifteenth-century architectural form. This form, Ormonde Hall reported in the *Graduate Chronicle*:

> ... was an anachronism as applied to a gymnasium and to a university devoted to the discovery of truth and to the training of minds and bodies fit for leadership in the tasks of today and tomorrow. Such architectural deception would kill the dignity and integrity of a war memorial. It would lack in spirit and could not significantly express anything – certainly not the spirit of the post-World War II student.[30]

Clearly these critics had in mind a particular approach to physical culture and sporting excellence which was to be expressed within and from outside the building, and it included a desire to memorialize in a 'modern' way the courageous struggles of soldiers lost in both world wars – the athlete/soldier/citizen about whom we spoke in Chapter 1. Ormonde Hall further suggested in his article that the determination of a contemporary architectural style was one of the most pressing problems facing UBC at mid century. Hitherto, he said, the campus had been tied to an (albeit 'mongrel' derivation) of a master plan 'commonly known as the grand composition' which attempted 'to corset the pulsating body of an unpredictable living creature within massive frames of stone and architectural fetters'. To him and others around him it was obviously out of harmony with modern thinking, modern education and the modern body.

This post-war moment of anxiety over traditional design was a precursor to an era of enthusiasm over what would be called high modernism, and an important wing of this movement appealed to the image of rationality incorporated in the machine. The eclipse of history by memory profoundly influenced modern commemorative architecture, and modernism, in its flight from tradition and history and pursuit of rational utility over past traditions. To be sure, modernism looked quite different depending on where one located oneself (and British Columbians often talked of their physical isolation and distinctiveness), but the modernist principles of scientific management and the imposition of rational order permeated societies on both sides of the Atlantic. The ruling ideology of the day was still forward looking and progressive as Vancouver modernist architects enthusiastically sought to adopt and simplify European modernist efforts to improve society through new applications of science, technology and the arts.

This was the positivistic, technocentric and rationalistic period when houses, apartment blocks and cities could be openly conceived of as machines for living in.[31] More broadly, many modernist architects of the time believed sincerely that architecture could and must assume a central role in the construction and enrichment of a new social order.[32] Their modernist ethos promised to address urgent social questions, as well as personal architectural aspirations, through the conception of the modern architect as a social engineer focused on equity, economy of form and construction, and community-building values.[33] Thus, in some respects, the modernist movement emerged as the accepted architecture of liberal democracies and welfare states, even though from some other points of view it would become little more than a thin veneer over a utilitarian box.[34] According to the President of the University, Norman Mackenzie, modern functional design would bring beauty, utility and health to the campus and it was no accident that the most notable modernist buildings were erected at UBC, the nursery for British Columbia and therefore Vancouver talent.[35] His appointment of Frederic Lasserre, mountain-climbing aficionado and former Navy officer as head of the new Department of Architecture and

Planning was directed toward that goal, and Ned Pratt, pioneer modernist architect, would help effect it.[36]

Lasserre, who had enhanced his architectural training in Zurich and the University of Toronto with practical experience at Tecton, the foremost modernist architectural firm in London, was lured to UBC from his position at McGill's School of Architecture. His ardent drive to promote modernist architecture in Vancouver was tragically cut short by his death in a climbing accident in the English Lake District in 1961 while on a Canada Council Fellowship to study British public housing. His influence, however, was substantial, and at his memorial service one of the speakers claimed that the War Memorial Gymnasium was a veritable expression of his personality, looking out as it did onto the mountains he had loved so much.[37] Through his eyes the modernist architect was a new kind of 'planner' for city and community – a builder of sound, economical structure and promoter of the cultural advancement of society. Modern, he had said, with an approving nod to the values of youth and progress, meant honestly expressing the needs of today through the frank and economical use of structure and materials – and he was determined to see this expression at UBC.[38] With Ned Pratt, partner in the firm of Sharp, Thompson, Berwick and Pratt, who was also an athlete and Olympic medal-winning rower, the gym took shape as the University was pressed to take a courageous stand for modernist architecture – a style that was to act as a metaphor for the modern bodies produced within it.

The architectural firm of Sharp, Thompson, Berwick and Pratt that had been retained by the University for many years was well aware of the international trend toward modernism, though found themselves in somewhat of a bind. In a letter to Fred Lasserre, and clearly worried by his public criticisms of his firm's recent work on the new Faculty of Applied Science building and the generally eclectic nature of many of their current designs, senior partner Charles Thompson tried to explain that the firm had been constrained for over 30 years by UBC's insistence upon collegiate gothic-style buildings (what Dean Sedgewick delighted in calling 'bastard' gothic). 'Modern architectural development', wrote Thompson, 'has quite naturally, during the interim, shorn itself free of these eclectic aspirations, and one of the major problems confronting us is to bring these somewhat conflicting interests into harmony. We feel that the break, if approved, should be evolutionary and progressive rather than abrupt.'[39] Lasserre disagreed, responding diplomatically but immediately by insisting on being included at the earliest stages of new designs at UBC. 'You must decide', he told Thompson, 'between imitation gothic or frankly and honestly modern.' Furthermore, he complained, 'I hate coming in at the tail end when the only consideration should be as to how quickly we can get started on actual erection.'[40] Indeed, Lasserre placed considerable pressure on President Mackenzie to embark on a complete reassessment of the University's

building plan and he worked diligently to actualize his views.[41] It was perhaps
not coincidental that the firm of Sharp, Thompson, Berwick and Pratt offered
the Department of Architecture $1000 for student prizes that year.[42]

The need for economy also contributed to the appeal of modernist
architecture, and not surprisingly, in the aftermath of war, economy seems
to have been a main concern. Gordon Shrum, in one of his many roles as
domineering head of the UBC grounds and buildings committee, pointed out
that in every (post-war) building on campus the keynote was on economy.
'Modern functional architecture must be applied', he said. 'Tile and
concrete finishing can be used ... factory type windows can replace other
types ... We should not put up buildings in terms of their lasting only 30
years, as they may well have to last 50 years.'[43] Harsh economic realities
certainly seem to have helped focus Thompson on the merits of modernism.
He turned over responsibility of the gymnasium to his more modernist
partner Ned Pratt, who, assisted by Fred Brodie, rejected Thompson's earlier
truncated neo-romanesque gym design and sought more current ideas about
swimming pools and gymnasia from the *Architectural Forum* and in
discussions with the Alumni association.[44] Pratt was particularly interested
in new design technologies, though when he wrote to a number of journals
for advice about reinforced concrete construction methods and gymnasium
and swimming pool design information he found it very hard to come by in
the aftermath of the war. Those cost comparisons with which he was
provided from other architectural firms showed the UBC gym estimates
coming in extraordinarily cheaply at 30 cents a cubic foot.[45] The resulting
design, says Windsor-Liscome, was 'a powerfully deliberate, functionalist
solution highlighting the four staircases, the clerestory gymnasium lighting,
and the glazed concourse/Memorial Hall'. The structure was a large
'floating pan' on slender reinforced concrete columns that resulted in
unobstructed sightlines from the bleachers on either side of the capacious
gymnasium.[46] But the inside was very bare indeed – shorn of its luxuries,
even its necessities for the functions it was expected to serve. Pressures of
budget, even Lasserre admitted, could substitute bleak utilitarianism in
place of enlightened functionalism.[47]

The War Memorial Gym thus became one of the first examples of
modernism on the UBC campus in 1951, a unique example of modernist
architecture heralding the emergence of a distinctive post-war movement in
modernist architecture in Vancouver led by a vigorous group of artists and
architects including Arthur Erickson as well as Ned Pratt and Fred
Lasserre.[48] From the point of view of its designers, the new gym was an apt
response to modernist enthusiasm. It was a superb statement of modernist
values, a lucid resolution of structure, plan and aesthetics.[49] The focus was
on light and space, the design hard-edged with stark lines, flush walls, right-
angled corners and bold geometric patterns.[50] In particular, the dominant

machine ethic was very apparent: hygienic and simple, stripped of ornament and reference to the past, memorializing yet erasing in one fell swoop. Memory, monument and modernity merged to become one:

> The inverted roof focuses spectator attention on the large springy floor. Throughout the $750,000 structure the emphasis is on glass which is both attractive and … cheap. Herculite doors, a ramp-like entrance, projecting stairs, and an over-all hangar-like appearance lend the gym an impression of striking modernity, which is in direct contrast to the staid conservative architecture of other campus buildings.[51]

Even today, 50 years later:

> The War Memorial Gym appears to float rather than sit rooted to the ground. The building's bulk increases as it rises, and its bottom circumference is painted a dark grey to make it 'disappear'. Different portions of the building can be identified from the outside. The stairwell looks like a boxy rectangle added on to the corner, and the entrance foyer is its own rectangle at the front. Great X-shaped steel trusses are visible through large swaths of window panes. They show how the frame structure places the building's weight on a few points.[52]

How, then, did this 'brave new world' of modernist architecture and its exemplification of the hallmark qualities of equity, efficiency and community affect the training of bodies in our gymnasium? Is it not the architect, says David Harvey, who has been most deeply enmeshed throughout history in the production and pursuit of utopian ideals and spatial practices … the architect who struggles to open spaces for new possibilities, for future forms of social life? Should we not be reminded, for example, that memorials reflect, not only communal remembrance, but also the memorial designers' own time and place, their training and values, as well as the fact that no architect is free of context or ambiguity?[53] While professional design discourse is an important part of the generation and propagation of ideas, the dominance of such discourse may not fully benefit the users in the proposed space. Architects may conventionally focus their attention on buildings as visible, substantial entities considered in isolation, but the places they create are palpable territories of social activities and meanings.[54]

The Influence of Le Corbusier

'Few photographs of Le Corbusier's buildings show people in them, and where they do, women almost never occupy the same space as men.'[55]

In particular, the aesthetic design of the gym owed much to the foundational influence upon modernist architecture of Le Corbusier, a French architect considered by some to be the most important of the twentieth century, though denigrated by anti-modernists such as Lewis Mumford as a 'crippled genius' and a sexist who warped the work of a whole generation.[56] Whatever one's leaning it seems difficult to understand architecture in the twentieth century, or Canadian modernism in particular, without first coming to terms with Le Corbusier. He dominated the architectural world from the 1920s until his death in 1965, and in his challenge to create a truly relevant form for the age he became the greatest influence on Canadian architectural students at mid-century. 'I am captivated', Arthur Erickson wrote as a student, 'by the cleanness, the airiness, the frankness of this new architecture.'[57]

Le Corbusier was convinced that the bold new industrial age deserved a brand-new architecture where technology would be the progressive force to restore harmony and order to the problems of contemporary urbanism.[58] I will throw out everything from the past, he declared in *L'Art Décoratif*, while in his numerous works he ruminated on the human condition in the modern age, believing he was helping to give shape to the thought and sensibilities of his times.[59] 'I bring into the domain of architecture propositions which call into service all the techniques of modern times, but whose final aim is to go beyond simple utility. The indispensable purpose is to give to the men of the machine age the joys of the heart and of health' (at the same time suppressing any notions of domesticity).[60]

In essence, Le Corbusier's legacy was to seek inspiration in traditional forms and translate them into buildings and materials that he thought were appropriate to a modern scientific and technological age – connecting, he hoped, the best of the new with the best of the old.[61] History, he declared, was his only real master, though Jane Jacobs, in *The Death and Life of Great American Cities*, has since deflated such pomposity. He flattered himself that he was designing for a new age, she says, although he was not. Rather he was merely adapting in a shallow fashion reforms that had been a response to nostalgic yearnings for a bygone, simpler life.[62]

Le Corbusier found his true beauty in geometry – the language of man. Indeed the notion that architecture arises spontaneously from the conjunction of utility and geometry was a characteristic Corbusian construction.[63] 'Geometrical figures are naturally more beautiful than irregular ones', he wrote in *Vers une Architecture*, celebrating the Parthenon as the supreme example of geometric comprehension.[64] Architecture, then, was a discipline that defined its boundaries according to the workings of orthogonality, that is the right-angledness of the line, and Le Corbusier was insistent in calling for the power of the right angle and the straight line in his designs. Human order, as he saw it, was a geometrical thing, a male product, the mark of great civilizations. 'The streets are at right angles to one another and the mind is liberated'[65] was one of his favourite sayings. By contrast, disorder, 'that medieval tangle of twisted streets and twisted roofs' showed only weakness and limitations. It was the right angle that was the sum of the forces that kept the world in equilibrium – the (male) regulating line that was a guarantee against (female) wilfulness. 'Man, by reason of his very nature practices order; that his actions and his thoughts are dictated by the straight line and the right angle.'[66]

In describing the configurations of modernity, Le Corbusier also expressed the architecture of modern sports training and the masculine culture in which the spatial rules of sport were defined and developed. Such a spatial configuration, according to Eichberg was related to a sportized, geometric, enclosed sense of space associated with a distinctively male version of nationality and a functional image of sport as a planned, controlled and regulated activity.[67] Such activity produces results in the cognitive hierarchy of strategy, tactics and technique, and once it is decided, the sportive way leads directly to the goal.[68] 'The human being steps straight ahead,' he said, 'because he has an aim. He knows where to go, he has decided on one direction, and he strides resolutely forward. The right angle is the instrument which is necessary and sufficient for action, because it serves to determine the space in a completely unequivocal fashion.'[69] 'Look about you – look beyond the seas and the centuries – and tell me if man has ever acted upon anything but the right angle, and does there exist anything around you but right angles.'[70]

Such statements underscored a preoccupation with the straight line and the right angle that was central to twentieth-century Nazi and fascist body culture, focused on impelling the race forward directly to their goal and avoiding curved lines which could be seen as dysfunctional, feminine and deviant.[71] In this view curves were simply a waste of space, time and energy and a potentially subversive element in the pursuit of power and the rituals of correct body training. Indeed, most extreme forms of technical-bureaucratic and machine rationality, notes Harvey, combined perfectly with the myth of Aryan superiority and the blood and soil of the fatherland.[72]

The modernists' statements about the human being, its straight lines and right angles were, in fact, based on societal practice and a notion of hegemonic masculinity in the world of sports and sports places at mid-century. To Le Corbusier and his fellow modernists, the widespread gothic style of gymnasium architecture on North American campuses could never be considered appropriate for athletic development in higher education. It was, he said, 'caged, chlorotic, and spiritless' – not in any way helpful in building supermen.[73] Modernist architecture, by contrast, invited the perpetuation of life itself, encouraging renewal, change, and rejuvenation. When sport and functionalism went hand in hand the most appropriate shape for a gymnastium or sports field had to be rectangular, incorporating the geometrical logic of Foucault's panopticism, the citadel or the prison, with their central perspective and their view of power.[74] Seen from this perspective, a modernist, rectangular gymnasium designed to promote organized movement and team sports was an inspired choice for a war memorial celebrating the virility and power of the young student/soldier/athlete who had gone to battle for Canada. Modernist design, in a Foucauldian sense, thus became one of the major disciplinary means of power by which modern bodies were to be produced. It may not be an accident, says Samuel, that 'the esthetic flourished in a decade which may retrospectively be seen as the Indian summer of the working man'.[75] To be modern was not a fashion, it was a state.[76]

Based on Le Corbusier's conceptions, with his passionate adherence to straight lines and Newtonian view of the body as a machine, a gymnasium logically had to be a machine for training the body in – and the shape of the gymnasium had to reflect this function. Man, as a geometric animal in a closed system could be viewed as a surrogate machine in an industrial age.[77] 'Our skeletons are alike, our muscles are in the same places and perform the same functions; dimensions and mechanism are thus fixed.'[78] And by machine, Le Corbusier meant anything used by man to perform a function, and whose function could be identified by its shape.[79] A house, therefore, was a machine for living in, just as an armchair was a machine for sitting in, and a gymnasium a machine for training the body in. The shape of his buildings were thus expected to reflect these mechanical functions precisely, and in *Vers une Architecture*, with its many mechanical metaphors and analogies, his functional aesthetic of modernism and the machine was most fully laid out.[80] 'We must invent the modern building like a giant machine … the house of cement, iron and glass, without curves or … ornament, rich only in the inherent beauty of its lines and modelling, extraordinarily brutish in its mechanical simplicity.'[81]

Taking what he saw as the possibilities inherent in the body machine he projected them onto his building designs for a typical, standardized, normal man, based of course on classical ideas. 'The Greek scale, the Greek measurement of man, the human presence in all the Greek works has stayed with me always', he said in one of his final interviews before his unfortunate death by drowning in the Mediterranean.[82] After all, it was in the gymnasium in Athens that a boy's body had been moulded, strengthened for manhood and ordered for the needs of the state. The Greek philosophy that enamoured Le Corbusier had visualized a complicated architecture of exclusion and difference on the split between public and private, inside and outside, men and women. The anatomical differences between men and women had been translated into the shapes of their living spaces – women's reproductive organs internal like their place in the home, men's genitals conspicuous and expressive of desire and aggression.[83] Geometrical regularity had been essential in the Greek stadium and in the straight lines of the gymnasium. Straightening the body meant shaping it and reflecting the desire for morality and control. Walking with long straight strides along straight streets and in straight buildings expressed manliness and dominance of the environment.[84] Thus guided by his passion for the Greeks and enthusiasm to restore natural order to urban chaos by using geometry and tradition in his designs, Le Corbusier sought in his modern machines to create forms of spatial perfectability premised on a pure male body type conceived of as the youthful, normal or classical body.[85]

Luis Carranza notes that by reading the architectural works of Le Corbusier through a feminist lens we can see how they were loaded with codes and systems of meaning that reflected his attitudes about men's and women's place (and space) in society.[86] Le Corbusier, he suggests, objectified and demonstrated an aversion toward women in his designs, seeing them as inferior and disregarding their needs in his architectural production. In his drawings and paintings, women are portrayed as large and muscular, their long hair hiding man-like faces. The female genitals are always disguised or absent. One can only tell they are women by their huge breasts and the titles of his compositions. By contrast, the male gaze was one of the driving forces that controlled his architecture. Modern architecture was the realm of men, and his portrayal of men reinforced stereotypes and attitudes about male virility, power and female subjection.

Underpinning the entire architectural programme of Le Corbusier was the universal proportional measure he proposed in the 'Modulor' – a system of measurements he devised in 1942 based on the ideal male body, which he identified with that of a six-foot Englishman. 'I first designed for the normal height of a Frenchman', he told an interviewer shortly before his death. 'Then all of a sudden I realised that the Anglo-Saxon couldn't pass through the modulor doors 1.75 metres high. So I made the doors 1.83 metres high.'[87] More accurately, Curtis suggests, 'the Modulor man was built like a Greek Kouros statue with bulging thighs and a slender waist, though he had obviously also just come from a few hours vigorous cycling around a roof-top gymnasium track'.[88] Essentially, the Modulor was supposed to be a harmonic measure to the human scale, universally applicable to architecture and mechanics, and it echoed Vitruvian, Renaissance and other famous systems of proportion. The 6-foot man with his arm upraised was inserted into a square which in turn was subdivided according to the golden mean. Various scales within the square allowed the Modulor to give harmonious proportion to everything from door handles to the heights and widths of urban spaces. More than a tool, it was a philosophical emblem of Le Corbusier's commitment to architectural order and the regulating lines of classical Greek architecture.[89]

But metaphorically what was being regulated was the male body. If a building was, for Le Corbusier, a machine for living in, then its occupants would logically have to be man-machines.[90] The machine, in Freudian terms, represented all that was male: activity and power. By claiming that his buildings were machines, and hence a mechanism for classification, Le Corbusier was able to assign to them a gendered distinction as male, since a traditionally designed house would be passive by nature and therefore female. Beatriz Colomina has nicely shown how Le Corbusier somehow always managed to imprison or 'hem in' the woman in his modernist designs. As an architect he liked to show the mastery of the feminized body as colonized territory – the prostitute as conquered by machine. Traces of domesticity in his designs were rare. Few photos of his buildings show people in them, and in those few, women always look away from the camera and almost never occupy as much space as the men.[91] His windows carefully enclosed and framed the landscape outside, allowing man to analyse and control it visually. 'A window is a man', he said. 'It stands upright. It allows the gaze of domination over the exterior world.'[92] Thus his buildings seemed to be specifically designed with an eye to those who respected order, governance and dominance over unruly (womanly) nature. Even the relationship to the ground on which they were built was oppositional, using pillars or stilts to impose order on an unruly and curvaceous landscape. The dominance of machine over nature (what Francis Bacon viewed as 'a common harlot' whose wildness needed to be squeezed and controlled) could be depicted by siting the buildings in a way that was as far removed from the natural flow of the landscape as possible. As a frame for a picture, then, the gymnasium could be seen as producing the picture by domesticating the landscape outside and classifying the views it collected within its spaces.[93]

Modernist architecture thus structured and defined the social spaces in which different gendered identities could be rehearsed, performed and made visible in the War Memorial Gymnasium. Gender needs space to develop, change or be reproduced, and one could see that, in many respects, the new 'brutalist' architecture, as some called it, was deeply masculine in its biases, woven into the very fabric of modernity and modernism. This was not at all surprising given that spatial and temporal practices are never neutral in social affairs, and sports as well as architecture are not neutral either, especially in relation to gender.[93] The human occupancy of the sports landscape typically reveals through its highly gendered character the dominance of men in sport and its organization.[95] Competitive sport, like warfare, is historically a masculine phenomena (even though women can, and indeed do, participate in this historical expression of masculinity). Brian Pronger says 'boys raised on competitive sport learn to desire, learn to make connections according to the imperative to take space away from others and jealously guard it for themselves'.[96] Basketball, for example, which was to become the central activity in the War Memorial Gym, is a sport where the quest to forcefully take and maintain physical territory by bodily invasion is central to the game. Sports landscapes can, therefore, be appropriately read as masculine landscapes, and it has to be admitted that when it was first constructed the War Memorial Gymnasium appeared to be a very male place. Its modernist designers were male. Its sporting intentions were male.[97] Its very appearance was quintessentially male.

'Power Geometries': Disciplining the Gendered Body in the Spaces of the War Memorial Gymnasium

PATRICIA VERTINSKY

'What gives a place its specificity is not some long internalized history but the fact that it is constructed out of a particular constellation of social relations, meeting and weaving together at a particular locus.'[1]

There is a Harvard convention that each department should have a unique identity and stand in its own building. Higher education at the University of British Columbia followed no such convention, though the buildings that stand now each tell their own disciplinary, political and educational stories. The triumph of modernism and modernist architecture in the post-war years, of which the War Memorial Gymnasium was an outstanding example, came to a symbolic end in North America, some say, when the Pruit-Igoe urban housing development in St Louis was dynamited in 1972 because it had become an uninhabitable environment for the low-income people it housed.[2] It was an expensive lesson for standardized, modernist urban housing schemes, some of which had proved to be disorienting, inhospitable and socially destructive – seriously damaging the urban fabric. Critics claimed that these building schemes epitomized the ability of modernist architecture to depress the spirits of those who inhabited them.

This was the nether side of high modernism, says David Harvey, where the subterranean celebration of corporate bureaucratic power and rationality, disguised as the worship of the efficient machine that would embody all human aspirations, meant that inhabitants could no longer modify their environments to meet their personal needs.[3] Following the heyday of modernism, there was an increasing feeling in urban design that architects might have more to learn from people in the context of their own landscapes than from abstract theoretical ideas. Perhaps it was time, some critics said, to build for people rather than for men and to reverse the surreptitious consolidation of conservative positions that seemed to have become entrenched through modernism.[4] Nor, they continued, was the straight line acceptable any longer as the one given rationality. It needed to make way for new forms of non-linear architectural strategies in an increasingly postformal, postmodern world.[5]

Modernism had reified a passion for large geometric spaces and perspectives, for uniformity and the power of the straight line. Le Corbusier had always thought big – big buildings, big open spaces, big urban highways.[6] And in many respects modernism had magnified the oppressive dimensions of the belief in linear progress, absolute truth and technical rationality. Fred Lasserre clearly had begun to think so, for he suggested that the modernist designs of educational buildings, like a number of new schools in Vancouver, might be pushing a fundamentally technical view of education too far. Discussing one of a series of newly built elementary schools in 1952, he worried. 'One will wonder why the building seems so impersonal, why it lacks childlike humour, and physical and psychological scale, and why it is so very diagrammatic ... so unlike the average child's whimsicality.'[7] The effects of a fundamentally modernist logic upon post-war educational buildings in the area were certainly inescapable. Edmund King, chief architect of the Vancouver School Board in the 1950s, embraced modernist designs with the enthusiasm of a convert, preferring massed rectangular buildings and standardized and economical materials. He believed that his newly built schools should mould as well as reflect the pedagogy within them. Embracing the broad acceptance of the technical efficiencies and economies embedded in modernism, he declared that schools 'should be efficient ... simplicity in design, without basements, attics and ornamentation ... utilitarian ... with fluorescent lighting units and tile on the floor'.[8] Back at UBC, an article in the student newspaper refused to cede value to this efficiency. Bemoaning the scholastic shortcomings of incoming students it blamed the high schools for becoming 'ever more modern, less effective'[9]

Sport architecture such as the War Memorial Gymnasium was just such a monument of modernity – a citadel in Le Corbusier's words in which a man could feel secure,[10] but a place nevertheless that increasingly lacked space for the burgeoning needs of sports and athletics at UBC. When the War Memorial Gymnasium was completed in 1951 it stood at the heart of the body of the Point Grey campus – a heartbeat away from the homely and popular Varsity stadium with its wooden grandstand, adjacent to McGinnes field (donated to the University as a memorial to fallen soldier William Eugene McGinnes by his father),[11] and not many steps away from the old gymnasium – soon to be rechristened the Women's Gymnasium. Its centrality on the campus, at the centre of men's athletics, celebrated Canada as a land of sports and sportsmen, and encouraged the public display of physical masculinities. This was where early, sports-minded leaders at the University of British Columbia, among them Sherwood Lett, Gordon Shrum, Norman MacKenzie,[12] Fred Lasserre and Bob Osborne expected to find affairs of the body – for a fit and sound body was central to those civilizing and elevating impulses required to educate Canadian citizens, mould their characters and harden their resolve for service and leadership.[13] It was where students flocked to see the

Thunderbirds vanquish their opponents on the basketball court, where they cheered the 'spectacle' of the visiting Harlem Globe Trotters and gaped at the wizardry of the Chocolate Co-eds (an All-American women's basketball team called a 'negro powerhouse' by the student newspaper).[14] Perhaps they met their future spouses at a Saturday night hop celebrating the crowning of the Homecoming queen. For them, in its early years, the gymnasium provided a 'sense of place' that reflected their particular ways of seeing the world and the stories they wanted to tell themselves about themselves.[15] It was a place that held a territory of meanings, representing the continued reproduction of proper places for everyone.[16] But it was also a place that restricted access to its spaces, limiting the educational, sporting and career opportunities of women – and others – in a variety of ways that we will now explore.[17]

Karl Raitz invites us to think of sporting places like gymnasia as a kind of theatre in which the behaviours of those who participate or watch alter both the nature of the activity and the place where it is practised.[18] The gymnasium, like the theatre, shapes the play, while also providing a context for different experiences and social interactions within and beyond it. In his many studies on sporting space, Henning Eichberg reminds us too that the nature of sport (and physical activity) has always, to some extent, been determined by place and space, and that it has itself produced specific forms of place and space.[19] Subject, context and sporting practices, then, all come together as necessary ingredients of a 'sense of place' in the changing landscape of higher education.

Places are made through power relations which construct the rules, define the boundaries and create spaces with certain meanings in which some relationships are facilitated, others discouraged – what Doreen Massey calls social relations stretched out. These boundaries are both social and spatial. They mark belonging and exclusion – who belongs to a place and who may be excluded – as well as the location or site of particular embodied and didactic experiences.[20] Spatial and temporal practices, we are reminded, are never neutral in social affairs. In the gymnasium, bodies and places are woven together through intimate webs of social and spatial rules that were made by and made embodied sporting subjects.[21]

So when we ask who produced the sporting and didactic culture within the walls of the newly built War Memorial Gym, and for whom, we must turn to the study of relationships, and when we ask why it was produced we must turn to questions of power.[22] Just as Eichberg has drawn conclusions about the patterns and dynamics of physical culture from historical changes in sport architecture, so we can usefully trace the 'power geometries' – the effects of multiple configurations of space and social relations within and around the War Memorial Gym which provided a sense of place in higher education. To speak of power geometries, then, is to focus upon the shape and structure of the spaces in which lives are given meaning in particular locations over time.[23] 'Power geometries are powerful forces, forces that are themselves continually transformed through unrelenting struggle, whether that struggle is open rebellion against the situations that govern our movement and give form to our thoughts, or the more mundane everyday accommodation to ongoing cultural, political and economic change.'[24]

Gendering the Spaces of the War Memorial Gym – A Process of Exclusion

'It's really quite simple. People use sport to connect with those with whom they share pre-existing common identities, whether it be class, religion, neighborhood, gender, race, cultural preferences and so on. They also use sport to distinguish themselves from those with whom they have little in common ... Sport is a site of social distinction.'[25]

Fred Hume, local historian of UBC Athletics, recently wrote nostalgically about the War Memorial Gymnasium in the Athletic department's student newspaper, *The Point*:

> Over the years, War Memorial has been the scene of many events and activities. But most of all it has been 'home' giving us that special feeling when rival players claim how difficult it is to beat the Birds when in the confines of the War Memorial. A tribute to those who gave their lives serving Canada, an example of what community initiative and participation can produce, the palace of sweat has been home to numerous heroes and champions ... War Memorial remains center stage at UBC.[26]

But while the gym gave a real sense of home to many, that 'sense of place' called home has also been the focus of much work by feminists who have seen 'home' as a site of disenfranchisement for women, just as the sporting arena has so often been. In its daily usage, the War Memorial Gym was not a place for everyone, and it was certainly not always home to many female students, athletes and staff who were excluded in many ways from the social and working spaces of the gym (except for the secretarial and janitorial work, that is, where women occupied a subordinate service role). Nor did it feel like home to many gay and lesbian athletes, students and coaches who felt pressed to hide their sexuality in the locker rooms, at team gatherings and even in the boardroom.

Feminist scholars have complained how built landscapes, the landscapes of homes, public spaces, and, not surprisingly, sporting and physical culture arenas, have been remarkable in their desire to confine, control and exclude women. Built environments have participated in the construction of gendered identities, often reflecting received wisdom about gender roles and reproducing the flawed logic of simplistic binary oppositions such as masculine/feminine, public/private, indoors/outdoors and home/work in the conception, allocation and meaning of spaces for male and female activities. Men first built a world for their own purposes, says Elizabeth Grosz, and in doing so they sought to take up all the space for themselves.[27] After all, a proving ground for masculinity can only be preserved as such by the exclusion of women from their activities, and this has been all too readily apparent in the world of sport.

From the beginning, the spaces of modern sports facilities such as gymnasia were sexed spaces involved in the construction of sexed bodies. In some respects, the indoor gymnasium was structurally related to and arose simultaneously with the prison, the asylum and the schoolhouse in the context of a spatial disciplining and functionalization of social life.[28] In schools and colleges, gymnasia were initially seen as a useful tool for securing discipline among particular groups of students and for sanctioning new styles of behaviour in a place set apart for sport and exercise.[29] They were starkly evocative of the ways in which gender boundaries could be policed through access to the facilities within, their design and placement, prescribed curricula, attitudes of coaches and teachers, and administrative and legal policies. When resources permitted, many educational institutions built separate gymnasia for men and women, though all too frequently the girl's gym was smaller, less well equipped, and lacking in spectator space.[30] Furthermore, of all the disciplines, physical education with its central focus on the body was the most strongly influenced by echoes of Rousseau's view of biology as the root of gender assignment and as justification for separate educational/physical and sporting arrangements based on male power and dominance and female frailty and constraint. Through sex-coded activities, physical educators were able to mark and patrol the borders between masculinity and femininity.[31] Hence perceived physical differences and abilities formed the bedrock upon which physical education programmes were constructed, as well as the spaces in which they were conducted, and they proved remarkably resistant to change.[32]

Marie Haidt, Director of Women's Athletics at Penn State University in Pennsylvania, complained bitterly and publicly about this lack of spaces for women's athletics. She was one of many women physical educators in North America to challenge male hegemony over sporting spaces in higher education in the early decades of the twentieth century. Painfully aware of the superior facilities and equipment that their male colleagues enjoyed, they were impatient with their subordinate status and the need to sustain their instructional programme by creative means. To effect their model of female physical education, women teachers needed a gym of their own.[33]

Campaigning fervently, like so many others, for spaces for women's sport and physical culture, Haidt demonstrated how women students' sporting needs in higher education were subordinated time and again to the men's:

> Women having physical education class in the Armory, men coming in for practice, women having to leave. Women exercising in the Dairy building, men coming in, women having to leave. Sure there were times and places set aside for women's activities. Hygiene classes in the Old Main, corrective class in the Home Economics Building, natural dancing in the Grange Dormitory Playroom. But women had to confine their athletic pursuits to specific times and they had no place to shower, and no permanent place to set up their equipment. Space for the girls was anything but a priority ... they had the activities ... but *where* the 1000 women on campus did them depended on where the 4000 men were not.[34]

Marie Haidt was more successful than many of her peers. When her lengthy campaign for a women's gymnasium finally bore fruit she triumphantly designated White Hall as a spot where men would never be by placing a sign in bold print on every entrance, 'Men do not enter.' Male students called it the 'house that hate built', but for Haidt it was her chance to rectify the many years that women students sporting needs had been subordinated to the men's. 'Work hard ... this building is for you girls', she said. 'Do everything you can not to let the men students' come in and take this over.'[35] And, of course, accommodated in their own special space, within their own gymnasium walls, women could then carry out their own apportioning of space and indulge in their own forms of separation and exclusion.

No Room at the (Men's) Gym

'If space is fundamental in any form of communal life, space must also be fundamental in any exercise of power.'[36]

Pressure for space was not so different at UBC. Writing in the *The Ubyssey* in 1946, Betty Stuart complained bitterly that,

> Contrary to rumors UBC women students are quite as interested in the Memorial Gym Drive as the men ... We women seem to get the small end of the stick rather often ... take for instance the hoop girls who sigh for a gym where they *and* the men will have a practice court apiece, and the little co-eds who struggle with their girdles in the cramped locker room. Were opportunity provided, might not many

more of our co-eds, reluctant to squabble over the gym floor, become fanatical sportsters and bring fame to the hall of our Memorial Gymnasium ... and remember boys, when you are making up those ambitious plans for the Memorial Gym, never underestimate the power of a UBC co-ed with a trophy just beyond her reach.[37]

Yet even before its official opening it appears that both students and the athletics and physical education staff largely accepted the idea that the War Memorial Gym was mainly a place for men's activities. Budget reductions forcing cutbacks in the initially planned activity spaces and facilities for women staff and students had led rather quickly to the acknowledgement that the old gym should be sufficient for women's physical activity needs. Not that access to even this space was automatic. It seemed to depend upon the women proving their specific need and enthusiasm for sporting activity. 'Once the new gym opens', Joan Fraser wrote in *The Ubyssey*, 'the girls, *if* they show enough spirit, will be able to take over the old gym'. 'But', she continued, 'that's a big if. Athletic lethargy among the women is a serious problem and if something doesn't happen between now and then all our plans might fall away.'[38]

Such anxieties were hardly surprising given the prevailing wisdom that catering to the needs of women was not a high priority at UBC.[39] In their daily experiences on campus, female students faced constant indications of their secondary status, and central among these was the notion that, as a minority, they were intruders in a male environment. This was especially true where sport was concerned.[40] 'It is evident', complained Jackie Shearman, that:

there is a serious minority problem in existence on this campus. This minority group has been shoved so far into the background that a great many people are unaware of its existence and if it does manage to force its way through the impregnable wall built up against it, it finds that its efforts are of no avail. The minority group to which I am referring is ... the 1841 women ... at this university, and especially those women who actively participate in athletics ... how about giving us a little space.[41]

In the years preceding the building of the War Memorial Gym there is evidence that women students had time and again been denied both co-educational opportunities and 'places of their own'. 'The lower ratio of women to men enrolled at UBC (for all but a short time during World War I) was at least partly due to an indifference, even hostility towards the higher educational needs of women.'[42] The Kidd Report of 1932, which condemned UBC as an unnecessary expense during the depression years, had further exacerbated and condoned public questioning about the value of higher education for women. 'Are they seeking an education or a thrill', complained a letter writer to the local Province newspaper.[43]

Central among the reasons put forward to deny women full access to the advantages of higher education were medical shibboleths about female frailty and ideologies concerning the potential dangers to femininity of 'unwomanly' activities. These anxieties had emerged during the late nineteenth century as part of the broad study of the science of sex differences and in response to female demands for emancipation and access to higher education and the professions. They were compounded by women students' efforts to participate in sport and athletics since both their unique anatomy and physiology, and the special moral obligations laid upon them by society to preserve their vital energy and womanliness for the traditional role of wife and mother, were seen to disqualify them from vigorous physical activity. The chief fear, surviving well into the twentieth century, was that physical exertion in vigorous and competitive sports would endanger female reproductive capacities and place their femininity in jeopardy.[44] Physicians were sure that 'menstruation hindered a woman; her lower weight, inferior strength and lighter bone structure made her more accident prone; intense physical activity displaced her womb making her barren', and so on.[45] Sports competition was believed to add to these injuries and introduce more emotional stress and unladylike elements. The sceptre of mannish female athletes, for example, was an emerging concern, inflated by unflattering comments from male sports writers such as Andy Lytle of the *Vancouver Sun*, who liked to describe women athletes as 'leathery limbed, flat chested girls'.[46]

Yet having fought to enter higher education, a number of active women students were determined to challenge such proscriptions and enjoyed sporting pursuits where they could. Changes to less restrictive clothing during the 1920s and 1930s helped considerably, as did the emancipating effects of women's work during World War I. Indeed their efforts to gain recognition in athletics and sport paralleled their struggle to establish their academic credibility on campus. While their games playing was often trivialized, frequently unsupported, and rarely acknowledged as an important contribution to the University or society in the early years of UBC's existence, women's sports clubs and teams developed and sometimes flourished.[47]

In 1923, a women's track club was formed despite the misgivings of the Dean of Women, who accepted prevailing medical beliefs that such activities were too strenuous for female students. Five years later, the women's athletics club insisted on joining the Western Intercollegiate Athletic Union, but in the face of only grudging support from the University's administration. When the women's senior basketball team was invited to compete for Canada in the Women's World Games at Prague in 1930 there was no financial support forthcoming from the Board of Governors as had been the case for men's athletic endeavours. Were it not for a public campaign to collect funds the team would have been unable to compete and then to win the championship.[48] Nor did women's basketball escape the continued objections of medical authorities. Females were believed to have particular physiological and psychological differences that influenced their participation in basketball.[49] Muscular strength was one concern, as was anxiety over their poorer physical endurance – which might result in excessive fatigue. Some physicians even made a connection between general body weakness from sport-induced fatigue and lung diseases, especially tuberculosis.[50] Playing during menstruation was another perceived difficulty, especially during the first two days.[51] Such was the concern that in 1935, the American Medical Association drew widespread public attention to the dangers of women's basketball in *Hygeia* by suggesting that 'basketball can make too heavy a demand on the organic vitality of a growing girl ... a great deal of excess energy is needed for the physical changes which are naturally taking place'.[52]

Twenty years later, the Research Committee of the influential American Division of Girls and Women's Sports was still issuing recommendations by women physicians to restrict girls' sports activity during the first half of their menstruation.[53]

Women's Rules – Separate Philosophies – Separate Gyms

'When women enter sports they are sports built by men for men.'[54]

In many respects, it was issues around girls' basketball rules and the stance against competitive sports for women which affected most immediately the displacement of women from the newly built War Memorial Gymnasium, and more broadly, the activities which were to take place in the spaces of the gym in the years to come. The familiar story of basketball's invention by former Canadian clergyman James Naismith at Springfield College in Massachussets in 1891 can be found in every North American sport history textbook, along with Senda Berenson's rapid adaptation of the game for women at Smith College. In an effort to prove that modified forms of basketball would not damage women's physiology or promote masculine characteristics through vigorous play, Berenson immediately disassociated the women's game from the men's. 'Rough and vicious play seems worse in women than men,' she said, and 'the excitement of the game will make our women do sadly unwomanly things.'[55] Indeed, the speed with which Berenson adapted Naismith's invented game for her women students spoke volumes about the ready acceptance by women physical educators of biologically based gender differences and the notion of separate spheres. The imposed differences in the game through separate girls' rules effectively eliminated the temptation for women to compete against men and kept them confined in their own carefully defined spaces.[56] Thus the price of the autonomy they came to enjoy within this separate sphere was the acceptance of polarized and rigid sex roles. This is not to say that women's sports were always seen as a pale imitation of men's or that women physical educators accepted without question women's proclaimed physical liabilities. Martha Verbrugge has shown how the views of many women teachers toward female physicality were at times highly nuanced as they were persuaded that sex differences could be both enabling and disabling factors in women's lives. In this way 'they could endorse femininity and heterosexuality, sustain the importance of their profession, justify separatism and equity, and still leave room for new ideas about womanhood and fitness.'[57]

To avoid physical roughness and overtaxing women's constitutions, as well as to promote team work, Berenson devised a series of rules which restricted the women players and constrained their space and freedom of movement.[58] The resulting game, announced as a 'New Game for the New Woman', combined the physical development of gymnastics with the abandon and delight of true play. Influential male physical educator Edward Hitchcock from nearby Amherst College gave his wholehearted endorsement. 'Women's basketball', he said, 'requires hardihood, alertness, quick perception and volition without the excessive energies of the men's game'.[59] For the men's game he agreed that 'her anatomical structure says no, her physiological functions say no, and her psyche says no'![60]

The success of Berenson's adapted game encouraged her to publish a set of girls' basketball rules in *Spalding's Athletic Guide* and these were widely disseminated and used in North America.[61] Other influential female physical educators such as Clara Gregory Baer from New Orleans modified the rules even further, introducing numerous ways to avoid the 'mayhem' of the male game and keep women's basketball ladylike and non-strenuous.[62] Like male sports, women's basketball games could thus be viewed as cultural performances, rituals that played out some of society's most deeply held assumptions.[63] Rule selection was particularly important since it reflected very particular philosophies about women's physical abilities and their role in society. Women physical educators found that they could use different versions of the rule book to promote their views on women's sport and exercise while discouraging selected negative aspects. Thus, wherever women's basketball was played different rules obtained, with the level of conservatism tending to be highest in the north-eastern and southern states of the USA. What was consistent, however, was the idea that the girl player's welfare (as defined by each group of physical educators) was all important. Basketball was understood to be an educational rather than a competitive experience for girls and women of such importance that Phebe Scott proclaimed 'so goes basketball, so goes women's sports'.[64]

The adoption of women's rules basketball in Canada followed a similar, perhaps even more convoluted path. Basketball was first introduced into Ontario schools in 1900 when Nora Cleary, a teacher in the Windsor Collegiate Institute saw a picture of a basketball in a *Spalding's Athletic Guide* and sent for a ball and book of rules from the company. The game she introduced to her students was strictly ladylike, slow paced, and moved at the pace of ping-pong.[65] Floor-length skirts or bloomers, together with the limiting floor divisions, greatly restricted movement, and since the game was often played on grass (for lack of a facility), it was largely a passing game.[66]

From this time, however, girls' basketball became ever more popular in Canadian schools, and communities from coast to coast increased their demands for gymnasium space, which by the 1920s had often come to be considered 'the boys' domain' for extracurricular activities.[67] It was, says Bruce Kidd, the sport of entry for most girls, as female sporting activity flourished in the aftermath of World War I.[68] Initially, the majority of teams across the country played the American Spalding Girls' Rules game. Even the famed Edmonton Grads women's basketball team, 'the greatest team that ever stepped out on a basketball floor', played girls' rules in their first years of competition.[69]

Writing about sport and physical education for girls in Canada, McGill instructor Winona Wood explained that the form of basketball familiar to a Canadian girl was determined largely by where she happened to live. Versions of girls' rules were more often found in central and eastern Canada. Westerners, she said, usually played by the Amateur Athletic Union of Canada men's rules since educational institutions in Eastern Canada, by virtue of their size and number, had been able to train qualified women instructors who used only girls' rules.[70] In Ontario, especially in Toronto, the more conservative female physical educators (most of whom had been trained in the United States) readily adopted the creed of the American Women's Division of the National Amateur Athletic Federation. This required strong opposition to competitive sport, play for play's sake – with the motto 'a girl for every team and a team for every girl'.[71] By contrast, the more modest institutions in western Canada with smaller staffs often had to depend on male instructors to handle the girl's programmes and the men typically taught five-a-side men's rules.[72] The result was that in spite of its great popularity, women's basketball and its methods of play were involved in almost constant disagreement across the country.

Some flexibility during the inter-war years was introduced by the Canadian Intercollegiate Women's Basketball League (a meeting of minds from Queens, Toronto and McGill), which introduced a set of women's rules somewhat less restrictive than the Spalding girls' rules. But no sooner had discussions begun to allow more scope for female athleticism than a major conference in the United States chaired by Lou Hoover, Vice President of the National Amateur Athletic Federation and wife of President Herbert Hoover, and attended by leading female physical educators in the USA, announced growing concerns 'over the general conditions surrounding the (robust and unladylike) playing of basketball and other sports for women'.[73] The result was the elimination of all inter-school and intercollegiate competitions throughout most states in the USA with a ripple effect into Ontario and Quebec, where influential female physical educators concurred with the decisions of their American colleagues.[74] The women's physical education section of the Ontario Educational Association decided in 1934 that 'Ontarians could do no better than to accept the rules of the Women's Athletic Division of the American Physical Education Association.'[75]

Helen Bryans, Director of Physical Education at the Ontario College of Education in Ontario was right onside with her American peers, and her views and influence are of particular interest to us here since Marian Henderson, the future Director of Women's Physical Education at UBC, was her student in 1930–31. They later accompanied each other to do graduate work at Texas Women's University. Marian thought the world of Helen Bryans, and Helen, says Bruce Kidd, probably achieved greater influence on Canadian physical education during the 1930s than anyone else, male or female. Her energy was extraordinary, her teaching innovations exemplary, and she virtually directed the hiring of female teachers across the country.[76] She was a passionate advocate of the girls' rules movement and the biologically deterministic platform of the American Women's Division that demanded that girl's and women's sport be non-competitive and adapted to their special needs and interests. To Bryans, an athletics programme was only successful when every girl was participating, with other girls, in all the 'purposeful' activities available; when it was educational rather than competitive, with any competitive activities carefully controlled; when it focused on skill and control rather than speed, strength and endurance; and when the welfare of the girl, along with self-control, initiative, good work habits and a neat appearance, took precedence over athletic achievements.[77]

This curious blend of protective and progressive impulses, middle-class rigidity and separation of women from men in their games, but with passionate attention to female fitness and the joy of sports and games participation, became Marian Henderson's guiding philosophy. In an interview with her at 90-years-old, Ann Hall tells how she recalled with enormous pride her years as a teacher at Oakland Collegiate in Toronto when she insisted that all girls wear gym rompers, eliminated all inter-school teams and instead formed 40 basketball teams and 40 volleyball teams – with every one of the 500 girls in the school playing on a team. Her driving force was to make the unskilled skilled, she said, hence the main purpose of a girl's physical education programme was to instil a love of physical activity for a lifetime in those less, rather than more, athletically gifted.[78] It was a goal characteristic of much progressive education at the time.

Thus, when Marian Henderson arrived in Vancouver in 1946 to direct the women's physical education programme at UBC, bringing with her Bryans' philosophy of women's sports and physical education that demanded girls' rules basketball and a non-competitive approach to women's sport, she was more than a little shocked to find many women students and high school girls playing boys' rules basketball. She determined then to demonstrate her passion for teaching girls' rules to women students, and set about organizing telegraphic meets and focusing upon the development of feminine attributes in her students. Although there were established women's basketball teams she organized a separate girl's team (see Figure 3.1) who played according to girls' rules against college teams from the north-western United States at weekends. They were able, she said with satisfaction, to have an entire weekend playing non-competitive basketball (see Figure 3.2).[79]

Far outweighing the simple physiological benefits of sports and physical activity were the women's goals she shared with other female physical educators from Ontario and the United States of 'learning skills, fun, emotional outlet, mental health and democratic living'.[80] Looking back over the years when she was much older, she wondered aloud whether she should have been more accommodating, more flexible in her attitude, especially where competitive sport was concerned.

Figure 3.1   'Women's rules basketball team at UBC' – Marian Henderson (Penney) is coach. (*Totem,* 1957.)

Figure 3.2   'Load of handling femme sport enthusiasms on the campus fell on head of pleasant Marian Henderson'. (*Totem*, 1950.)

It was this difference of opinion about the merits of competitive sport for women and the collision between girls' rules basketball and full-court play which exacerbated tensions between Bob Osborne and Marian Henderson, respective heads of men's and women's physical education in the early years of the War Memorial Gymnasium. Bob Osborne was a champion basketball player, one of Canada's best. As a student in 1930 he had been a member of the UBC basketball team that went on to become the Canadian intercollegiate champions. He was soon Captain of the team, President of Men's Athletics, and, in 1936, a member of Canada's Olympic basketball team. Even after graduating to become a local high school English teacher he continued to play, returning in his spare time to coach the women's Varsity basketball team. When Gordon Shrum recruited him to become the Head of Men's Physical Education in 1946 it was for his athletic stardom and abilities as a coach, not for any academic or professional training as a physical education specialist.[81] Prominent among his new duties was the position of head coach of the men's basketball team, and in 1948 he showed his worth by becoming national coach to the Olympic basketball team – taking six of his star UBC players with him (see Figure 3.3).

Figure 3.3   'Thunderbirds coach Bob Osborne with his winning
basketball team'. (*Totem*, 1947)

Called the 'Wizard of Oz' for his basketball coaching skills,[82] Osborne
(see Figure 3.4) was comfortable coaching the women's teams as well as the
men's. The women he coached, as well as most of those who taught
women's basketball in the high schools, did not play Canadian girls' rules
either (see Figure 3.5).[83] A clash of philosophies and professional practice
between the two directors was almost inevitable.

Working alongside Marian Henderson in the women's physical
education programme, fellow instructor May Brown was very aware of
the difficulties that were developing between Bob Osborne and Marian
Henderson over the latter's women's sport philosophy. Complaints were
beginning to be heard from high school physical education teachers who
felt that Henderson was holding back the women's sports programme by
her insistence on girls' rules and an extreme anti-competition stance. The
teachers sent delegations to Bob Osborne and tried to persuade the other
women physical education instructors at UBC to support their
complaints. The student-run Women's Athletic Association also worked
to neutralize Henderson's efforts to dampen sports competition but were
prevented from doing so by the Dean of Women.[84] 'We were very torn',
says May Brown:

> and the complaints got under Bob Osborne's skin quite a bit. Some of
> us in the faculty felt caught in the middle because we could see their

Figure 3.4   Bob Osborne. 'Headaches untold faced Osborne as head of Athletic Department but many problems will be ironed out with the new Gymnasium'. (*Totem*, 1950)

(the teachers') point. In a way I felt that Marian was not getting into the BC thing enough and appreciating the kind of female athletes we were turning out. I saw both points of view for I was trained at McGill where we played women's rules, and I had also played basketball in BC high schools and was comfortable playing men's rules. But, overall, we felt we must stick with Marian. She was determined to support the women in her own way and she constantly spoke up for them and their needs. Men taking over the big gym – now that was really not right.[85]

Brown was referring to Osborne's earlier decision to cut back the women's facilities in the War Memorial Gym and to the growing rift between the two Directors that would eventually demote Henderson (who had far more formal physical education credentials than her younger male counterpart) and leave Osborne in charge of the School of Physical Education. The loss of seniority, which showed up without fanfare in the University records of appointment in 1954 as 'change of title – no longer Director for Women', should not have surprised Henderson given the history

Figure 3.5   'Boys' rules
basketball'. *Totem* (1958)

of women academics in higher education, and especially in physical education, though she apparently attributed her demotion in part to the fact that she had recently married.

She might usefully have looked back at the McGill School of Physical Education where decades earlier Ethel Mary Cartwright, an indefatigible pioneer in developing physical education training programmes while Physical Director at McGill's Royal Victoria College, had been subordinated to her younger and less trained male colleague, Arthur Lamb. Lamb, who had been appointed Physical Director of McGill while still a medical student, was promoted to Director of Physical Education in a newly organized department that controlled both the men's and the women's physical education and athletics programmes. Although she had helped found and successfully nurture the physical education programmes at McGill for years she was shuffled aside by a man many years her junior and with considerably less professional experience. He personally chaired the committee responsible for women's physical education and even denied her a role on the executive committee of the School on the grounds that it was inappropriate to have a woman make decisions about men's athletics.[86] 'Dad' Lamb apparently liked to recount with glee that he was once called 'a moss-backed archaic diehard', but he always stood by his principles and was lionized by his male physical education colleagues for this virtue.[87] 'Carty', as she was affectionately known by her students, eventually resigned her position and retired in 1927 (albeit temporarily) to the country to raise chickens.[88]

'Sorry Girls – You're Not Moving'!

Particularly galling to Henderson's female faculty colleagues at UBC was their general lack of power in preventing the initial cutting of the women's facilities in the War Memorial Gym, for they could see that they were being increasingly cut off from the decision-making which allocated the gym's teaching and playing spaces. 'My recollection when we first saw the cuts', said May Brown,

> was that all the women's facilities, the extra gym, the dance salon, the studios, the staff changing rooms were chopped. I can remember that we were livid. Everything they had been telling us was going to be for us was absolutely gone. Clearly they had made a decision to secure the big basketball court, and we said, 'Fine, you are saving your bleachers, and your courts but we have been wiped out.' And when we started to get ready to move to the new gym, all of a sudden they said, 'Sorry girls, you're not moving.' So the men moved, and we stayed behind in

the old gymnasium. Soon a new sign was put up at the old gym saying 'women's gymnasium', and for many years after that the War Memorial Gym was simply known as the men's gym. As far as we were concerned at UBC, a War Memorial implied a place for men, and so men belonged in the War Memorial Gym – women didn't (except to go and watch games of course.)'[89]

The whole episode was remarkably reminiscent of leading US physical educator Eleanor Metheny's story about the struggles in higher education for women's sport, space and place told at the annual conference of the Western Society for Physical Education of College Women in 1958. Marian Henderson was almost certainly there listening, for she regularly attended these professional meetings on the west coast of the United States – sometimes encouraging other women faculty members to go with her.[90] Indeed she became chairman of that association for two years. Metheny's story, entitled 'Will we save our tennis courts?', was an allegory about a college faculty collectively faced with a drastic cost-cutting exercise in facilities. The debate over what to cut, she said, began:

> with the scientists looking bold and self-conscious ... assured of every consideration ... they were already studying the blueprints for an atom-smasher that would fit nicely on the women's tennis courts. ... The School of Education looked less assured ... The Humanities were smugly self-conscious of their own traditional virtues, muttering ... we don't take up much space you know ... The men's physical education faculty was sitting with the coaching staff from the department of athletics. They seemed slightly elevated above the rest of the faculty because they were sitting on money bags.

Metheny went on to point out that a few money-conscious administrators had already begun to realise that athletics in higher education did not necessarily make money, 'though it is generally believed that it does, which can be just as effective'. The men from athletics, she continued:

> did not even glance in the direction of the women's physical education department ... Why should they? They did not identify themselves with the women ... They scarcely knew them. Occasionally the Director of Athletics, who was also the Chairman of the Division of Physical Education had to meet the head of the women's department but it always turned into a hassle, with the woman making outrageous demands and getting angry when her demands were refused. ... (Anyway), who cared about women's physical education? They had no athletics teams and it was said that they were just plain opposed to competition.

The issue, then was how to persuade the College Faculty of the merits of saving the women's tennis courts, and Metheny approached the problem as David to Goliath 'armed only with a tennis racquet and ball'. 'Girls can learn to move', she said:

> only by moving, and they need space in which to move ... move in a variety of ways, for a variety of reasons, in ways ... that will be meaningful in their lives ... and I shall continue to argue on those grounds until they drag me kicking and screaming to the small gymnasium where hordes of girls are huddled together doing exercises ...

With David's skill to find the right answers, she concluded, the women could save their courts, though we are left with the strong impression that the women did indeed lose their tennis courts (just as they were soon to lose theirs at UBC), further reducing their sphere of influence and performance within the zone of higher education.[91]

In practice, the women at UBC were very happy in their own gymnasium, albeit a smaller, older and more modest structure than the War Memorial Gym. They did not yet know that they were to lose the nearby tennis courts to the Faculty of Arts as well as their newly gained gymnasium. Marilyn Russell, student athlete and later a faculty member in the School, said that for the time it belonged to them it was a wonderful gym for the women to work in. Students and faculty remember that, prior to the men moving to the War Memorial Gymnasium, the old gym had been extremely crowded, and the women's classes had often been pushed out to the field house, or a small portable activity room called the 'bandbox', or into the Varsity stadium where male students tended to gather in the bleachers to eat their lunch, socialize and watch the female students practice. Complaints by the women faculty about intrusive male spectators had yielded a compromise that students could sit and watch but not speak, but there was always an audience for the women's classes. Once the War Memorial Gym was in use, the women took over most of the offices in the women's gymnasium and were afforded more teaching space and practise time.

Even so there was overcrowding and the women would find various ways to sneak into the men's gymnasium for certain classes. It was not uncommon, said May Brown, to have a class scheduled but with no specific place to go. You simply had to take your class to any vacant space you could find and get on with it. Scooping up her courage, one day, Brown tells how she took her class to the War Memorial Gym and persuaded the attendant to let her in through the back door. 'We were in there for eight weeks of class before anyone noticed. I didn't even tell Bob Osborne I was in there, though it sure was a nice floor for teaching.'[92]

In the women's gym, Marian Henderson worked to establish a women's physical education programme patterned after the Ontario model, keeping women's sport as separate from the men's and as feminine as possible. True to her training, and teaching and coaching experience, she worked assiduously to de-emphasize inter-scholastic competition and focus upon participation, play days and telegraphic meets. Her students called her a stern taskmaster and a dedicated teacher with a constant concern for appearances. 'It was very important how you looked', said a former student. 'You had to wear a short skirt, basketball boots or long shorts, and always appear clean and pressed … though as students we could see what she was aiming for. She tried to make us more feminine, help us appreciate that being a woman's physical education teacher was different from men teaching boys.'[93] Although she had very little support from her male – and some of her female – peers, others she worked with felt that she had a wonderful vision of what a physical education programme should look like. Academically oriented, they noted that she was quite lonely on campus, finding women friends in other faculties and, until her marriage, returning to Ontario to spend her summers there. 'Even though she wasn't always easy to get along with, she was a wonderful teacher', remembered one of her students and colleagues. 'Her ideas in curriculum were extraordinary and she always had some interesting new plan to run the badminton unit or organize swimming classes.'[94] Another of her students, Barbara Schrodt,who later became a long-term faculty member and highly successful field hockey coach, remembers her as a strict and vigilant disciplinarian who focused with more intensity upon the posture, appearance and neatness of her female students than upon their athleticism.[95] It was not Marian Henderson but Bob Osborne who was so impressed with her superb sports and coaching skills that he approached her later to become a faculty member of the School of Physical Education.

Women on the Move – The Demolition of the Women's Gym

'The project ahead is to return women to those places from which they have been dis-or replaced or expelled, to occupy those positions … partly in order to show men's invasion and occupancy of the whole of space as their own and thus the constriction of spaces available to women…'[96]

Although the women had their own gymnasium, they knew that they did not play a large role in the affairs of the School of Physical Education. 'We didn't really have much of a voice. We did our jobs, we loved our students, and we loved what we were doing', said May Brown, despite the fact that without warning she had been swiftly denied a promised faculty position upon becoming pregnant in 1950. 'We were very congenial and we enjoyed the men's staff at social occasions, but you couldn't say we had a voice. Our strength was with the students and the camaraderie we had with them. Even in our crowded little gym we used to have a great time.'[97]

These 'relatively' good times were to end in the late 1960s when the women's gymnasium was slated for demolition to make way for an addition to the Faculty of Arts.[98] Details are confusing regarding the planned demolition and the arrangements to replace the facility. As early as December 1964 a warning shot was heard when President John B. Macdonald set up a committee to work with University planners on the future role of athletics and physical recreation in the University and their requirements with respect to facilities. Both Bob Osborne and Marian Henderson were on this ten-man (and two-woman) committee, which was told that 'all land west of a line formed approximately by the east fence of the Stadium was now reserved for academic purposes only'. The idea, outlined at a Board of Governors meeting was to remove all physical education facilities on the East Mall to the south campus so that 'all the foreseeable requirements of physical education could be accommodated on the Wolfson Field … in a phased development'.[99]

Construction was soon begun there on a new physical education building. Unit 1 of what would later be named the Osborne Center was designed to accommodate teacher education classes, student athletics and an expanding School of Physical Education and Recreation, which now boasted a graduate degree, a recreation degree option and a growing faculty and student complement. Discussions about a replacement for the women's gym, however, soon stalled, and when the Senate voted to demolish the women's gymnasium in 1969 there were still no firm arrangements for a replacement and no formal plans around the issues of women's space and facilities. The women students and the women's athletics committee (which was housed in the women's gym) were particularly upset at losing their facilities, said Marilyn Russell. They talked about making a human chain around the building and lying down in front of the bulldozers coming to demolish it. Avoiding a potential confrontation, the administration stepped in to propose a replacement for the women's gym with a second unit in the Osborne Center.

Coupled with the anguish over losing their gymnasium was a vigorous move among the women's athletic committee to forge a more equitable partnership within men's and women's athletic activities and to unite the men's and women's physical education programmes. In a feisty delegation to the Board of Governors, several members of the Women's Athletic Committee roundly rejected the principle of simply replacing the women's gymnasium and insisted upon co-educational facilities throughout the campus. There was a need, they said, in a forward-looking presentation, for all groups on campus concerned with physical recreation facilities to unite to determine the type of facilities which would best serve all groups and to allow men and women to play together as well as to learn together. In particular, they wanted the spaces of the War Memorial Gym to be rededicated to general recreational needs at the heart of the campus – as had been the original desire of the men and women students who funded it.

President Walter Gage listened to the delegation and responded politely. While commending the Women's Athletic Committee for taking a long-term view, he nevertheless recommended a short-term solution – a gymnasium to be built on the south campus primarily for the use of women students at a total cost not in excess of $500,000.[100] In a letter from the School of Physical Education dated 24 February 1970, Bob Osborne showed his support by following up the President's recommendation and insisting that a new gymnasium must be completed as soon as possible and that the 'needs of the ladies' be kept in the foreground. One cannot help comparing the ceiling of $500,000 for 'the ladies' when, only a year or so before, a new football stadium had been financed by the university to the tune of more than twice that amount. The new Thunderbird Stadium (now far from the centre of the campus), accommodated 3,000 spectators, as well as several dining rooms, press and TV facilities, a fully equipped training room, offices and a wrestling room.[101] With the addition of this expansive new stadium Bob Osborne was quoted in *UBC Reports* as saying, 'we know of no University in North America with more acreage committed to athletics'.[102]

What university administrators and planners were being pressed to realize was that physical education in higher education and the role of athletics within it was changing with the times. The bulldozing of the women's gymnasium, and the emerging if not yet well accepted concept of equality of opportunity and funding for women in sport and physical education, occurred around the same time that a schism was widening between the profession and the discipline of physical education – a schism which was to have an enormous impact on the future conduct of the School of Physical Education and the nature of activities in its home in the War Memorial Gym.[103] Furthermore, second wave feminism brought with it a rejection of 'separate spheres' and new demands for gender equity.[104] Physician Evalyn Gendel was just one of many pointing out that the unladylike connotation so frequently applied to physical exertion by the female was 'an historical and societal hangover from other times that was on its way out'. 'Being female', she said, 'implied no inherent biological deterrent to physical activity'.[105] The deliberate segregation of men's and women's activities according to preconceived notions of appropriate sporting activities was thus increasingly open to question in terms of the limitations it imposed on both sexes.[106] Many women physical educators no longer wanted to be isolated in their own separate, often 'lesser' facilities, and the women students increasingly clamoured for more sporting and co-educational opportunities and a greater share of the men's sporting spaces.

The notion that 'Canadian girls were expected to play well enough to be pleasant playing companions for the male, but never to be a threat to his superiority and never to be more interested in her own achievement than his' was rapidly fading.[107]

Nor were women's rules in basketball the divisive issue they had once been, now that the dominant women physical educators of Eastern Canada had decided to abandon them in 1966 and switch to the full court men's game that had been played in Western Canada for decades.[108] Their decision, resolving one of the most divisive issues in women's sport in Canada, was helped along by UBC physical educator Helen Eckert, whose scientific study of women and competitive basketball brought to light no ill effects among girls and women from high-level competition.[109] In any case, the women's rules basketball team at UBC had already been put on a trial basis due to lack of student interest in the team.[110]

The new rules agreement was but an echo of the larger press in Western Canada for a national organization for women's intercollegiate athletics. Rebuffed in their attempts to join the men's CIAU at a meeting in Banff in 1969, the women went ahead anyway and formed their own Canadian Women's Intercollegiate Athletic Union.[111] Marian Henderson (Penney) thought that this was absolutely the wrong way to do it. 'I always will, of course', she said 26 years, after her retirement in 1973. But her sports-minded colleagues, such as Marilyn Russell (Pomfret) and Barbara Schrodt, were very much part of the changing and energetic scene of women's sport and physical education. Marilyn Russell became the first President of the Canadian Women's Intercollegiate Athletic Union with the goal of increasing the level of female intercollegiate competition and improving the public image of women's sports across Canada.[112]

In fact, this would be an uphill job at UBC given the information revealed by the campus media that, of the $5 athletic fee collected from every student to support extramural sport, $4.20 went to the men's athletic committee leaving just 80 cents for the women's use.[113] Despite the fact that they now constituted almost 40 per cent of the student body, women athletes, with their annual budget of $29,600, were still chronically short-changed, and conditions for their training were second class compared to those for the men.[114] Their team travel had to take place by bus and train, no money was available for uniforms or accident insurance, scanty first aid supplies were offered and during sport practises they contended constantly with inadequate, crowded facilities (including only six hours of practise time a week at the War Memorial Gym).[115] Over at the men's athletic committee, debate centred around three station wagons that had been offered by Vancouver businesses to make the men's team travel more comfortable.[116] They too deplored the unfair and sweeping belt tightening that was cramping men's athletics, and their inadequate budget was

$114,000, even though they regularly ran up a deficit which was periodically excused by the Board of Governors.[117] Expenses for their football team (which generated a miniscule revenue) equalled the entire women's athletics annual budget.[118]

Despite the problems to be solved, many saw these years as the beginning of a real turning point in the fortunes of women's athletics and physical education at UBC, and welcomed the fresh breezes of equity initiatives such as Title 1X in the United States and the recommendations of the Report of the Royal Commission on the Status of Women, which in a sense marked the beginning of institutionalized feminism in Canada.[119]

Faced with more immediate concerns, such as the loss of their own gymnasium, the Women's Athletics Committee worked to renegotiate their way back into the men's sporting spaces and to press forward with their reconceptualization of physical education and athletics on the campus. In a substantial brief to the President and the Board of Governors they pointed out that 'all space is University space and satisfaction of academic needs alone cannot make a campus'. They showed how the facilities of the War Memorial Gym had become restricted to the extent that 'their use by the general student population now took place only on noon hours' and complained that a 1964 Senate Committee on Recreation, Athletics and Physical Education advocating the return of the War Memorial Gym to the students for their original purpose had never been acted upon. Though exercise answers fundamental human needs to dissipate energy in a creative and wholesome way, the brief noted, when blocked from healthy recreational pursuits the students were seeking less desirable outlets. Even the Dean of Women was now ready to testify to the advantages gained by sporting women. Women students who participated in athletics on campus rarely appeared in her office among the troubled and disturbed.

Turning to the issue of a replacement for the women's gymnasium (which the brief said had, in any case, been in a deplorable condition of neglect), the Women's Athletic Committee offered a series of suggestions to be taken up by a planning and a users' committee for the second phase of the Osborne Center. The users' committee requested that any facilities distinguished on the basis of the sex of the user be minimized; that spaces within new facilities be designed as combinable subspaces rather than divisible large spaces; and that design efforts be focused on making the new facility attractive to approach, easy to enter, congenial to stay in and convenient to navigate and use. To these features were added other design ideas, such as covered walkways leading to the structure, several small and open doorways rather than a few monumental ones, and the provision of sheltered resting or lounge subspaces – all features notably lacking in the War Memorial Gymnasium. And in a final comment they asked that 'architectonic' considerations (for example, purity and simplicity of form) be subordinated to provisions for heterogeneity, diversity, flexibility and sociability. The proposed external forms for the facility, they reiterated, did not need to conform to a-priori conventions with regard to appearance, building materials and technologies. 'There is no dictum on this campus', they said, 'that building surfaces must be planar or meet at right angles.'[120] Were they questioning, perhaps, Le Corbusier's desire to design for a Newtonian world where 'every body left to itself moves in a straight line'?

Unit 2 of the soon-to-be-named Osborne Center was completed in 1972, in the same year that the modernist Pruit-Igoe urban housing development was demolished in St Louis, but for a number of reasons a complete move to the new facility by the School never took place.[121] 'It wasn't as if a decision was ever made *not* to move there', said one of the former faculty, 'it just didn't happen'. It was a controversial building put in a controversial location by an architect who had been hired from elsewhere to reconfigure the campus. It was not a good teaching station. There were no offices built in the first phase of the building so the staff never moved there. Furthermore, it was isolated, far off on the south side of the campus. 'No one would hang around a place you had to walk a mile to', said another.[122] 'The location of the Osborne Center was just wrong, wrong, wrong. It didn't work – nobody went there.'[123] Thus the War Memorial Gymnasium continued to be the home of the School of Physical Education and Recreation, and hub of an increasingly diasporic community, while changes in campus design following the rapid expansion of higher education in the 1960s and early 70s rendered it ever more peripheral to the academic core on campus.

Recreating the Student Body:
The Bowling Wars

STEPHEN PETRINA

'Bowling', argued that the University of British Columbia (UBC) student Ron Bray, 'is *recreation* rather than *sport* and should not necessarily be confined to a Gymnasium'. The Alma Mater Society (AMS) President played his recreation card to counter a series of false promises made by administrators. Although bowling alleys were included in the 1947 blueprints for the War Memorial Gymnasium, the fate of bowling remained undecided in 1955. Almost annually, the bowling alley's fate swung back and forth between students and President Norman MacKenzie's office. By 1955, the AMS held the UBC President accountable and demanded action. The students wanted what was promised prior to the opening of the War Memorial Gymnasium in 1951: they wanted to bowl. The AMS President placed his finger directly on the problem. Was bowling a recreation or a sport? However moot the difference may seem today, at mid century administrators were reluctant to admit new forms of leisure, such as bowling and billiards, to either the halls of academia or athletics. If it was recreation, would bowling's pagan culture soil the sacred temple of sport? If a sport, how serious could it be if players could be seen competing with a pint of beer in the hand and a cigarette in the mouth? Situated comfortably in leisure, bowling culture was somewhere between recreation and sport, playing one off against the other. Of course this bubble could not last, as students taxed the principles of leisure time beyond limits of normality with recreational drug use and sexual athletics on campuses during the 1960s.[1]

When bowling alleys were finally installed in the War Memorial Gymnasium in 1957, the decision revolved around revenues and only peripherally concerned principles. When the alleys were removed in 1968, the game had changed beyond recognition. Thus the story of the bowling alleys at UBC neatly captures how culture and power circulated in the machinations of university governance and student life during the 1950s and 1960s. They represented a convenient, though not altogether unique, site in which administrative and student politics – mundane interests concerning class, gender, labour, money and technology – could circulate. Indeed, this story is merely one that unfolded again and again in relation to the interior spaces of UBC's recreational and sporting domains. Buildings and spaces have their politics, and, in many ways, these politics wear into the very fabric of what it means to be academic. Those who come to universities seeking enlightenment quickly discover that it is premises rather than principles that provide memories and bring these institutions to life. As we shall see, the memories and politics built into campus gymnasiums and student unions are part of the larger processes of the commodification and embodiment of leisure time and recreation since World War II.[2]

The removal of the bowling alleys from UBC in 1968 marked the end of an era and the demise of bowling. But bowling is suddenly in vogue again. In the late 1990s, the convergence of nightclubs and bowling alleys created a new hybrid known as 'cosmic' or 'extreme' bowling. New $10 million bowling multiplexes were built for the new club scene. Bowling proprietors who survived the bowling bust of the past two decades reinvested in the late 1990s to transform their alleys into extreme clubs with black lights and digital sound systems. Michael Moore's movie *Bowling for Columbine* plays to packed houses. Whilst Moore documents the sinister nature of particular liberties in the United States, he also demonstrates how commonplace the bowling culture is, despite the glamour of the bowling revival. This chapter addresses the details of this culture.[3]

'Bowling Goes to College'

Irritated with the rejection of a bid to expand recreational activities such as billiards and bowling in 1949, the students had little recourse but to seek vengeance through their mighty pens. 'Puritanical', the student newspaper called the decision, adding sarcastically, 'imagine the state our great university might get into if this single thin edge of the wedge were to invite all manner of vile debauchery to sweep away the ideals of educated thought'. The students knew a contradiction when they saw it. 'Just how much better, or worse, for public relations is a bowling alley like the one planned for the basement of UBC's War Memorial Gymnasium?', *The Ubyssey* editors pointed out. 'What a wonderful cloak those words "war memorial" must be', the editors reasoned, 'that they can sanctify a bowling alley'. Thus the students recognized early that bowling could be sanctioned as a form of university sport but not as a form of recreation.[4]

Enticed by the increasing post-war popularity of recreational activities, many students were in the habit of frequenting the bowling alleys and pool halls in downtown Vancouver during weekday and weekend nights. Difficulties with bus services to UBC after midnight and with other forms of transport inspired students to seek ways to bring popular recreation to campus. By the late 1940s and early 1950s, a number of students participated in bowling teams and billiard tournaments. Some of the female students competed in an intercollegiate telegraphic bowling league, arranged from the Commodore Lanes and LaSalle Recreation on Granville Street. Male and female students also had the option of participating in intramural competition in the six downtown bowling centres. By 1950, they could bowl in 25 establishments in the Greater Vancouver area, and could choose from a dozen more that were opened throughout the decade. Bowling alleys were different from other recreational facilities, such as playgrounds and swimming pools, in that few were municipally owned. University and fire station alleys accounted for the few non-commercial establishments.[5]

In the early 1950s, bowling was Canada's most popular organized recreational activity, with more players than curling, golf and tennis combined. In an era of increasing popularity of spectator sport and 'leisure' time, bowling offered a form of participant recreation to the entire family. In some establishments, 60 per cent of the bowlers were women. Junior bowling leagues provided an opportunity for high school students to develop their early habits in the game. Industrial leagues continued the bowling interests of Canadian men, mostly cultivated on military bases during the war. Over a million Canadians casually bowled each year, and a fair percentage were members of bowling teams. Across the country, about 1,200 bowling centres offered a combined 7,000 lanes on which to bowl, marking a 40 per cent growth in these businesses. Bowling was a thoroughly commercial, modern trend, and alley construction leaned toward spacious, swanky palaces streamlined with a striking decor. The club-like, clean, wholesome bowling establishment was truly a fabrication of the late 1940s, however, as bowling proprietors increasingly created a new image for what had been a vulgar activity typically offered in the smoke-laden basements of beer pubs and hard-liquor parlours.

Despite the new spin that proprietors and equipment-supply companies worked to give bowling, the old image was not easily overcome. In the early 1950s, many Canadian parents and teachers remained unconvinced that bowling was entirely innocent of undesirable influences. Public bowling's early reputation had been earned through associations with bookmakers, booze, dice players and hustlers. It was considered to be a rough, working-class game, and many Christians and social reformers assumed the Devil itself was at work in bowling alleys and billiard parlours. Between the 1920s, when prohibition liquor laws placed the sustainability of public bowling in question in the United States, and the 1940s, when volumes of young men joined the armed forces, bowling-product manufacturers and proprietors combined to reform bowling practices. To attract a customer base, bowling was reformed to appeal to women and offered as a decent form of entertainment for the entire family. Bowling 'alleys' became 'lanes', 'gutters' became 'channels' and bowling became a 'proper' recreation for white, middle-class consumers.[6]

Generally, in the late 1940s and early 1950s hours spent at work dropped as 'leisure time' increased. The number of families with middle-class incomes rose sharply and levels of disposable dollars nearly doubled, although expenditure in the so-called leisure market (such as alcohol, casual dining, pleasure travel, recreation, sports, etc.) lagged behind family incomes. Indicative of the appeal of middle-class pursuits, many low-income families were spending beyond their means. Sedentary pursuits, such as listening to the radio and reading, were in decline while active recreation, such as bowling, was the preference of middle-class families. The desire for active recreation clearly required leisure time, disposable money and facilities, and where bowling palaces and swimming pools were available the sales of corresponding sporting goods increased. This relationship, quickly recognized by proprietors and equipment vendors, fuelled the market for leisure-time activity and expenditure throughout the 1950s. Design for leisure was a new industry and 'leisure studies' a new academic interest. Analysts of the times attributed the reduction of hours in a working week and the increase of leisure time to automation. Liberal welfare politicians saw an opportunity to extend the power of governments to recreational citizenry. Psychologists applauded the additional time for recreation, and suggested that the new opportunities for self-expression and emotional outlet counteracted crime, ill health, labour unrest, mental instability and poor hygiene. Some bowling alleys hired sociologists to calculate the relationships between leisure time, spending money and community. Physicians prescribed recreational exercise such as bowling for people from eight to 80, certain that bowling could tone up flabby 'office muscles' and provide a nervous release from the stress of daily work. Anticipating future increases in leisure time, these analysts looked to schools and universities to provide proper socialization in leisure and recreation for easing the transition into modern adulthood.[7]

Physical educators were among the most ambitious in their attempts to provide a curriculum that would satisfy the demands of a new era of leisure. They took philosopher John Dewey at his word: 'Education has no more serious responsibility than making adequate provision for enjoyment and recreative leisure.' 'Preparation for leisure' thus became the new mantra in physical education after World War II. In British Columbia, a programme of recreation, or 'pro-rec' as it was popularly called, was instituted in response to the government's National Physical Fitness Act of 1943. Pro-rec promoted the organized extension of physical education beyond the school curriculum to entire communities. Signifying changes in the importance of leisure-time activity, a degree programme in physical education was established at UBC in 1946 and the School of Physical Education was opened in 1952. Six years later an undergraduate programme in recreation was added. Indeed, as early as the late 1940s, physical education and recreation had been considered an essential part of university education for all students. However, the expansion of physical education into recreation required more than the adoption of new programmes and facilities, for it tested the very foundations of the subject which was solidly based on athletics and sport. At UBC, as we shall see, recreation had to take a back seat to athletics and sport in physical education during the 1950s and 1960s. It was not easy for many educators to accept that the three Bs – bowling, billiards and bridge – were as important as basketball, football, hockey, or swimming.[8]

Whether physical educators included bowling in their curriculum because of its popularity, its anticipated positive effect on students, or out of a sincere commitment to recreation, the game of rolling a ball at pins was made a course option on college campuses across Canada. In the USA by 1950, 117 college and university campuses had installed or were installing bowling alleys, and most of these offered bowling as a physical education course as well as an intercollegiate, intra-fraternity, intra-sorority and intramural competitive sport. The University of New Brunswick was the first in Canada to provide bowling alleys in 1950, and over the next few years most other Canadian universities followed their lead. Bowling went to college in a big way and became an institution in student unions and sporting facilities. In most universities it was readily accepted that the administration's attraction to bowling alleys was extra-curricular: efficient management and marketing of the alleys could guarantee a steady income of revenues.[9]

'The Deal is Off', 1947–51

The desire for bowing alleys at UBC was hitched early on to the design of the War Memorial Gymnasium. In the first design stages of the project, AMS officials appealed to administrators to consider the educational and extra-curricular value of bowling, and the university architects acted quickly on the requests made by the gymnasium's planning committee. A six-lane bowling alley was proposed as yet another facility in the living memorial to the fallen soldiers of World War II. Controversy would follow, however. Already appearing to some critics as a 'luxurious playground for school-boys', with its proposed addition of saunas, whirlpool baths, and bowling alleys, the War Memorial Gymnasium seemed in danger of becoming a 'pagan temple to the glory of the human body'. What the critics had trouble seeing was that this 'pagan temple' was being funded primarily through student fees and fund-raising initiatives; students deserved at least some say in what would go on in the temple. A financial statement in early 1950 showed that students had underwritten 65 per cent of the funds for the entire gymnasium project through student fees and loans, athletic contests, beauty pageants, fashion shows and rummage sales along with a door-to-door provincial campaign. Yet, when the War Memorial Gym opened its doors in 1951, it was clear that numerous cuts had been made to the plans. The students were unimpressed to find that the bowling alleys had not yet been installed and their fate hung on an administrative fiat.[10]

In an attempt to force a move by the university officials, the AMS held a referendum to see if students were in favour of providing a further $8,000 investment in the construction of the bowling alleys. This might act as a down-payment, in anticipation of recovering that amount over the course of four years from revenues. Prior to the referendum, John de Wolfe, President of the stuffy Literary and Scientific Executive debate club, had objected that bowling, like billiards, would detract students from their studies. And, as if on cue, de Wolfe touched on nearly all of the 'puritan' concerns sounded by cautious administrators and parents. Nevertheless, of the 20 per cent of the student body that showed up at the polls, 704 voted in favour and 257 voted against the referendum question. The alleys were approved in principle, and the Board of Governors as well as the School of Physical Education gave their tentative approval. All that remained was the approval of the administration, which seemed sure to be forthcoming. Immediately, proposals began to roll in from managers of local establishments and bowling manufacturers offering to ship, free of freight charges, finance and install the necessary supplies for the War Memorial Gym bowling alleys.[11]

News of the proposed bowling alleys travelled quickly to parties with vested interests, mainly through *The Ubyssey* and the *Vancouver Sun*, which noted that the university was interested in leasing the space to a commercial bowling alley manager. British Columbia distributors for National Bowling and Billiards Ltd and the Brunswick-Balke-Collender Company of Canada mailed in detailed specifications and contracts, and local establishment owners also responded. Saul Lechtzier, manager of the DeLuxe Bowling Centre on Hastings, took AMS officers to lunch, but it was Vic Huckell, manager of Abbott Bowling Alleys and two other successful lanes in the downtown area, who was given tentative approval to 'strike it rich' by the AMS and university administrators. Huckell estimated that gross profits could be $4,000 per year, and promised the AMS 40 per cent of this to pay off their investment. Suddenly, the War Memorial Gymnasium's humble six lanes for physical education and recreation was big-time culture. *The Ubyssey* painted a glowing picture of the new bowling culture:

> The PE Dept plans to use the alleys for a large part of the day to give instruction in the art of bowling. Most evenings there will be leagues of student and faculty organizations. The alleys will be fitted with the latest innovations. Bowlers will no longer be able to sneak even a quarter of an inch over the foul line as there will be automatic electric

eyes that will light up large red lights whenever anyone crosses it. Before the ball rolls down the rail it is dusted off and when it reaches the rack a hydraulic stop slows the ball down and deposits it gently in the rack. To help you line up the ball there is a set of range finders imbedded in the alley. The strategically placed markers make it easy for those who can't see as far as the pins. There will be lots of room for spectators in the three rows of settees behind the alleys.[12]

The Brunswick suppliers assured the AMS that students would have 'the most modern and up-to-date set-up of any establishment in Canada, and far ahead of any university presently operating alleys in Canada'. With their Yellow Pine and Canadian White Maple bowling alley beds, Nu-Peg Pin Spotters, Safe-T-Ball Returns, Triple Duty Pit and Foul Lights, Red Crown King Fibre Bottom Pins, Tri-Colour Mineralite Balls, Reversible Pit Mats, Doubles Score Tables (see Figure 4.1), Snack Bar, No-Scuff Shoes and various sundries, Brunswick was offering a facility that made the basketball court upstairs in the WMG look as if it was designed in the Dark Ages. But before the popular bowling culture could transform the subterranean space of the WMG there were still two hurdles to negotiate.[13]

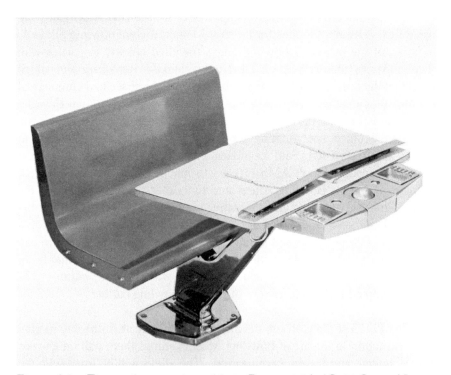

Figure 4.1   The modern scoring table in Brunswick's 'Gold Crown' Line aided in designing striking interiors. *(The Gold Line Catalogue*, 1958.)

The first hurdle was to finish the basement area so that Brunswick could install the alleys. The architects had left the space intended for bowling basically untouched. They requested an additional $16,284 to provide the brickwork for the walls, ceiling finishes, cement for the floors, electrical fixtures, heating and ventilation systems, and paint. Neither students nor administrators were happy with this unfinished business, feeling they had been nickel-and-dimed throughout the contract process. Other demands, such as $29 for three flag holders, $239 for doubling the pumice block walls in one room, $398 for stiffening corridor walls and $1,220 for adding extra 2x10 joists over the bowling alley room left the AMS unable to pay, even after using the customary 6 per cent withholding of architect's fees to cover unanticipated changes. The additional amount necessary to finish the bowling alleys again hinged the fate of the bowling alleys on an administrative decision.[14]

Final approval of the AMS's proposals for bowling had to come from UBC President MacKenzie and the Board of Governors as the AMS had 'assumed all the liability' that they could on this project. Urging the President to set aside funds to finish the space and 'provide bowling facilities for the student body', AMS President Vaughan Lyon appealed, 'The space is there, now standing idle, the demand for this healthful form of recreation is present on the campus, and money is available to put the alleys on a self-liquidating basis.' Three days later, after reviewing the estimates for bringing the bowling alley room up to standard, the Board of Governors delivered an unexpected blow to the students. While 'sympathetic, they said, no money is available for this project at the present time'. In a letter to Lyon, President MacKenzie explained that the Board of Governors was operating on a fixed budget and that all of their funds had 'already been committed'. The President promised to keep the bowling alleys in mind and give them 'sympathetic consideration whenever further monies are forthcoming'. Insiders were sure that there was indeed money but the impending British Empire Games now seemed to be the only game in town. Hosting the games in 1954 would generate a British Empire grant and revenues for university coffers even though a regulation, Olympic-sized swimming pool would be required. Bowling alley funds, and funds originally targeted for certain fixtures and rooms in the War Memorial Gym, were thus diverted to the construction of the new swimming pool and surrounding premises. While not as committed to the British Empire event as the senior administrators, the students were caught between wanting the bowling alleys and the pool. However, once the administration admitted to have 'paid the out-of-pocket expenses of the university' for hosting the Empire Games, AMS officers felt forced to contact Brunswick, Huckell and the contractors in early 1952 to cancel plans. We 'had hoped that some of the university's friends and advisors would have agreed with our plans', they wrote. 'Respectfully,' they added, 'the deal is off'.[15]

'A Shocking Commentary on the University', 1955–57

In October 1957, *Canadian Business* declared that 'bowling is by far Canada's biggest participating sport'. The same was true in the USA. In Canada, bowling was a $52 million industry with 3,000 lanes in 900 establishments scattered across the country. There were over a million bowlers in Ontario alone; Toronto had more bowling alleys than New York and Philadelphia combined; and Windsor and Vancouver had the highest number of alleys per capita. *The Financial Post* noted that 'bowling alleys boom along without regard to recession, region or remoteness'. Up to 25 per cent of all revenues in the business was profit. Bowling leagues were running the establishments at full capacity six evenings a week. 'Drop-in' bowlers, taking advantage of their leisure time, kept the lanes busy during afternoons and late nights. In Vancouver, 'Bowl-A-Parties' for women's organizations and the 'Ladies-in-Waiting' league expanded the customer base for entrepreneurial proprietors. Bowling palaces with bars, cosmetologists, laundry services, nurseries and restaurants exploited the appeal of recreation and sport to the entire family. The Canadian Junior Bowling Council, formed in 1957, quickly spread across the provinces to promise the business of habitual bowlers well into the future. Physical education courses in bowling, along with intercollegiate and intramural competition, seemed to guarantee that the next generation of parents was properly socialized into the middle-class recreational and leisure pursuits.[16]

In more ways than one in the mid 1950s, UBC looked completely out of step with the rest of the country. It was not merely that UBC did not have bowling alleys. The university's entire athletic, physical education and recreation programme appeared under-funded, understaffed, under-supported, and without adequate facilities for both male and female students. Total student enrolment in the 1950s increased from 7,960 for the 1950/51 school year to 14,899 in 1957/58, an 87 per cent increase, making UBC the second-largest university in Canada. Enrolment had far outpaced the expansion of facilities which had been inadequate for years. In 1949, for example, students were 'appalled by the lack of recreational facilities' at their disposal. At the start of the year in 1953, a special alumni committee had been appointed to assess the condition of athletics and recreation on campus. The committee recommended an 'immediate extension of recreational facilities such as playing fields, ice arena, a swimming pool and squash courts, together with the completion of the gymnasium'. When recreational space per student was assessed, UBC appeared to be in a 'much worse position' than 20 years before. A student committee set up by the AMS in 1957 made almost identical recommendations to those made in 1953, but now the tone was politically harsh and demanding. The War Memorial Gym was in use for 15 hours each day, they complained, leaving little time for women's physical education, intramurals, or casual recreation. Some students had to return to the university to attend physical education courses late in the evening. The maintenance man was overwhelmed by the volume of demand, giving the gym the reputation of a 'filthy building' that was 'poorly maintained'.[17]

Speaking directly of athletics, the students argued that 'it is deplorable that the administration would not be concerned about the loss of extramurals from the curriculum of UBC'. The annual contribution of administration to the athletics programme was about $5,000, while the students were kicking in $31,700 through an AMS grant to athletics and the School of Physical Education ($24,000), athletics cards ($6,500) and gate receipts ($1,200). The administration's contribution paled next to other Canadian universities and the students' contribution well exceeded that of other student bodies. By 1957, the students who had underwritten a large percentage of the original cost of the War Memorial Gym had paid off the balance and were now in the process of paying for an extension to Brock Hall ($5 from each student's fees). They realized, in fact, that they had paid for at least one-eighth of their university's $25 million total investment in facilities. To bail out the athletics programme from a dangerous deficit in March 1957, the AMS proposed an extra $5 athletics fee per student to top up the $19 AMS fee for all student activities and recreation. Since 21 per cent ($24,000) of these fees was already going to men's athletics and 3 per cent ($2,800) to women's athletics, many students thought that their contributions were high enough. They could see that a good part of their fees were going to support the 5 per cent of the student body involved in university sport. Furthermore, the administration's idea of raising tuition fees to generate more funds was a distasteful option to students. With fees among the highest ($240 per year) of Canadian universities, UBC had a reputation of a 'rich man's university'. According to analysts, its athletics system was 'bush league'.

Sports journalist Allan Fotheringham wrote an honest but damaging series of articles on UBC's conditions in early March 1957. Fotheringham began by saying that, despite some of UBC's merits, this university's sports programme was 'strictly bush league'. 'Desperately in need of money, and without adequate facilities or staff,' he continued, UBC could not 'go on much longer under present athletic conditions'. Attendance for football fell from 12,000 per game in the early 1950s to 4,300 per game in 1955. In 1956, student attendance was about one-ninth of the total enrolment. The homecoming game, which was the only game the Thunderbirds won in 1956, drew only 1,258 spectators. Alumni attendance was extremely low, and alumni donations to UBC were the lowest of the ten major Canadian universities. Attendance for basketball games in the War Memorial Gym dropped from 8,400 in 1952 to 6,700 in 1955. 'No UBC sport pays for itself', Fotheringham observed, 'or even approaches black ink'. Men's basketball and football, the two sports with the greatest revenue-generating potential, were the biggest financial losers. Expenditures on these sports were $14,399 and revenues generated were $8,256 in the 1957/58 calendar year. Athletics programmes in smaller universities across Canada were operating with twice the total budget of UBC's programme. UBC offered 22 varieties of sport, by far the most diverse and extensive of Canadian campuses, yet it was the least organized. While there was an increasing apathy toward spectator sports, there was an increasing interest in recreation and participant sports. Nearly half of the full-time undergraduates, men and women, participated in intramural sports programmes and paid a $7.50 fee to sponsor a team. With this tense climate for UBC athletics, proposals for any form of recreation that smacked of interference with the existing sports programme had to be politically finessed.[18]

Playing on the politics of UBC athletics in late 1955, the AMS President Ron Bray contended that 'bowling is recreation rather than sport': alleys did not have to be in the gymnasium. In November of 1955, the AMS surprised university officials by proposing that bowling alleys be included in the design of an extension to Brock Hall, which was essentially a student centre. The AMS requested that bowling alleys, pool tables, ping-pong tables and a barber shop be among the recreational facilities that would allow them to recover their investment. Caught by the proposal, UBC's President quickly responded. It was more 'sensible and economical' to reconsider the War Memorial Gym's spaces, MacKenzie wrote to the students, and he hoped that the existing 'difficulties might be overcome by cooperation' between administration and students. He played directly into the students' hands. The AMS was prepared with two proposals for Brock Hall: one with and one without bowling alleys. Bob Osborne, Director of the School of Physical Education, also played into the AMS's hands and gave his faculty's preferences away in the process. Up to this point, he said he had been opposed to the bowling alleys, since the faculty felt that the unfinished gym space could be used for another men's locker room or an exercise room. He agreed, however, that between Brock Hall and the gym, the latter was the best choice, and he qualified his agreement with the caveat that faculty members were reluctant to recognize bowling as a physical education activity if it was not organized in a sports facility. In the War Memorial Gym, bowling would be more properly a sport, or at least it would have the aura of a serious recreation. Furthermore, it was estimated that the cost of installiing alleys in Brock Hall would be $74,500 compared with $41,610 for the War Memorial Gym. At a planning committee meeting in late December 1955, members voted down the proposal to place bowling alleys in Brock Hall, with the three dissenting votes coming from the student members. The Board of Governors did the same at a meeting the following week.[19]

Left with a student mandate and an alternative plan, the AMS went to work on securing the Gym for their bowling alleys. In a poll taken by *The Ubyssey* in December 1955, while 68 per cent of the students questioned opposed the inclusion of bowling alleys in Brock Hall most of them did want bowling alleys and thought they belonged in the Gym. Co-ed Daphne Williams summed up the situation by pleading with Bray: 'Please Santa, give me a six-lane bowling alley for Christmas.' Bray made his final case to the Committee on Revenue Producing Recreational Facilities, whose interest was piqued by the possibilities of a money-making proposition. An investment analyst predicted that the alleys could pull in an annual gross income of $11,529 and a net profit of $4,944. A Bank of Montreal loan would cover the initial costs to UBC in the installation of the alleys ($20,375) and the completion of utilities and details in the gym space ($15,000). Local Vancouver alley proprietor Stan Curry would manage the alleys and either lease the space for $4,000 per year for five years or operate the alleys as an employee of UBC. The AMS knew that money talked in this dire financial and recreational era. In addition, MacKenzie and the Board of Governors were feeling obligated to the students on this issue, and somewhat embarrassed about the empty, unfinished gym space.

On 27 August 1956, the Board approved the AMS's plan for UBC to borrow money, complete the gym space, install the alleys and hire a manager. MacKenzie immediately anticipated the heat he would receive for this decision. To counter any criticism from the provincial government, he wrote to his friend Robert Bronner, the Attorney General, confiding that 'superficially it appears fantastic to spend money on bowling alleys when we so desperately need residences, classrooms and laboratories'. Dormitories were over-packed and 'temporary' army huts housed a number of courses. He hoped that Premier William Bennett and the Social Credit government would lend their 'sympathy and understanding' to the difficult decision. MacKenzie also anticipated a routing *The Ubyssey*, which liked to 'criticize the powers that be' for his decision to fund recreation. Short of a move to 'shut it up', which would cause more of a fray, there was nothing he could do. At the next Board of Governors meeting, MacKenzie recommended that the bowling alleys 'be deferred' until funds were available. Nevertheless, in the January and February meetings in the new year, the Board reaffirmed their decision.[20]

'Recreation Increased', read the top headline in *The Ubyssey* on 22 February 1957. Although anticlimactic for the seniors, the students anticipated that they would be bowling at the end of the academic year. For the AMS, the results of their drawn-out agitation were bitter as well as sweet. On the one hand, it appeared that the battle was won. On the other, the administration planned to direct revenues, above those necessary to pay-off the loan, to the expansion of athletic facilities, which would not provide the students with a 'kick-back' of revenues from 'concessions for chocolate bars, soft drinks and cigarettes, fairly substantial in bowling alleys'. The Brunswick company's branch manager assured UBC officials that the addition of the lanes to the 'handsome' War Memorial Gym would provide a 'sporting outlet' for students and a recreational benefit to the university district. 'Recreation serves a two-ply purpose', the Vice President of Brunswick's Bowling division assured administrators, since 'it offers students an opportunity for a well-balanced life and it provides the college or university with students who are better equipped to do their work'. No sooner did contractors finish placing utilities and details in the gym than Brunswick installed their specially customized, modern Centennial Bowling Alleys (see Figure 4.2). During the third week in May of 1957, the alleys were finally open for business.[21]

On the day before the alleys were opened, a big, orange, neon sign that spelled out 'BOWLING' in bold letters was hung on the south wall of the War Memorial Gym and plugged in, to the dismay of administrators and faculty. Arriving on campus, the Head of the School of Architecture, Fred Lasserre, was 'taken aback' to see the large, undignified sign hanging on his prized War Memorial Gym. Going directly to the UBC President, Lasserre

Figure 4.2   Brunswick's 'Centennial Bowling Alleys' as designed for and installed in UBC's War Memorial Gymnasium (with temporary furniture).

argued that it was a 'shocking commentary on the university if the first thing the visitor to the campus sees is a glaring sign advertising bowling'. The 'visual impact' was massive, and he was 'sorry to see a neon sign on campus'. Fearing that his good name might be 'associated with the decision to make it as large as it is and to place it in such a prominent location', he wanted to go on record as having had nothing to do with it. Thoroughly annoyed, MacKenzie unloaded the volume of complaints on the Buildings and Grounds director. He was curious why such a huge sign could not spell out UBC or WMG instead of BOWLING. Now, MacKenzie continued, the first impression 'visitors coming along University Boulevard get is that we operate bowling alleys!'[22]

'The Bowling Alleys were being used to capacity', 1957–63

When the students returned to campus in September of 1957, the neon sign was still hanging on the wall of the War Memorial Gym – UBC was indeed open for the business of bowling. Through the summer, Curry did what he was hired to do, which was to put the business of bowling in order. The Board of Governors approved Curry's business plan, including the rates for drop-in and league bowling. For drop-in play, Curry charged 25¢ per game or, in the bowling vernacular, per line. For league play, students and faculty paid 75¢ for three games if bowled before 7 p.m., and 85¢ for each set of three games bowled between 7 p.m. and 11 p.m. League times were scheduled for weekdays and Saturdays from 3 p.m. to 11 p.m. 'Women only' leagues were scheduled from 1 p.m. to 3 p.m. each day. Intramural leagues were given a rate of 20¢ per line and were scheduled for 18 hours per week during times allocated between 12.30 p.m. and 7 p.m. Leaflets were spread across campus advertising the lanes and sent to clubs, fraternities and sororities to recruit league teams. Bowling proprietors placed priority on filling their establishments with league bowlers, as this guaranteed a steady flow of revenues. Drop-in play was sporadic and unpredictable, but allowed for an informal introduction to the game. In the case of educational bowling, students were given an introduction into the discipline and excitement of the game, providing the motivation for drop-in and league play. Students enrolled in bowling courses at UBC could bowl, free of charge, between 8:30 a.m. and 12.30 p.m. each day.[23]

The bowling programme in PE was such a 'popular option' that administrators speculated that the 800 students electing bowling would pay a fee if one were levied. Already in the fall, the UBC President was facing the question of expanding the physical education bowling programme into revenue-generating hours. Students complained that the bowling blocks in physical education quickly filled to capacity, and intramural league players were jealous that the fortunate students who selected the bowling option had the opportunity to bowl free of charge. The demand for the bowling option surprised Osborne, but his faculty were prepared with the rich curriculum materials developed by their US and Canadian colleagues. Many physical educators considered bowling 'the ideal carry-over sport, admirably suited to maintaining physical fitness long after an individual's active playing days' in other sports were finished. It was the best form of recreation for socializing students into a middle-class culture of leisure. Physical education students were provided with detailed instruction on the etiquette, regulations, rules, and techniques of bowling. There were fundamental body movements that had to be learned and repeated for successful bowling. Stances, footwork and methods for the release of the balls formed the skill-based component of the curriculum. Skill-wise, the objective was rolling the ball so as to make strikes and spares. The objective was to roll a high score, and final grades were primarily based on comparisons with national bowling norms. Kinesthetic knowledge was developed to counter the problem of gutter balls. Instructors posed problems in self-discipline for students. 'Have you noticed whether you swing your arm freely? Or do you force or push the ball out on delivery? Does your arm move in a pendulum-like manner or does it sweep forward in a wide curve to the left (for a right-handed bowler)? What does that do to direction?' In addition to pointers, students were taught common bowling terminology. What was an 'alley ball', 'barmaid', 'creeper', 'dead wood', 'fish', 'foul', 'frame', 'kick back', 'king pin', 'kitty', 'mother-in-law', 'pocket', 'powerhouse', 'turkey', or 'working ball'? A positive disposition to bowling etiquette was crucial. Simple manners made or broke the modern bowling alley experience. 'Do not talk to a bowler who is delivering her or his ball', instructors stressed. 'Control your temper and refrain from abusive language.' Etiquette was formed to alleviate what were called 'mental hazards' in athletic parlance. Although etiquette was the same whether bowling in Vancouver or anywhere else, an entire tradition of Canadian five-pin bowling was defended at UBC.[24]

About 90 per cent of Canadians preferred their five-pin bowling to American ten-pin, and UBC students were no exception. Whilst in the early days of student agitation for the War Memorial Gym alleys there was talk of ten-pin lanes, when the installation was finally made in 1957 interest was solidly with five-pins. Canadian five-pin bowling was invented in Toronto in 1905 and by the 1940s was the standard across Canada. In five pin bowling, the pins are a height of about 7 inches and have a rubber ring round their mid-section. The pins are spotted in different places and a bowler is allotted three balls to roll per 'frame'. Bowlers must knock down the left corner pin to get a score in an individual frame. Canadians argued that pins in the American-style game were more abundant, larger and easier to knock down with the large ball; Americans argued that with three balls per frame in five-pin, the Canadian game provided a handicap. Brunswick was happy to oblige Canadians with five-pin lanes, but would have rather introduced the more lucrative ten-pins into Canadian leisure habits. In the 1950s, Double Diamond Bowling Supply introduced a line of bowling alleys to convert Canadians to their national bowling culture. The problem with five-pin in 1957, however, was that automatic pin-setting machines had only recently been developed and were expensive.[25]

One of Curry's immediate challenges in the War Memorial Gym was keeping a reliable, steady supply of 'pin-boys' to set pins during drop-in and league times. Pin-boy wages were typically the largest expense for bowling alley proprietors. For example, in Curry's business plan, pin-boy wages were estimated at $2,000 per year (40,000 lines at 5¢ per line). Curry counted on local boys from Lord Byng Secondary School, but, as he found out, teenage boys were not always available during afternoon league hours. The hiring of teenage pin-boys had its own set of problems, but these boys would work for low wages. Pin-boys in the War Memorial Gym and Vancouver alleys had the reputation of being a tough bunch. They were known to harass the bowlers from the 'pits' (area behind the pins), often intimidating the learner bowler and irritating the experienced. Nasty bowlers who rolled hard balls at the pin-boys paid the price. For these bowlers, pin-boy etiquette flew out the window and pins were spotted forward or back to cause splits. Child labour critics cautioned against the hazards of pin-setting and against the late hours that proprietors required pin-boys to work. The legendary 'Lemieux gutter ball', a ball thrown in anger that knocked out a pin-boy cold in Vancouver's Commodore Lanes in the 1930s, provided an example for labour activists through the 1950s. University students, who might have been more cooperative, were reluctant to work for 5¢ per line and felt that the job of setting pins was beneath their dignity. Already in early October 1957, Curry reported that the 'alleys were being used to capacity and the only limiting factor was the availability of pin-boys'. Students were being forced either to set their own pins or postpone their games. To assure that there were no further reductions in 'the sum of calculated revenue figures', Curry recommended that UBC invest $24,000 for six of Double Diamond's new automatic pin-setting machines. The automatic pin setters would allow six bowlers per lane, as opposed to five, and speed up league play.[26] Despite Curry's recommendation, automatic pinsetters were not purchased at this time.

Fraternity, sorority, residence and intramural team leagues and parties occupied the bowling alleys during the afternoons and evenings, leaving very few opportunities for drop-in bowlers to practise. The lack of pin-boys aside, the only deterrent to additional team play was the lack of bowling facilities. UBC's six-lane alley was small for the size of the student body when compared with the downtown alleys of 40 or more lanes. Each year during the mid-1960s, there were 50 to 60 teams of five bowlers per team participating in league play at any given time. The intramural leagues, with 50 teams, presented the largest challenge to the bowling facilities during the fall, and the intramural programme in general taxed PE equipment and facilities. There were 3,500 intramural participants, amounting to nearly half the full-time undergraduate student body. The high participation rate reflected the function of the programme to 'encourage students to make sport and recreational activities a daily habit and an end in itself'. By 1957, intramural sports for male students included badminton, basketball, bowling, boxing, table tennis, volleyball and wrestling. The intramural programme for female students was the same as for the males, with the exclusion of boxing and wrestling. Women demonstrated a strong interest in bowling, and there was a tradition of intramural and telegraphic bowling leagues for women that began in the mid 1940s. In the late 1950s, there were often as many as 30 women's teams competing in the intramural tournament. The only co-recreational sport in the intramural programme during 1957/58 was bowling. Bowling was viewed as a sport that was not a test of muscular strength, hence female students could compete head-to-head with the males.[27]

Although the women showed a high interest in bowling, and could compete with their peer male students, the women's leagues were allocated only about ten afternoon hours per week. Afternoon hours in bowling alleys were typically reserved for women by commercial proprietors. The response was overwhelming and bowling quickly became the most popular form of recreation and the largest competitive sport for women in Canada and the USA. Many proprietors considered the interest of women bowlers to be the biggest factor in the bowling boom of the 1950s (see Figure 4.3). Eager to capitalize on this interest, equipment manufacturers and proprietors transformed the traditional notion of bowling alleys into community centres for entire family recreation. 'Bowl for health, beauty, exercise and recreation' and 'Keep that girlish figure' were slogans for the women. While women were generally expected to integrate bowling with familial responsibility, there was a feeling of independence and liberation for some female bowlers. Bowling could be a refreshing social form of recreation and for others an opportunity to flaunt sexuality or demonstrate a competitive streak. The Women's Bowling Pro Tour was established in 1959 as a response to the rapid growth of the Women's International Bowling Congress throughout the 1950s. Intercollegiate competition for women was more popular than that for men until the late 1950s, mainly due to the Intercollegiate Telegraphic Tournament held in Canada and the USA. However popular, UBC was reluctant to sanction a women's bowling team for intercollegiate competition. This was a result of the overall lack of support for women's athletics which, by 1963, was considered 'meagre'. The Women's Athletic Association felt that although their mandate was to provide 'maximum opportunity for recreation and competition', the mandate could not be met. They were struggling to support the existing 11 women's sport teams. One more team, even for a popular, inexpensive sport such as bowling, would not be supported.[28]

Figure 4.3 'Marilyn Taylor aims for a strike while Maureen Thompson, on the next lane, demonstrates good bowling etiquette.' (*Totem*, 1959)

The men's bowling club was initiated in 1959 and the following year was transformed into the Thunderbird bowling team. In 1960, the bowling Thunderbirds were actually a conglomerate of two teams of six men per team. Expenditure necessary to support the team, basically for bowling shoes and shirts, amounted to $190 in 1960 – compared with $13,848 for the football team. Through the mid 1960s, there were as many as four teams, or 24 team members. Trials began in September of each school year, and those who averaged 200 or better over 12 games became team members. A home league was formed annually through the bowling club, and provided an opportunity for the team to practise competitively. Under the direction of coach Curry, practise sessions were held in the War Memorial Gym lanes every Tuesday from September to February. A series of exhibition matches was often scheduled with senior teams from downtown Vancouver and other local lanes. In 1960, UBC hosted the First Annual Intercollegiate Telegraphic Meet, a tournament that the Thunderbirds topped each year for five consecutive years. The UBC team dominated intercollegiate competition through the mid 1960s, winning the Western Canadian University, Canadian College Singles and Team titles year after year. Inspired by local competition and the Pacific National Exhibition Tournament, in 1962 the team hosted 300 of BC's best bowlers in its First Annual Five-Pin Invitational. Amateur and professional bowling competition was fierce across Canada. When the Plaza Lanes team of Sault Ste Marie, Ontario, won the American Bowling Congress Masters ten-pin tournament in 1966, Canadian bowlers went wild.[29]

Bowling continued to boom at UBC through the early 1960s, reflecting the 'big business bonanza' of bowling throughout Canada. Lavish bowling palaces, with 40 to 60 lanes and complementary cocktail lounges, continued to be constructed, but now in the shopping centres of suburbs such as North Vancouver. As one journalist put it: 'A bowling alley is, of course, essentially a one-purpose gymnasium, but what has happened is that some elements of the Turkish bath have crept into it. It is now a multipurpose palace of rejuvenation.' Brunswick sold about $4.5 million worth of equipment, and Phillips sold $8 million of their Bowlamatics (automatic five-pin setting machines) each year in the early 1960s. There were 18,500 lanes in Canada, or one lane for every 1,000 Canadians, and 148,535 lanes in the USA in 1962. Two million Canadian bowlers spent $200 million on fees alone and generated $60 million profit per year for proprietors at this time. Total investment in bowling capital was $85 million. Brunswick was fond of saying that 'no sound is so inspiring as the triumphant shout of a bowler, and no sound is so sweet to a bowler's ear as the CRASH of the pins when a strike is heard'. What proprietors heard was money pouring into the cash register. However, administrators at UBC were ambivalent about the revenues generated from their six lanes. Gross revenues were about $16,500 and after total expenditures were subtracted ($14,000 in wages for pin-boys, maintenance, and the manager), net profits did not pay off the original loan as quickly as predicted. With the original investment in the War Memorial Gym bowling alleys nearly paid off in 1963, changes were quickly made. In May 1963, the Board of Governors approved UBC President John MacDonald's decision to transfer the control of the alleys to the School of Physical Education to be used for 'academic purposes only'.[30]

'Hardly anyone goes bowling any more', 1964–68

Since the bowling alleys were 'not a money-making proposition' as far as administrators were concerned, the transference of their management to the School in 1963 was a move of fiscal convenience. The leagues were abolished and, predictably, administrators eventually lamented the fact that, in effect, the alleys were 'not put to full use'. Osborne felt that the installation of automatic pin setters might renew interest in bowling 'without the necessity of running the bowling lanes as a commercial establishment'. However, his main commitment was to the physical education programme. 'The principal reason for the installation of these machines', he argued, is that they 'will provide for a much more satisfying experience for the students who are taking instruction in bowling'. PE was compromised when students were forced to do the work of pin-boys. Despite his attempt to reconcile athletic foundations with leisure by calling bowling a 'recreational sport', Osborne had no intention of supporting the recreational side of bowling. He drastically underestimated the importance of Curry or a similar manager in generating and maintaining the business of bowling. Surprisingly, in July of 1964, the Board of Governors approved Osborne's proposal for automatic pin setters. In the summer, six 'Ready to Play Bowlamatics' were installed. The university agreed to charge students 10¢ per game and turn these revenues over to National Bowling and Billiards, Ltd. for the lease of the six pin setters ($5,600 per lane). Osborne anticipated that 50,000 games would be bowled each year. When the aggregate number of games reached 250,000, the machines would be UBC's to keep. But by this time students had waited so long for the pin setters to arrive that the anticipation had all but worn out their inclination to bowl. The installation of pin setters six years after the alleys were installed – years after most other bowling alleys across the country had automatic pin setters – was a horrible case of too little too late. Two years after their installation, due to infrequent use of the lanes, the automatic pin setters were removed. Even as control was transferred to PE in 1963, Osborne and his faculty wanted the alleys removed altogether to make room for physiological experimentation laboratories.[31]

Although it appeared that the School had little interest in managing the business of bowling, most analysts attributed the decreased interest in bowling to the 'lack of a social atmosphere offered by a gymnasium'. Despite the discipline of physical education expansion, facilities such as gymnasiums were still viewed as suitable for athletics and sport, not for recreation. By 1963, when the UBC Student Union Building (SUB) was being designed, the planning committee's consensus was that 'if bowling alleys were located in a SUB where there would be generally a better atmosphere and a concentration of students, the bowling alleys would receive much more use'. This option looked attractive for revenues. 'Bowling lanes in student union buildings at American universities', UBC administrators were told, 'earn an average revenue of $900 to $2,400 per lane, the median being $1,700'. In 1963, the cost of five-pin lanes and equipment was about $4,500 per lane, or $10,000 per lane with automatic pin setters. In a SUB, unlike a gymnasium, bowling appeared to be a money-making proposition. 'Bowling is always more popular in a union', administrators were told. Nevertheless, student interests in the early 1960s were different from their interests in the 1950s.[32]

The student market had quickly changed and, as the 1960s proved, was unpredictable. In a sample survey in 1962 of 1,564 students (12 per cent of the 12,972 total enrolment), 57 per cent favoured the idea of placing bowling alleys in a SUB. Only 19 per cent considered them an essential addition. Bowling alleys were nineteenth on the list of facilities regarded essential, below a snack bar, theatre, swimming pool and auditorium. Recreational areas for table tennis ranked 26, handball ranked 27, bridge ranked 30, and billiards was low on the list at 34. Of the 464 women surveyed, 43 per cent felt that bowling was a desirable addition to a SUB as opposed to 37 per cent of the men. The overall interest in bowling at UBC had dwindled from three-quarters to one-half of that of the 30 other campuses surveyed. In spite of this relatively low interest in bowling, the SUB planning committee worked to persuade administrators: 'Bowling will serve in bringing together students from all residence units and undergraduate societies. It is one of the forms of active recreation most popular elsewhere with both college men and women, and this may prove to be true also at UBC once attractive, accessible facilities are provided'. The SUB committee anticipated that physical education students would be charged for morning use. Similar to the design process of the War Memorial Gym, bowling alleys were part and parcel of the SUB. In the case of the SUB, however, students were not so unified.[33]

'Hardly anyone goes bowling anymore', *The Ubyssey* editor wrote in the fall of 1967. This seemed to capture the sentiment of a majority of the 25,878 students now on campus. A week after this 'Spare Us' editorial appeared, the results of *The Ubyssey* survey of students were published.

When asked what recreational facility they would like to see placed in the area that was to house the bowling alleys, a large majority of students favoured things like a giant sandbox, pub, or swimming pool. The following week, Jon Strom, President of the Bowling Club, spoke out in defence of his chosen recreation and sport. 'Hidden in the cellar of the gymnasium', he reminded his peers, 'are six lanes now serving 200 people a week'. 'Bowling is not a dying sport.' In early November, the AMS student council voted to retain the lanes in the SUB plans despite the 'speculation that the popularity of bowling is subsiding'. *The Ubyssey* staff countered, noting that 'whether the students like it or not' the War Memorial Gym lanes were to be moved into the SUB, and when the SUB officially opened on 26 September 1968, the bowling alleys were installed. A few weeks later they were open for business. Once an 'emporium of athletic prowess' in the War Memorial Gym, the bowling alleys were now reduced to a mere emporium of recreation (see Figure 4.4). The SUB's 'Games Area' was, strictly speaking, a rec-room for billiards, bowling and table tennis.[34]

Figure 4.4   Ex-AMS President Shaun Sullivan breaking in the renovated War Memorial Gym alleys in the SUB in 1968. Note the social atmosphere.

Through the 1960s, not only had the student market changed but the very nature of students changed as well. Student recreation in leisure time was intensified, but not in the way anticipated by the discipline of physical education. For example, an AMS 'mixer' held in the gym on 17 September 1965 was a sure sign of the times to come. Osborne was furious and lodged a 'vigorous complaint' about this particularly disastrous party. The condition of the gym was, according to Osborne, 'absolutely intolerable as a result of people being ill and vomiting following drinking what must have been considerable quantities of liquor judging from the empty whiskey bottles found on the premises'. The gym and bowling alleys were trashed. The janitor was so distressed that he was 'fed up and ready to quit – there was such a mess'. The result resonated with the War Memorial Gym critic who feared the gym would be a 'pagan temple'. When the lanes had been installed in the Gym in 1957, bowling etiquette underwrote basic rules that regulated what bowlers wore and how they acted in the alley. When the SUB was opened in 1968, the rules for the bowling alleys reflected new issues. The SUB Games Area was for recreation and had few pretensions to sport. The new etiquette reflected the new student. 'Drunkeness, and Pot and Hash and who the hell is that with the glue and his head in a plastic bag? NO, NO, NO, that is a No No down here. This is not a moral or ethical question, nor is it a social judgement. It is a problem of responsibility.' If in the 1950s, Brunswick could emphasize to administrators that 'in the Bowling Alley Business, the main thing the operator sells is *time*', in the 1960s administrators had financial reason to panic when stoned bowlers lingered, taking up to two hours to bowl a single game. The student body was recreated in the SUB, but not at all to the satisfaction of administrators.[35]

The bowling alleys in the SUB were adequately successful in terms of revenue. An evaluation of the use of the facilities found that the bowling alleys were 'fairly heavily used'. Monday night leagues, intramurals and everyday social bowling kept respectable revenues flowing to the satisfaction of administrators. But by the early 1980s, revenues in the order of $15,000–$20,000 per year paled next to the money generated by the new electronic games. A single electronic game generated $1,000 per week with little upkeep and surveillance. It was not that students became increasingly individualistic, or were 'bowling alone' in the SUB. Rather, if the SUB is an example of the commodification of leisure time, administrators defined what amusement and recreation would look like. In February of 1986, the SUB lanes were removed because of lack of revenues. The Games Room remains to this day a video arcade. Games like Arachnoid, Baby PacMan, Comet, Donkey Kong, Double Dragon, Gauntlet, Iron Maiden, Tempest, Tron and World Cup provided opportunities for a lucrative, consumptive and virtual recreation. Revenues generated from 100 games (video and pinball) amounted to $330,000 for the 1986/87 fiscal year. Leisure time and recreation, it seems, were capital ideas.[36]

The popularity of bowling continued to decline across Canada throughout the 1970s. Only one out of 22 Canadians older than 14 years bowled in 1976 as compared with one out of eight in the early 1960s. About 61 per cent in 1976 considered bowling to be their favourite sport, but few actually bowled. Once again, similar to the 1940s and earlier, Canadians were more likely to play golf or hockey, or go skiing and swimming rather than bowling. In British Columbia in 1976, people were much more likely to spend an afternoon or evening jogging, walking, or doing yoga than participating in any of the recreational sport activities. However, the most significant changes between the early 1960s and mid 1970s were in outside-the-home versus home-centred leisure-time activity. By this time, 83 per cent of Canadians surveyed watched television for four or more hours a week. This activity combined with listening to the radio (71 per cent) and to records and tapes (40 per cent), marked the increasing popularity of home-centred, consumptive recreation. Activities reserved for affluent families in the 1950s (such as listening to records and tapes, and watching television) were consuming significant amounts of time for all families in the 1970s. This was not due to the 'golden age of great achievement' in culture anticipated by the Canadian government any more than it was due to a long trend in the commodification of leisure-time recreation. By the end of the 1970s, corporations such as Sony, which anticipated the convergence of home-centred activities (listening to tapes) with outside-the-home activities, succeeded in making something as innocent as walking a consumptive form of recreation. Cultural elitists, radicals and religious fundamentalists alike were stumped. Was this the devil finding employment for idle hands?[37]

Recreating the student body, if the story of the bowling alleys in the War Memorial Gymnasium has a moral, required more than the compulsion of capital and the Devil. During and after World War II, the power that circulated through the student body worked to establish bowling as a UBC institution. Administrators wanted the student body to be busy, and overcame the contradictions of academics and athletics with recreational desires by calculating financial interests. Revenues and premises overcame principles. By surprise, in basically out-politicking their superiors, the students were recreated, yet not entirely in a way they expected. Though Brunswick and bowling proprietors commodified leisure time and recreation, they were not successful in anticipating the rate at which students would alter their consumer preferences. Physical educators worked to overcome the subordination of the body to the mind in academia, responded to the new leisure-time market and capitalized on student desires for recreation. Yet when pressed, these educators were more than willing to abandon recreation for their traditional market of athletics and sports. Pin-boys, exploitable and unpredictable as they were, worked to make or break the bowling experience for students. The gym, with its non-social atmosphere, unhygienic appearance and limited space, constrained access and made evident the contradiction between sport and recreation. More than capital and the Devil, recreating the student body required the mundane, political interaction of a variety of actors, actions and performances.

Bowling alleys never transformed the War Memorial Gym into the 'palace of rejuvenation' that characterized other bowling venues throughout North America in the 1950s and 1960s. Even with the addition of bowling alleys and whirlpool baths, the Gym never fully became the 'pagan temple to the human body' that critics feared. As innocent a practice as bowling was at that time, the bowling alleys nevertheless emerged as a site of desire and bodily performance. Despite their promise of liberation from the confines of academics and athletics, like other spaces on campus, the bowling alleys regulated performative culture. Student bowlers embodied fairly standardized rules of performance and etiquette, much like their professors who put on a face each day for acceptance, or like the basketball players and fans in the bleachers on the main floor of the War Memorial Gym. The pleasures of consuming the bowling experience were rarely without the constraints of performative culture. Bodies were recreated at the university, yet not unlike academics and athletics for most students, the performances and pleasures were not all that memorable.[38]

Gold-Plated Footballs and Orchids for Girls, A 'Palace of Sweat' for Men

BECKI L. ROSS AND ERIN BENTLEY

Regarded as both an era of socially conservative values in the West, and a presage of 1960s liberatory social movements, the decade following World War II embodies a complex nexus of cultural retrenchment and resistance. In North America, this period signifies the cold war – a period American military analyst Rebecca Grant suggests is illustrative of a troubling corollary between repressive gender norms and national security.[1] This historical epoch is concurrently associated, in official Canadian history, with the burgeoning welfare state and accompanying notions of 'caring and sharing ... [as] ... central to our Canadian identity'.[2] However, these sentiments appear incongruous with other local and national realities: the ongoing cultural denigration and residential school abuses inflicted upon many First Nation peoples; the displacement of African-Canadian women from hard-won factory positions occupied during the war;[3] the 1946 inception of Canada's McCarthy-esque national security regime – the Security Panel – which would subsequently purge the Canadian military and civil service of hundreds of gays and lesbians;[4] and the hegemonic (re)production of idealized wife/mother subjectivities for Canadian women – read: Anglo-Celtic, bourgeois and (hetero)feminine.[5]

In the wake of war-related trauma, death and social upheaval, the marriage rate in Canada exploded, while the nuclear family was extolled by social scientists as the most stable, mature arrangement of domestic relations. By 1956, the age of marriage had plummeted: on average, women married at 21.6, and men at 24.5. 'Especially for women', Doug Owram argues, 'the completion of [high] school, engagement, marriage, and the birth of the first child were more or less consecutive events'.[6] Moreover, a mere 6 per cent of Canadians between 18 and 24 pursued post-secondary education in 1950.[7] Those who did attend Canadian universities in the post-war period were predominantly white, from the middle and upper classes. Male students significantly outnumbered female students, and politicians and university brass made special accommodations for veterans returning home from service after World War II.

The post-war university, as a site of nation-building, occupied real and imagined spaces within which processes of national identity formation were constituted. And athletic endeavours on campuses (and off) became intimately associated with national archetypes: the athlete equals the citizen, the soldier, the ambassador (see Vertinsky, this volume).[8] Given that these nationally sanctioned identities were almost exclusively associated with and available to men, and sportsmen in particular, how did sporting women at the University of British Columbia (UBC) make their mark? If, indeed, they were portrayed as 'delicate parodies' of the 'true' (male) athlete,[9] what kind of welcome did they find on the fields, tracks and gymnasium floors of UBC?

In this chapter, we seek to examine the material and discursive conditions under which female athletes strove for sporting excellence at UBC between 1945 and 1955. We explore how institutionalized administrative ambivalence (bordering on hostility) towards funding women's sports, the negligible reportage of women's sports in the student newspaper – *The Ubyssey*, and the ideology of separate spheres for separate (and unequal) sexes, contributed to the construction of the post-war female athlete as a trespasser on men's sacred terrain. Part of men's terrain at UBC included the War Memorial Gymnasium, which played a central role in the production of hetero-gendered and racialized subjects. Both before and after the Gym's official opening in 1951, white (heterosexual) male athletes, coaches, and teachers were summoned as its rightful occupants; women were summoned as spectators and side-line/half-time boosters of men's mighty feats.

Although the outright elimination of support for women's athletics at UBC was not an option, and paradoxically women's elite teams were often highly successful during the immediate post-war period, sporting women learned that their place on collegiate playing fields was provisional – their sporting practices were most often configured by those in positions of authority as a footnote to the hegemonic narrative of men's athletics.[10] According to historian Lee Stewart, 'Women in sports [at UBC] were clearly seeking an ideal of physical excellence that, like higher education, was historically a male pursuit.'[11] In particular, those women whose sports demanded rigorous physical strength, body contact and speed, were subject to suspicion, and, in some quarters, disdain. Women were not supposed to sweat profusely; some etiquette manuals submitted that ladies did not sweat at all. By contrast, other female performers on campus – fashion models, cheerleaders, majorettes (see Figure 5.1) and beauty queens – were prized for their (hetero)sexual – often semi-nude allure – their ability to lift men's morale and their compliance with highly conventional, idealized notions of female desirability. These women performed femininity very differently from female athletes whose non-traditional passions and sheer corporeality placed them in tension with increasingly rigid scripts for normative womanhood.

Figure 5.1   'Majorettes practise one of their many intricate routines, which provided colour and spirit on the gridiron.' (*Totem*, 1948)

The first decade after World War II at UBC was marked by processes of negotiation by female athletes and administrators, and was a time shot through with contradictions. On the one hand, (white) female athletes, and female co-eds more generally, were urged to become fit for (maternal) service to the nation, and during World War II, two hours a week of physical fitness training was mandatory for all co-eds. An explicit objective of the plan during and after the war was to instruct commitment to fitness as a patriotic duty. On the other hand, fitness for women was imagined within exceedingly narrow parameters. Between 1945 and 1955, top-level female athletes could not expect facilities and equipment to enable their athletic excellence. Even intercollegiate women bowlers at UBC were refused official team status, while their male counterparts formed the Thunderbird team in 1960 (see Petrina, this volume). However, at the same time, female athletes, coaches and sports administrators talked back and struggled to wrest greater control and resources from men who called the shots within varsity athletics.[12]

Getting the Short End of the Stick

In a 1946 editorial on the sports page of *The Ubyssey*, Betty Stuart vented her frustration at the unequal allocation of funds, equipment and practise space to female athletes. She also expressed hope that plans for the new War

Memorial Gymnasium, originally planned for opening in 1950, would improve the situation:

> We women get the small end of the stick rather often. Take, for instance, the case of the Women's Rifle Club who long for a decent range on the campus; the hoop girls who sigh for a gym where they and the men will have a practice court apiece, and the little co-eds who struggle with their girdles in the cramped locker rooms ... Were opportunities provided, might not many more of our co-eds become fanatical sportsters and bring fame to the hall of our Memorial Gymnasium?[13]

Several months later, in February 1947, Jackie Shearman penned an angry letter to the sports editor of *The Ubyssey*: 'The lack of publicity for women's sports is an utter disgrace ... How about giving us a little space ... and steering an occasional sports reporter in our direction?' Shearman, an accomplished member of the women's basketball team, stated that the 'minority group' of 1841 female co-eds faced 'an impregnable wall built up against it'.[14] Female athletes, she continues, lacked opportunities to 'bring up as much silverware as the men'. In the same issue of *The Ubyssey*, the associate sport editor, Chick Turner,[15] addresses Shearman's complaint by blaming the uneven coverage on the disappearance of the 'slim contours of the female reporter', and then consoles the 'sweet chicks' with his moral: 'Send us the news, and you shall see some Feminine sport in *The Ubyssey*.'[16] Two years later it appeared that little had changed.

In 1949, Chick Turner was appointed as a one-man commission by the President of the Alma Mater Society (AMS) to prepare recommendations regarding the potential inclusion of the Women's Athletic Directorate (WAD) on the governing council of the AMS. In his 'Report of the Investigating Commission on the Position of the Women's Athletic Directorate' (1949), Turner spelled out 'the differences' between men's and women's athletics:

> Women's athletics have suffered from lack of publicity. This can be traced almost entirely to the fact that feminine sport lacks the spectator appeal of men's athletics. Again, the reporters for The Ubyssey dislike intensely the job of reporting women's events and more often than not, they will pass up the game or match altogether. The sports editor has tried repeatedly to enlist the help of girl reporters, but they stay only long enough to get a date![17]

In this passage, Turner acknowledges that female athletes practise and compete for UBC in virtual obscurity. However, he accounts for this by invoking common-sense views of 'feminine sport' as a much less desirable commodity than men's athletics. Here, he implies that men's bodies in general are more valuable than women's, and that men's sporting expertise in particular is inherently superior, and hence deserving of paid spectatorship: men's sports have limitless exchange value, women's sports have none. Beneath Turner's dismissal of women's athletics as unworthy is the late nineteenth-century medico-moral mythology that women were deficient in competitive instinct and the drive to excel, *and* that they were burdened by unstable hormones and fragile, easily damaged reproductive systems.[18] Only 15 years earlier, in 1935, Mary Louise Bollert, the first Dean of Women at UBC, had 'opposed a proposal by university women to form a track team, arguing that the sport was too strenuous for women without close supervision of their activities'.[19] Similarly, in 1938, Maryrose Reeves Allen, the Director of Physical Education for women at Howard University, wrote that 'the heavier sports ... have no place in a woman's life: they rob her of her feminine charms and often of her good health'.[20] Health experts, both men and women, made female sporting bodies the object of observation and surveillance – in Foucauldian terms, they exercised bio-techniques of power to specify the contours of normalized femininity.

Rehearsing a familiar refrain in his 1949 report, Chick Turner naturalizes the sports editor's contempt for women's athletic achievements and absolves him of responsibility for dodging attendance at games and matches. Painting the editor as a model of (white) chivalry, Turner champions his exhaustive efforts to recruit female writers, to whom he refers as 'girl reporters' with sexist relish. Lastly, he both laments and mocks the women who show up at the newspaper's office as capricious, if not desperate co-eds with one thing in mind: heterosexual courtship, and its logical extension, the MRS degree.[21] Elsewhere in his report, Turner contends that 'smaller budgetary needs of the Women's Athletics Association offset the lack of spectator appeal'.[22] Taking for granted the impossibility of paying spectators, Turner justifies the already institutionalized status of women's sports at UBC as unequal, impoverished and undeserving of resources. Not surprisingly, spectators at men's sporting events were charged $1.00, while spectators for women's events were charged 25 cents.

In Iowa during the 1950s, against all odds, revenues from women's basketball games underwrote the expenses of 16 other interscholastic women's sports.[23] During the impressive reign of the Edmonton Commercial Graduates, or The Grads, it was not uncommon for 10,000 spectators to pack gymnasia wherever they competed.[24] And, in 1951 at UBC, it was reported that a weekend of varsity women's volleyball in Powell River, BC, drew more spectators than the boys' games.[25] So it was never a foregone conclusion, everywhere, that no one was willing to pay to watch women compete.

Gendered Segregation

Men's and women's athletics at UBC had long been segregated into separate men's and women's athletic associations (and budgets), and men's and women's sports. Upon the official opening of the War Memorial Gym in October 1951, the bulk of the women's athletic programme was relocated to the Old Gym, as we have seen. Archival and ethnographic research suggests that women, and women's athletics in particular (including dance), were not especially welcome at the War Memorial Gym.[26] Although female students participated wholeheartedly in fund-raising campaigns for the Gym they quickly learned their place.[27] A former athlete active in women's sports at UBC recalled that men belonged in the War Memorial Gym, women didn't: 'In my undergraduate years, I got to be in there once, about 1953, to do formal gymnastics.'[28] In 1946, J.D. Penn McLeod, Executive Director of the Gym's fundraising campaign, wrote that 'the hall of heroes will be dedicated to the fallen sons of BC. The names of every BC soldier, sailor, and airman who died in Wars I and II will be inscribed in an honour roll.'[29] Not only was the War Memorial Gym erected primarily as a tribute to the 'great loss of young men in World Wars I and II', with often no, or irregular acknowledgement of women's war efforts; it was designed primarily to furnish a living shrine to the spectacle of male sporting heroism at UBC.[30] The Gym was imagined as a showcase for male virility, and as a source of much-needed revenue from men's widely lauded athletic prowess.

Women's athleticism was rarely judged newsworthy leading up to the inauguration of the War Memorial Gym. In 1949 a sports columnist at *The Ubyssey* claimed that 'few girls on campus' expressed any 'interest in athletics'.[31] In 1950, during a crisis in athletics funding at UBC, events were planned throughout the fall by the AMS, engineers and student political groups to promote men's athletics on campus. Focus on women's sport was confined to one day, 'Women's Day', organized by a sorority and the Women's Undergraduate Society.[32] So, men's sense of entitlement to institutional investment in a robust athletics programme was buttressed by the common-sense perception that women were unwilling or unable to mount credible, parallel claims to entitlement. In 1951, *The Ubyssey* reported that the AMS had passed a proposal to increase funding for the Men's Athletic Directorate (MAD) from $10,500 in 1950/51 to $17,200 in 1951/52 – an almost 72 per cent increase.[33] At the same time, the Women's Athletic Directorate (WAD) suffered a loss in funding, from $1,900 in 1950/51 to $1,700 in 1951/52. Between 1945 and 1955, the WAD operated on a budget that averaged 13.5 per cent of the men's budget – a staggering disparity.[34] And though all athletes at UBC were required to subsidize the costs of team travel, the women's programme was acutely impoverished. In 1951, Sheila Kearns wrote: 'we've got a winning [women's] basketball team here, but they couldn't stretch their money to cover any road trips'.[35] As a result, female basketball players became accustomed to local games in city-based community leagues in high school gymnasia, rather than intercollegiate play out of town. Women's varsity basketball games were routinely scheduled for 6 p.m., while men's games were at 8 p.m., which (a) exemplifies protectionist assumptions about women's safety at night and (b) confirms men's basketball as the preferred prime time spectacle.

The Phantasmatic Second Gym

In a UBC report from 1950, the author notes that facilities such as a 'small second gymnasium for women, a dance studio, and squash courts' were planned as a block at the end of the War Memorial Gym.[36] Again, the stated intention to add a 'small second gymnasium for women' betrays the standpoint that female athletes' needs were not a priority, and might only be accommodated, though on a reduced scale commensurate with beliefs about what (little) they merited, at some unspecified future date.[37] In fact, the small gym was more phantasmatic than real: the additions never materialized, and throughout the 1950s female athletes were reminded of their abject status as disenfranchised subjects with restricted claims to decision-making power and resources.[38] The War Memorial Gym promised largely white men the freedom, in the absence of women, to coach and be coached, and to amass accolades from a loyal, home-town crowd. Men's sports, it was argued, would bring in much needed honour and prestige to the university, and make the province swell with pride.

Although women students composed one-third of the student body in 1950 and had participated in fund-raising efforts to finance the War Memorial Gym – hailed as 'the greatest student project in the University of BC history' – little effort was made to include them in the building as anything but spectators of men's competitions.[39] Concerns about women's stake in the Gym, such as those outlined sharply by Marian Henderson, the Women's Athletics Director, were ignored (see Vertinsky, this volume). A 1951 press release states that, 'The building seats approximately 3,600 and holds within its walls, the Physical Education Department offices, Men's Athletic Directorate offices, gymnasium, weight-lifting room, lockers, dressing rooms, and a coffee shop.' In documents written to describe the new Gym, a primary, and often first-mentioned property of the facility is its 'reinforced concrete bleachers'. The concrete columns that support the 'floating pan' roof are invoked as functional structures built to steer spectator attention to the gymnasium floor. 'Spectator seating is arranged for excellent obstruction-free vision of events with provision for future fold-away bleachers on the Main Gym floor.' Mention is also made of a control booth for broadcasting and sound equipment necessary for future media coverage – the important 'spaces of publicity' (see McKay, this volume). The objective to make male sporting bodies visible (and audible), from every scopic vantage point, was reflected in the transparency of the Gym's modernist architectural forms.

In the fall of 1954, according to *The Ubyssey*, the UBC Athletics Department signed a contract with a local television station, CBUT, to televise 16 sporting events at UBC.[40] Television – a symbol of the new scientific and technological age – would vault UBC's athletics into unprecedented public consciousness and support. In the wake of ardent public enthusiasm for the British Empire and Commonwealth Games in Vancouver, broadcasters spent an estimated $3,000 to show five football games, five basketball games, and six other events, including English rugby games. All of the planned telecasts profiled men's athletic contests and contributed revenue to UBC's coffers; TV coverage of women's varsity sport did not rate serious consideration, and was non-existent.

The event that (un)officially opened the War Memorial Gym was a men's basketball weekend, 23–24 February 1951, against the Eastern Washington University Savages and the Whitworth College Pirates of the Evergreen conference. It is noteworthy that the gift of the 1951 graduating class at UBC, presented at this opening game, was a pair of glass backboards for installation behind the basketball rims in the new Gym – a gift donated by male and female graduates that would, for many years, almost exclusively benefit male hoopsters.

In February 1952, female basketball stars at UBC, such as Eleanor Cave, Eleanor Nyholm, Mimi Wright and Dorreen Cummings, were permitted an exhibition game at noon in the new War Memorial Gym against the Roamers from the USA, who, like the Chocolate Co-eds (see below), were touted as a female version of the Globetrotters. To promote the event in *The Ubyssey*, Jan Crafter, a forward on the UBC women's basketball squad, highlighted the (hetero)sexual appeal of the players – tall 'blondes', a 'sparkling redhead who is good to look at', and 'fast-breaking brunettes' in 'blue satin shorts' – as a ploy to attract 'the fellas' on campus. Crafter makes brief mention of women's 'brains' and 'skill' at the end of her article, but she clearly understood that female athletes' talents were no match for the marketing cachet of feminine beauty. Beyond the gates of UBC, Canadian figure-skater Barbara Ann Scott – Olympic, European, and World champion in 1948 – was widely depicted in the sexist mainstream media as a dainty, doll-like, sweet, blue-eyed, blond beauty on blades.[41] And several studies of *Sports Illustrated* confirm the historic treatment of women as pin-up models rather than athletes, most graphically evidenced in the magazine's 'Swimsuit Issue', introduced in 1964.[42]

One sporting event at UBC that did generate considerable attention was the exhibition game between the women's basketball team, the Thunderettes, and the Chocolate Co-Eds, an African-American women's team from the southern USA, modelled after the Harlem Globetrotters.[43] It would seem that the Chocolate Co-eds' winning record against men's teams across North America made them a 'novelty'. More importantly, we suspect that the women's 'defeminizing' pursuit of professional basketball, their status as (paid) touring entertainers (away from the daily grip of family and community), and their racialized otherness,[44] were factors that combined to draw spectators, even though the match was played at noon on 1 March 1950, and not in the evening.[45] Between 1945 and 1955, few high-performance female athletes at UBC were non-white women. We can only speculate about the additional barrier of racism (both covert and overt) that faced athletes of colour – Black, Asian, South Asian, Latina and First Nations – on UBC campus, and off.[46]

Cheering On the Boys

Like other abject peoples, female athletes haunted the edges of the big primary Gym, territorially expelled from full inclusion in the gendered and racialized spaces of the living monument to dead military men. And yet they were obliged to support the public exhibition of men's athletic achievements, as were other female co-eds (especially the girlfriends/wives of sportsmen), cheerleaders (see Figure 5.2), secretaries and female cleaners, both within and beyond the Gym itself. In other words, the future of men's sporting excellence at UBC depended on a loose social consensus that men were best equipped, and the most obvious constituency to entertain sports fans. The future also depended on the occupation of women in an array of auxiliary, subordinate roles. For example, in 1949, the Men's Athletic Directorate presented tiny gold-plated footballs to the 'first fifty girls' who each 'lured' five men to the game against Central Washington College as a tactic to increase ticket sales. The slogan of the contest read: 'Girls – Get on the Ball!'[47] A year earlier, in 1948, the first 400 members of the 'fair sex' were wooed to the football stadium's grandstand the day of a big game by promises of chrysanthamums and orchids.[48] Recruited as bait to promote men's athletic endeavours, 'girls' at UBC were expected to use their (hetero)sexual charms to snare male fans and to assume responsibility for filling stadiums and gymnasia to capacity. It is noteworthy that no such schemes were invented to reward men for being tempted by female co-eds to pay for the spectacle of women's sporting competitions at UBC.

In 1950, *The Ubyssey* reporter Sheila Kearns announced that the female grass hockey team at UBC invited 200 men to 'squire' 200 college women, in Vancouver for the Pacific Northwest Grass Hockey finals, to a weekend

Figure 5.2   'Knit One, Purl Two, UBC Yahoo seems to be on the lips of
these enthusiastic cheerleaders.' (*Totem*, 1955)

dance.[49] Here, unlike the enticement of female fans to men's football, the
focus on dating and dancing erases the woman as elite athlete, and women's
grass hockey as legitimate sporting spectacle for both men and other
women. Men, or 'blind dates', were commandeered for the socially
sanctioned role of escort, a move which underscored the prized status of
heterosexual courtship rituals on university campuses during the baby boom
era.[50] A woman who dared to attend the weekend dance alone, or
accompanied by her female lover, would have ruptured the heterosexual
pact and faced censure, if not worse.

In the absence of men's company (or older women's watchful eyes),
young female co-eds were commonly thought to be careless about their
safety, and at risk of harm. The varsity women's grass hockey team (see
Figure 5.3) travelled annually to tournaments in the north-western United
States (though the players paid their way and used their own transportation),
and they were accompanied by a chaperone.[51] By the early 1950s, university
administrators had voted to make chaperones mandatory for all female
athletes' out-of-town trips. In 1956, Charlotte Warren of UBC's Women's
Athletic Association wrote to the Director of Physical Education for women
at the University of Alberta to disclose her university's policy, and to seek
advice for ways to cover the costs.[52] (It was also university policy to forbid

female students, unlike male students, to share rental accommodation unless at least one of the women was 25 or older.)[53] None of the men's athletic teams appear to have had chaperones, which betrays yet another gendered double standard: female athletes required surveillance while male athletes did not. Presumably, the scrutinizing activities of older women hired to safeguard the security of 'their girls' would protect the innocents from unscrupulous men and all varieties of unladylike behaviour, including predatorial homosexual advances (see below). White, middle-class, educated women were, after all, expected to keep themselves pure for marriage and motherhood. Hence the moral regulatory investment in the full-time policing duties of chaperones – ideally mature, married women – could be defended as a sound investment in the future health of the nation.

Female athletes at UBC whose sports crossed gender lines disrupted middle-class prescriptions for refined, respectable femininity, and courted rancour; women whose (hetero)feminine beauty was judged as the main event, reinscribed normative prescriptions and were rewarded.[54] Specifically, female beauty contestants, models, cheerleaders, baton twirlers and stripteasers[55] enjoyed enormous popular appeal (see Figure 5.4), in part because they were assumed to embody, and to act out, men's voyeuristic fantasies of feminine heterosexiness.[56] The Women's Undergraduate

Figure 5.3   'Grass Hockey Team, Varsity.' (*Totem*, 1946)

Figure 5.4   'Mardi Gras Ball, three "small girls".' (*Totem*, 1946*)*

Society's annual fashion show (see Figure 5.5), which typically featured women in bridal gowns, negligées and bathing suits, was a staple event on the UBC calendar, sure to 'capture men's eyes'.[57] In all, female performers who bolstered the efforts of male athletes (and male students, including veterans) were praised in boldly nationalist discourse: 'It's the ladies who stand behind the men who will mould Canada's future.'[58]

Although cheerleading was regarded as an activity exclusively for men in the late 1800s, by the 1940s it had become dominated by women, with men deserting the practice in large numbers.[59] In October 1948, an article on the sports page of *The Ubyssey* trumpeted support for the men's football team: 'Cheer Leaders Denny Pierce and Ruth Genis will be on the sidelines this week to lead spectators in their enthusiastic cheering to help build up the morale of the team on the field.' Two years later, in October 1950, *The Ubyssey* reported on a 'revived' team of twelve Drum Majorettes in preparation for Homecoming celebrations, and future trips in support of men's athletic teams: 'The troupe will carry on after Homecoming to add a little cheesecake to the football game and various other sport events ... where a show of feminine frames is most appreciated ... Working with a lack of equipment, poor facilities, and without cooperation of the weather man, the dozen stalwarts have done very well.'[60] Not only does the reporter lewdly refer to displays of scantily clad baton tossers, and heterosexualize his appreciation of their assets, but even female performers like the Majorettes could expect to 'strut their stuff' without adequate attire or equipment.

Figure 5.5   'Campus Fashion Parades showed latest styles in formal and bathing suits. At right is Mary Taylor, 1951 Queen.' (*Totem*, 1951)

Every year, beauty contests were held on campus for Faculty Queens, Sorority Queens, Mardi Gras Queen, Homecoming Queen and Totem Queen, and the queens were invited to sporting events 'to supply the pulchritude'.[61] The Homecoming Queen was chosen from an average of ten candidates at the annual Saturday afternoon Homecoming football game in October. Off campus, similar contests were popular cultural events at country fairs, snow carnivals, national exhibitions, rodeos and the federal civil service.[62] In January 1949, the sports editor of *The Ubyssey* announced: 'The sultry beauty of UBC's Totem Queen Jan Olsen will grace a number of athletic events on the campus.' The article mentions that she will 'kick off' a rugby match and commence a basketball game by 'throwing the ball in'.[63] Later that month, a sports reporter salivated: 'A touch of sex will be added today when the Vikings battle the Birds in the gym at noon hour. Just to give the male section of the hoop fans their large charge for the week, vivacious

Jan Olsen ... will be on hand.'[64] In both instances, Olsen was installed as an ornamental accessory whose public-spirited duty it was to stimulate and titillate both male athletes and male fans.[65]

While women competed against each other in the glamour sweepstakes, gladiatorial men in heavy football pads and helmets reminded returning alumni, chiefly other men (with deep pockets), of the symbolic and real import of 'hit, crunch, and burn' to the spirit, and indeed the political economy, of UBC.[66] To cultural critic Varda Burstyn, football players were 'trained in the values and conventions of the workaday world of factory or office, and [were] prepared for exercising violence in the service of nation and empire'.[67] That so many intercollegiate football players suffered injuries and the shameful humiliation of defeats in silence, only served to stoke the mystique surrounding stadiums as staging grounds for patriotic hypermasculinity.[68]

Focus on hyperfemininity at UBC extended beyond women's most public, blue-ribboned presentations of self at beauty pageants, fashion shows and fraternity stag parties. In 1950, the fashion editor of the *Vancouver Province*, Marie Moreau, enthusiastically commended UBC women for 'good grooming' and for 'dressing better than most college girls'. In an interview, she noted that she was glad 'the sloppy look' was gone forever.[69] Here, Moreau's championing of the neat and tidy, obedient girl is hinged to, and contingent on, the disavowal of her ill-kempt, unruly and hence untrustworthy other.[70]

Female Athletes 'Played', Male Athletes 'Competed'

In the post-war era, most men at UBC seemed happy to consume women's performances as beauty queens, fashion models, cheerleaders and 'exotic dancers' on campus, but they were infrequently prepared to watch and support the performances of female athletes.[71] Part of men's indifference is linked to the recurring myth that women played at sports, whereas men competed, and as such women's sports were perceived to be void of the drama and suspense synonymous with win/loss contests.[72] Prominent female sports administrators across Canada, influenced by trends in the eastern United States, sought to protect women from 'overly aggressive' boys' and men's sport, and emphasized participation over competition.[73] At UBC, Marian Henderson, the women's athletic director, defended girls' rules basketball because she believed strongly that women had no business playing boys' basketball.[74] However, modification of rules fed the fiction that games and sports played by women were inferior to those played by men, and that women were not serious participants.[75] Intramurals at UBC were promoted rather than intercollegiate teams in the Women's Gym as an avenue 'to meet new people'.[76] References are repeatedly made in *The Ubyssey* to women's sports clubs such as the Girls' Swim Club,[77] and to luncheons hosted for visiting women's teams in Brock Hall,[78] which seem to reinforce notions of women's sports as non-threatening, domestic and fun, and something altogether other than the smorgasbord of dog-eat-dog masculinity on the gridirons, ice rinks and courts of UBC.[79] And the presence of women at the luncheon as cooks and servers, and the athletes playing the part of hostesses, would have instilled an unthreatening element to women's athletics.

Lesbianism: Play It, Don't Say It

The spectre of 'evil lesbianism' dogged all women involved in athletics, both white and of colour, and made spectatorship of women's sporting contests a complicated affair.[80] Since the late 1800s, sexologists such as Richard Von Krafft-Ebing had associated women's pursuit of 'manly sports' with lesbianism.[81] In the late 1940s and throughout the 1950s, sportswomen in basketball, baseball, grass hockey, ice hockey, and track and field were suspected not only of encroaching on men's terrain of competition but of acquiring mannish characteristics. From 1943 to 1955, subtle and blatant messages were communicated to the 'amazons' who joined the All American Girls Baseball League (AAGBL) in the USA. Susan Cahn observes that, 'The AAGBL advocated a unique "femininity principle", deliberately contrasting players' amazing "masculine" baseball skills with their "feminine" attractiveness, an appeal accentuated by league-mandated pastel-skirted uniforms, make-up, long hair, and strict standards of off-field dress and behaviour.'[82] In her book *Girls of Summer*, Lois Browne notes that many of the baseball players were lesbians (and 10 per cent were Canadians), though in the Hollywood film version of the story, *A League of Their Own* (1993), actor Tom Hanks is showcased as the drunk/coach, and all references to the gay demi-monde are smothered.[83]

In an era of dichotomous gender roles and the pathologization of homosexuality, it is likely that silence and shame shrouded the identities of lesbian athletes at UBC whose bodies, ironically, interacted and performed in gender-segregated settings imbued with homoerotic possibilities. As Susan Cahn explains, the suspicion of lesbianism functioned both as a homophobic repellent and as a magnetic sexual force field in women's sport.[84] Locker rooms, showers, passageways and playing surfaces of gymnasia offered opportunities for same-sex bonding, yet women who loved women were compelled to heed the code 'play it, but don't say it'.[85] Between 1951 and 1972 at UBC, the segregationist containment of women's sports – both intramural and intercollegiate – in the Women's Gym, probably enabled both same-sex experimentation and loving relationships. It is also probable that the long-awaited completion of women's residences in May 1951 – named Wesbrook, MacInnes and Bollert – meant yet other women-only spaces for same-sex intimacy and sexual relations.[86]

While the pages of *The Ubyssey* make no overt mention of lesbians, this silence is not attributable to a dearth of debates regarding women's sexuality. Lively discussion at UBC followed the release of the 'lewdly sensationalist' Kinsey Reports, *Sexual Behavior in the Human Male* (1948) and *Sexual Behavior in the Human Female* (1953).[87] At the same time, the medico-moral pontifications of homophobic sexologists and psychologists were widely circulated, and legal prohibitions against homosexuality were enshrined in the Criminal Code.[88] In addition, the 1940s and 1950s was a time of extensive state-sanctioned surveillance and interrogation of gays and lesbians in the Canadian military and civil service, led by the RCMP.[89] In Vancouver as in other large urban centres, lesbians and gay men had begun to establish above-ground social networks in bars such as the New Fountain, Vanport and the Castle, as well as at house parties and cruising sites.[90] Their visibility sparked lurid news reportage and stepped up policing and societal ostracism at the same time that it made gay people knowable to each other.

A new genre of dimestore paperback, the lesbian pulp novel, also became enormously popular. The ideological purchase of these fictitious tales hinged, in large part, on their stereotypic description of the inherent iniquity and lascivious wickedness of the anti-heroines within. Titles such as *Strange Sisters* (1955), *Halo In Brass* (1949, 1950) and *Warped Women* (1951) reveal a great deal about hegemonic discourses regarding women's sexualities in this era.[91] Though predominantly built around the caricature of the lesbian as a sexual predator, these books nevertheless represented – for many lesbian and bisexual women – an entrée into a conceptual lesbian community. Moreover, they caught the attention, and aroused the ire, of North American state officials. In 1952, the pulp novel *Women's Barracks* (1950) by Tereska Torres was found to be obscene by Canadian judge A.G. McDougall, and its distributor, National News of Ottawa, was fined $1,100.[92] That same year, *Women's Barracks* was condemned by the House Un-American Activities Committee.[93]

Clearly, then, discussions of normative versus deviant female sexualities were, to a considerable degree, played out in the public arena. In short, the accessibility of these notions renders conspicuous the silence of *The Ubyssey* on these matters, since it is reasonable to speculate that some students at UBC would have been at least marginally aware of these debates, the ideologies informing them and the actual existence of lesbian and gay communities in Vancouver and elsewhere. The potential, combined effect of the 'masculinized' sportswoman and the 'dark threat of lesbianism' trope is not inconsiderable. Indeed, as Kane and Lenskyj suggest, such notions have historically placed immense pressure on both heterosexual and lesbian athletes to camouflage themselves in hyper-heterosexual roles – wife/mother – or in hyper-feminine styles of dress and behaviour.[94] This cultural obligation to perform a *mea culpa* significantly placed the female athlete in an abject position, thereby assuring and amplifying her subordination. Indeed, those female athletes most vulnerable to the malignant smear of mannishness were likely to be under constant pressure to prove their heterosexual credentials to male suitors, as well as to straight friends and family. Hiding in the closet must have provided some much needed protection, but routine tactics of deception, together with efforts to stem the tides of judgement and hatred, exacted a high price.

Conclusion

In the socio-politically conservative climate of the post-World War II era, female co-eds at UBC were constantly reminded of their role as men's helpmates on the sidelines and behind the scenes, as well as their moral, familial obligation as the nation's future wives and mothers. Gendered, racialized and heterosexualized limits placed on women, and female athletes in particular, assumed countless discursive and material forms, though resistance to the conventions of normative, reproductive femininity also took shape. Women enrolled at UBC pursued dreams of higher education and trained for white-collar employment, and some broke new ground in the professions; by the late 1950s, some acted on the politics of the Beat generation and civil rights organizing in the USA.

Sarah Banet-Weiser acknowledges the 'pleasure and desire experienced by beauty pageant contestants' who were not 'victims of false consciousness' trapped in 'repugnant rituals of feminine objectification'.[95] At UBC, beauty queens, cheerleaders and baton twirlers were disciplined according to hierarchized standards of physical attractiveness, and they reaped benefits from their roles as boosters. Female competitive athletes, by contrast, stirred varying degrees of derision and indifference among men (and non-athletic women) across the UBC campus. And though some reached their personal and collective goals and glory, they did so with grit, spit and sweat in spite of a myriad of institutional barriers that constrained their self-expression and athletic excellence. Chronic shortages of physical spaces, training and coaching personnel, financial resources, media coverage in *The Ubyssey* (as well as the *Vancouver Sun* and *Province*) and the lack of consistent moral support from fans, made sportswomen marginal to the arenas wherein men competed and were rewarded as the rightful recipients of the university's largesse.

Female student athletes, even white, able-bodied, economically privileged ones, could not lay claim to the tripartite athlete/soldier/citizen; the character to be built in gymnasia, on ice rinks, at stadiums (and on killing fields) – obedient, loyal, disciplined, productive, heroic – was reserved for men. The modernist vision of progress and enhancement of the body implanted in the War Memorial Gym was, as has been shown, white, masculinist and heterocentric. Sportswomen at UBC learned very quickly to settle for scraps and crumbs as administrators, funders and fellow students wrestled to reconcile the physical strength, speed and competitive drive women needed to win with cultural imperatives of hetero-feminine beauty, nurturance and self-sacrifice.

Fifty years later, the UBC Athletics Programme sports one female coach – varsity women's basketball coach Deb Huband – and 21 male coaches. Women's basketball games are still scheduled for 6 p.m., while the men's basketball team owns the coveted 8 p.m. slot; cheerleading squads, mascots and marching bands are fixtures at the men's games and not the women's. In addition, men's sports continue to outnumber women's sports on campus, news reports of women's sporting feats in *The Ubyssey* remain uneven and men's sports command a larger portion of the overall athletics budget. Outside the University's gates, the sports pages in mainstream North American newspapers systematically ignore most women's sports, especially football, soccer, hockey, wrestling and weight-lifting. And concern about sporting women's appearance and the 'taint' of lesbianism works to discipline players, coaches and administrators.[96] Assessing the cultural arena of the Women's National Basketball Association (WNBA) (1997–present), Banet-Wiser claims that the WNBA is 'clearly about normative femininity, hetero-sexuality, maternity, and perhaps most importantly, respectability'.[97] Though campus beauty contests have been abandoned, and the Totem Queen no longer 'kicks off' rugby matches, female intercollegiate athletes at UBC and elsewhere still compete on playing surfaces haunted and constrained by stubborn, bourgeois cultural anxieties about gender, race, sexual identity and nation-building. These athletes' victories and defeats are experienced as passionately as they were in the 1950s. But sportswomen never compete outside capillaries of power that maintain they don't belong, don't measure up and don't merit the same status and resources commonsensically afforded sportsmen, whose activities today stoke the myths of male sporting excellence, credibility and deservedness of tomorrow.

Designing Discipline:
The Architecture of a Gymnasium

SHERRY MCKAY

Memory, architecture and the tyranny of the past

> The particular force of memory comes from its very capacity to be altered –
> unmoored, mobile, lacking in any fixed position
>
> (Michel de Certeau, 1984)[1]

Theoretically, modern architects, identifying social memory with history and hence perceiving it as an impediment to original design and more generally to progress, discounted the role of memory in the conception of their buildings.[2] The architects of the War Memorial Gymnasium were no exception; nor would it seem were the students and officials who commissioned it. As one architectural commentator expressed it in 1944, 'the past is a distraction and a tyranny'.[3] It was a sentiment echoed by a contemporary UBC student who wrote of the burden, deceit and anachronism of architectural styles seeking to recall the past. But then, how might a modern architecture – of glass and concrete, of a vocabulary of forms intentionally stripped of any associational or literary aspect and entirely bereft of the symbolism and rhetorical figures of ornament – compel a recollection of anything beyond itself with any specificity or predictability? How could architecture, in this instance, bring to mind those who had served and died in a modern war, and their sacrifices and aims? Can social memory, denied a role in the conception of modern architecture, circulate without these architectural supports? Architecture served the individual in negotiating the here and now, of reuniting the feel of the modern world with the instrumentality of its production. If modern architecture was about forgetting – about steeling itself against the 'distractions' and 'tyranny' of the past – what purpose would it serve in housing a war memorial? Is the relationship of memory and architecture then, as Adrian Forty has recently asserted, 'less straightforward than some recent discussions might lead one to suppose'.[4]

The conventional monument, a venue that had once encouraged the exploration of social memory, was not available to the designers of the War Memorial Gymnasium: the building was to be a 'living memorial'. Society had begun to cast aside monuments, favouring the socially useful and future-oriented over anachronistic codes and the backward gaze. Hence the conventions of architectural commemoration were denied to any potential architectural eulogist by a society no longer stirred by them. The task of the War Memorial Gymnasium's design was therefore to memorialize without representation or recall of a past time or place, and to situate bodies in the here and now, to fuse the space of occasion with that of the quotidian (see Figure 6.1).

Although the ability of architecture to incite social or 'collective' memory with any reliability or durability has been questioned, other agents of recollection have been identified. Many now propose that social memory is instilled by the orchestration of bodies.[5] Ceremonies, codes of behaviour, rituals and repetition are deemed the source of 'collective memories' and their attachment to specific places.[6] The commemorative service held on Remembrance Day would be one such ritual; upon its performance memory resides in the Memorial Hall. Games and spectators also have their rituals. The body, whether mourner, player or bystander, moves in response to the script offered by the architectural plan. And modernists had at least granted a cognitive role to memory, a role activated by the body moving through space. However, neither the scripts, the bodies solicited, nor the memories recalled need be the same.

The Memorial Hall is both a mundane entrance foyer and an exceptional space of occasion, a space of daily passage and a place of annual ceremony. One might expect this simultaneity of seemingly opposing functions, the adjacencies of a space seeking to call forth the incorporeal with another dedicated to the enhancement of the body, to provoke a certain *frisson*. For some modernists, such a seemingly unforeseen juxtaposition might evoke Lautréamont's praise for the simultaneity of unrelated things: 'beautiful as the chance encounter of a sewing machine and an umbrella on an operating table'. That is, the possible strangeness of the pairing of a gymnasium and a war memorial might provoke memory in that aleatoric way in which memory is now thought to work. For Michel de Certeau today, Walter Benjamin in the 1930s and others in the decades in between, to fix memory is to claim a past, to institutionalize and to distort; but to free it, to under-stand it as a process 'unmoored' from objects, is to free it from the prescribed meaning of hegemonic history. The success or failure of the War Memorial Gymnasium as a memorial, monolithically fixed or pluralistically polyvalent, determinate or indeterminate, also positions it within debates on modernism contemporary with its construction – debates about whether architecture is a liberating or disciplining apparatus.

There were those in the late 1940s who commented on the juxtaposition of memorial and gymnasium, perceiving it as inappropriate rather than strange, however. David Brock, son of those commemorated by UBC's

Figure 6.1   War Memorial Hall, War Memorial Gymnasium.

Brock Hall, wrote to the President of the University, informing him that he did 'not think a gym will remind anyone of wars and men who die in them .... To admit that it is only partly a memorial is to admit it as no real memorial at all.'[7] He was, as he admits, of the 'minority opinion', in believing that:

> [t]he fact that their deaths were supremely useful and an economy besides which all other economies pale does not mean that a so-called 'useful' memorial is actually useful in reminding us of anything in particular. The gym will be a symbol of fun ... and what an excellent and necessary thing fun is, to be sure, but not necessarily a good symbol of death to anyone except a mystic, which basketballing students are not.[8]

That Brock was correct in judging his a minority opinion was clearly confirmed by the President of the University, who retorted: 'there has been a revulsion of feeling against the useless and, in many cases, ugly, memorials erected at the end of the last war' and 'it is necessary that a change be made in memorials'.[9] The President of the University was also of the opinion that they should honour those who served as well as those who died. His was the increasingly popular opinion. By 1951, when the Gymnasium opened, a war memorial that was also a gymnasium was a commonplace, a 'natural' occurrence. And if 'basketballing' students were not to be understood as mystics in the 1950s, they could at least be understood as the embodiment of modernity, of dynamic balance and torsion, and the natural expression of character.[10] The simultaneity of a memorial, a gymnasium and active bodies meeting, if not on an operating table (as Lautréamont might envision) but in a modern building unprecedented for its time and place, suggests an investigation of memorials, modernism, gymnasiums and bodies is in order.

Memorials

In 1944 *The Architectural Forum* addressed the urgent issue of 'Living Memorials' and 'How to honour the war dead'.[11] It was here recognized that 'in the eccentricity of modern thought, we were finally confronted by the principle that people and things are better forgotten. The new philosophy of architecture has been preparing us for the idea. It has no provision for enduring things, no solitude for posterity.'[12] In contradistinction to this new belief, the author argues that architecture, because of its very material nature, offers the 'vividness' of a physical symbol lacking in the printed word. While recognizing some of the current modernist critiques of memorials – their usually reactionary style, their misrepresentation of the past, or new ideas of war – the author counters the modernist conception of utility. He argues that 'If for example, a gymnasium be a pressing community need, it should be satisfied as a direct civic obligation. To take unction from the process by claiming for it the merit of a war memorial is a hypocritical sort of economy which [can be] likened to the disingenuousness of presenting a pair of rubbers to a child at Christmas.'[13] The author deemed it impossible to protect such living memorials from 'disedifying intrusion'. And in allowing that a memorial should be not only instructive and uplifting but also be 'an addition to civic beauty', the author opened up the issue of aesthetics and hence the possibility of a distraction from, as well as the transcendence of, the horrors of war.

   While *The Architectural Forum* debated the merits of living memorials, the popular press, *Saturday Night* in this instance, was convinced by the polls that the general public overwhelmingly preferred living, useful memorials, such as recreational community centres and playgrounds to 'monument monstrosities, ugly statues and cannons'. 'Democratically planned and operated', such living memorials were seen as a bulwark, not only against future wars, but also communism 'which minimized the sacrifice of its soldiers' and fascism which 'glorified war, monuments and parade grounds'. 'Recreation in our sense that aimed toward self-expression of the individual, is unknown to both communists and Fascists.' The author goes on to claim that it is 'generally recognized that people lacking facilities for self-development are the easiest prey for agitators trying to spread those doctrines'.[14] Clearly, ideology played an important role in determining what was to be remembered, with even the form that it took assisting in its political representation. It seems that the living memorial was intended to refer to not only a past war but also a contemporary cold war. There is another assumption here as well – the necessity of self-expression through the natural movement of bodies encouraged by playgrounds and recreational facilities. That a gymnasium as a war memorial would appear 'natural' was the result of a rather intense government and institutional effort in the early 1940s.

Modernism and Memorials

> Memory may well yet prove to be a short-lived architectural category – and one inherently alien to architecture. (Adrian Forty)[15]

If memory is 'inherently alien to architecture' as Adrian Forty claims, then it is something of a paradox that the War Memorial Gymnasium would be the site for both a memorial and the victorious ascension of modernism on the UBC campus. Modernism's preoccupation with the new, the *tabula rasa* and the future made it dismissive of the past, antithetical to history and suspicious of social memory. And while there were memorials built by modernists – Gropius' 1917 abstract May Monument in Weimar, or Lubetkin's 1942 monument to Lenin in London, for example – these were rare occurrences, and sculptural rather than architectural.[16] Even modernist architectural pedagogy with its emphasis on 'learning by doing' and 'starting from scratch' discounted the role of social or collective memory as embodied in architectural precedent or continued in architectural production; one was to forget past forms and their embodied memories. Those interested in the workings of memory in the twentieth century, cultural theorist Walter Benjamin and surrealist artist André Breton, for example, disdained the modernist rhetoric of progress and were largely dismissed in return, while Sigmund Freud was at best serendipitously heeded by the canonical modernists such as Le Corbusier, Walter Gropius and Lubetkin.[17] And, it is these canonical, progress-advocating modernists who provided the theoretical and ideological foundations for the architects of the War Memorial Gym – Ned Pratt of Sharp, Thomson, Berwick & Pratt and Fred Lasserre, director of the fledgling School of Architecture.

That the past was to be dismissed, overwhelmed and forgotten in the rush to adopt new principles, unconventional architecture and innovative techniques had its advocates at UBC. One such advocate of the new wrote in *The Graduate Chronicle* in 1948 supporting such a 'clean break toward … the advancement to new principles of a new architecture in contemporary techniques of planning and construction'. He believed that 'the most forceful way in which any university can express its current spirit to the community and to future generations is by the construction of well laid out beautiful buildings, consistent with the highest principles of Architecture'.[18] Modernism was not only an enthusiasm of design professionals: the above quote comes not from an architect, but from a student. And he was not alone, for he was joined by 'the courageous stand for modern architecture in the new War Memorial Gymnasium taken by the student building committee'.[19] Students, the initiators, 'clients' and future occupants of the War Memorial Gymnasium were also and clearly advocates of modern architecture. It was students, as founders of the 'Pre-Architectural Club in 1945', who pressed for the establishment of a School of Architecture based on modern principles and regional needs. It was students who supported the invitation of the renowned, Los Angeles-based but European-trained modernist Richard Neutra to speak at the campus, and it was students who joined the campaign for modern architecture at UBC. They quickly forgot their initial 1946 conception of a 'neo-gothic' gymnasium to wholeheartedly lend their support to the modern version of 1947. As Ormonde Hall, the student quoted above, wrote in his editorial: 'The determination of a precise contemporary architectural style for new college buildings is one of the most pressing problems facing the University of British Columbia.' The existing buildings (see Figure 6.2) and campus plan, the very space and form of the campus were considered an attempt 'to corset the pulsating body of an unpredictable living creature within massive frames of stone and architectural fetters'.[20] Modern architecture, it is implied, would free the body from its architectural 'corsets', allowing liberated movement. But the touted modern architecture was also in keeping with 'the rapid development of our technological age' and 'today's age of industrial production, research, and social democracy' and therefore reliant on the predictable and disciplined and hence possessed its own disciplining apparatus.[21]

In language echoing that more politically resonant rhetoric of *Saturday Night*, *The Graduate Chronicle* insisted that a modern War Memorial Gymnasium would be more in keeping with the function and spirit of recreation for twentieth-century men and women. Only modern design, it

Figure 6.2   The 1929, 'Old' or 'Women's' Gymnasium.

argued, would be consonant with 'a gymnasium and university devoted to the discovery of truth and to the training of minds and bodies fit for leadership in the tasks of today and tomorrow ... Only modern architecture could express the spirit of the post-World War II student.'[22] From the perspective of this student representative at least, modernism and the gymnasium were complementary in their task of training minds and bodies; liberating but also disciplining, making present but also casting into the future. Hence some purchase on the rules governing the relationship between architecture and the 'training of minds and bodies fit for leadership' can be gained by looking at the gymnasium as a building type.

The Gymnasium

> Without place types of some kind we could not know or act; ... We would have no way of structuring space or practices in space. (Schneekloth and Frank, 1994)[23]

What was the 'truth' of the modern gymnasium (see Figure 6.3). The history of spaces dedicated to sports and recreation, it has been argued, might be structured as an oscillation between open and enclosed spaces, between architecture and landscape design, between the body in commune with healthful nature and the body improved by precise determinations in controlled environments.[24] There were the open-air gymnasiums of the 1840s that marked a return to nature and that left the specially built houses for aristocratic ball games abandoned. There were post-Revolutionary spaces of public festivals inaugurated in France in1789 that were held in the open air, legitimized by nature and a political rhetoric that saw inclusiveness in the transparency in these wall-less venues. The playing field was a hybrid of sorts, open air but enclosed in the pedagogical initiatives that defined it. Advocates hailed the playing field a 'simulacrum of the world'[25] and 'analogue of the free market with potential for untrammelled competition'.[26] The playground could be either a recreational or a reformatory space. Whether the games learned and the sports practised were recreational or disciplinarian, based on the etiquette book or the machine, was a matter of class and gender.[27] Whether spaces for sport were open or enclosed also became a matter of the market as the need to delimit – for the purposes of private profit – spaces for a whole host of sports activities arose.[28]

Figure 6.3   War Memorial Gymnasium.

Henning Eichberg has observed the architectural ramifications of this sport space dilemma: notions of the body restored by nature will produce the garden city; those of the body improved by culture will produce the controlled, 'immured' architectural environment.[29] Both will claim the new body. It is perhaps because of the ascendancy of the garden city and City Beautiful models, especially prevalent in Vancouver, that nature will remain a reference, either as a view or as the application of green paint intended to disguise the artificiality of walls. Such reactions are perhaps, as Eichberg might have it, signs of bad conscience, an embarrassed abandoning of the foundational claims of modern gymnastics and sports as 'out door movements'.[30] And if current histories of early modern architecture are to be believed, there would seem to be no specifically modern typology for the gymnasium or any canonical exemplar – a sign of conflicted opinions about the nature of the gym.

Gymnasia do not appear as a specific building type in Pevsner's classic *Building Types through the Ages* (1976), nor are they highlighted in Thomas Markus' more recent Foucauldian, *Buildings and Power* (1993). The Avery Index to Architectural Periodicals lists just two in Canada, eight in England and some 47 in the United States as being of any architectural import for the whole half-century prior to the construction of the War Memorial Gymnasium. The gymnasium does not appear to have been a building type with which early modernists had much experience, yet they did bestow upon it a certain exemplary status. Recreation was deemed important enough to be one of the four functional components of Le Corbusier's 1922 *Contemporary City* and was a category of most major urban plans of the modern era, although the gymnasium specifically did not materialize there. Instead, the gymnasium existed as a kind of dream-wish, inserted on the rooftops of private homes and insinuated in appended terraces.[31] Rooftops and terraces were like satellite sanitaria, extensions of public health initiatives. Publicity photographs show residents doing callisthenics on balconies and in open spaces in Ernst May's Rommerstadt housing complex, while Soviet propaganda celebrated exercise breaks in Russia's new constructivist factories. These active bodies served to register the benefits of modern architecture; they were seen to produce each other. Every modernist project was a gymnasium of sorts – a space that was measured and regulated according to the dictates of the architectural game, of optimal light, space and air for the delineated activities of the modern body engaged in the game of modern life. Modernist housing and industrial complexes were surrogate gymnasiums – they were spaces of exercise, expressions of obsessions about healthy, effective, well-functioning, disciplined bodies.

Modernism did not expunge entirely the disciplinary and segregationist tactics worked out in the nineteenth century. Nor did it eliminate the tension between the body as the paragon of discipline and the body as the tool of uncharted experience, liberty and selfhood defined by 'untrammelled competition'. By the mid twentieth century, in both architectural and educational rhetoric, the body continued to be both the site for self-expression and the apparatus through which competition and cooperation could be trained and character honed. The balance between the supply of liberation or discipline was adjusted to the demand for industrial workers or recreational bodies.

The gymnasium transformed the open space of the impromptu and unspecific that was the playing field into the articulated space of the classroom. It frequently even added the amenities of the men's club. As a building type, the gymnasium's forms, spaces and social relations are not 'natural'. They are the result of specific body politics, body experiences and body ideals that were formed in the course of the modern era. This evolution is clear if we turn, by way of comparison to our present day expectations, to the pre-modern, 1889 brief for Providence's Brown University Gymnasium:

> [The building] is to contain a gymnasium with the usual appliances: running track, rowing-machines etc. It is to have two dressing rooms with 200 lockers and rooms for more if necessary. Shower and sponge baths and a dry-room with four or five baths; two private rooms for the Professor; billiard-room with three tables; bowling alleys, three if possible. Cage for baseball practice, sparring room, a piano, water-closets, three or four rooms for repairs and supplies and for the janitor; large swimming-bath if possible.[32]

Twenty-five years later the gymnasium was considered a well-defined type in North America about which general statements could be made about its form, space and function. It was a consensus only won after much experimentation.[33] By 1915 the gymnasium had become 'a very important factor in school planning'. Modern primary schools 'almost invariably' had one and high schools were 'practically never' without. Obviously, gymnasia were still not universal, and judging from Newark, New Jersey's 20 School Board gymnasia built in a mere five-year period the boom in gymnasia construction was recent in 1915. Perhaps pertinent here is the fact that the description of the gymnasium has all the specificity of the code book – down to the recommended height of the windows and dimensions of radiators, the gender-conscious distinction between locker rooms and shower facilities. Running tracks, seen to be passing out of favour, received less attention, while basketball, judging from the detailed instructions about its accommodation that it was felt necessary to provide, was clearly novel and in the ascendancy.

By 1931 the gymnasium had become a highly recognizable building type, its spatial structure more tightly codified (and social relations, as a consequence perhaps, increasingly 'normalized'). In that year the Technical

News and Research section of *Architectural Record* published a lengthy account of 'Gymnasium Planning', replete with 16 bibliographic references.[34] By this date the directors of physical education in colleges had set norms for gymnasia. Basketball courts were ranked highly; dance, banquet and stage facilities were not. Part of the evaluation of the gymnasium facility was based on the efficiency of space use, judged by 'square feet per player per game', 'square feet per player per day' and 'minimum standard square feet per player per game'.[35] Such body-space definitions would no doubt ring an accord with modern architects taught to think of space and body relationships in terms of efficiency as revealed by time and motion studies and cost per square foot. Space was scrutinized in terms of time (hours utilized) and volume and area assessed in terms of bodies (numbers of spectators, numbers of players) functionality (requirements for light, temperature and ventilation), and machines (dimensions of apparatus). In the tabulation of 'all round value' (maximum number of users in minimum amount of space), swimming ranked highest, with tennis, football and basketball all tying for second place. Golf, boxing and volleyball were placed slightly lower; dancing ranked near the bottom, marching scored the least.[36]

To understand the programmatic requirement of the gymnasium, architects could look to the discipline of education.[37] It is here in educational spheres, rather than the more prosaic and descriptive writing of architects, that much of the specific social text of the gymnasium is made explicit. Texts such as 'Gymnasiums in Public Schools: Physical Education a Great Factor in Promoting Health, Order, Discipline and Stability of Character' by Harry R. Allen, and 'Critic Teacher of Physical Training, School of Pedagogy, Philadelphia', appeared in *The American City* in 1912.[38] Gymnasia were, this author argues, a key defence against the degeneration brought about by urban life. It was an idea shared by modernists, such as Le Corbusier who was to offer his *Ville Contemporaine pour 2,000,000* as a virtual gymnasium ten years later. Gymnasia as the antidote to character degeneration brought about by urbanization would also become a common, almost deafening refrain in the community centre campaigns of the post-World War II years in North America and Vancouver. It is evidenced in a lengthy article published in *Architectural Record* in 1949, which began:

> Out of the formerly accepted idea of athletics as an extra-curricular scholastic or collegiate activity, or as a bit-time professional spectacle, there is emerging a concept of athletics, recreation, physical and health education all closely inter-related, closely tied into all phases of community life and planning. In such a concept the provisions of an industrial concern for its workers, of a community for its members, of a city park department, a school district, a college, all have importance.[39]

And in keeping with the inclusiveness and economies of the day, basketball had become the defining feature of a gymnasium – 'gymnasiums: planned to house basketball courts are adequate to provide for all activities in the normal school or recreation program'. This authoritative but reductive notion of the gymnasium was the outcome of 'a recent movement to coordinate the aims and findings of educators, planners, recreation, and health organizations'.[40] Their ideas, categories, definitions and assumptions had been entrenched in the resulting 'Guide for Planning Facilities for Athletics, Recreation, Physical and Health Education' of 1947.[41]

These notions, distributed via *Architectural Record* and comparable publications, also circulated in Vancouver and among architects, including the firm of Sharp, Thompson, Berwick & Pratt. Similar sentiments about the relationship of recreation to community living were echoed in the Vancouver Art in Living Group, which attracted the sympathy of Vancouver's design community in the 1940s. It was perhaps the perception of the new developments in gymnasium design, and the lack of local precedents or personal experience, that led Ned Pratt to request information and examples from the National Recreation Association in New York and the Portland Cement Association in Vancouver.[42] The bibliography compiled by the former lists ten publications (1938–47) and suggests six journals, including *The American City* and *Architectural Record,* where 'Articles on design, construction and equipment of recreation areas appear from time to time.' The Portland Cement Association referred Pratt to eight works that might be 'of some inspiration'. These included a gymnasium – Armoury, four auditoriums including a Memorial Auditorium, a field house, one gymnasium proper and 'even a CBS Transmitter's Station [which] might intrigue their interest'. Clearly, with so few examples, the gymnasium, as a specific building type, had not yet experienced the zeal of modernism's attentions.

A fervent investment in gymnasia had, however, been made elsewhere. There were high hopes for recreation in Canada. An association between recreation and the sacrifices made for the war effort was cultivated in the early 1940s. In 1942 a new national programme supporting the construction of recreation facilities was launched with the slogan 'Fitness for Freedom'. Facilities, such as gymnasia, were a perceived means of 'stepping up greatly the productive capacity of men and women war workers by increasing the height of their morale, their will to work and their physical ability to do so'.[43] Hence the link between recreation and the nation, the body and productivity was updated and firmly established in the 1940s. At the very end of the war, Major Ian Eisenhardt, the National Director of Physical Fitness, brought the same logic and rationale to the discussion of recreation in peacetime. He also brought the war memorial to the gymnasium stating that: 'the best memorials will be those that will allow for the growing up of a physically fit, mentally alert, and spiritually disciplined coming generation'.[44]

A gymnasium, with its potential accommodation of a variety of sports, often equipped with a stage for theatrical events, commonly housing leisure activities such as bowling and dancing, was similar to the community centre. Planners, recreation specialists and civic organizations had made substantial rhetorical investments in community centres in the early 1940s as well. In 1944 the Arts and Letters Club Committee on Reconstruction commented that there was a national need for them because: 'The war has generated a restlessness, an expectancy, among our people. They are ready for something. They anticipate important changes in the post-war world. If this expectation is defeated, chaotic conditions will prevail. We shall have, as in the depression years, a widespread discontent, a drifting of the population from place to place, a steady deterioration in morale.'[45] Memorials which made use of gymnasia or community centres as living memorials could therefore serve as the focus for a 'a new order, a better society'.[46] Gymnasiums would keep people in place.

One wonders, however, if settling down and contentment were the expectancy of the students who initiated the building of the War Memorial Gymnasium? Were they knowingly participants in the disciplining effort? Was their enthusiasm for a modern building also an enthusiasm for the control, surveillance and normativity that has been so often attributed to modernism's stark forms, hard surfaces and industrial scale, cold to the touch, unaccommodating to the body, relentlessly repetitive? Did these young eyes and supple bodies have a different notion of navigating this modern space? What is clear is that they were dissatisfied with the old gymnasium.

The 'Old' 1929 gymnasium was a timber and lath-and-plaster version of the collegiate neo-gothic (or 'Scottish Baronial') style of the neighbouring Library.[47] Similarly, its massing and symmetry were a more rudimentary expression of the design principles that established the academic buildings and the campus master plan. Its spatial configuration was straightforward – entry was at grade and on axis, bilateral symmetry apportioned interior space, and a simple foyer served to distribute users to gymnasium, bleachers and activity rooms. There were few thresholds and mediating spaces. Movement between the outdoor Memorial Tennis Courts to the gymnasium, to the activity rooms or to lockers was direct, the foyer perhaps allowing the chance encounter of the chess player and the gymnast, the kitchen crew and the basketball team.

The 'old' gym building derived something of its meaning from its location within the hierarchical space of the campus master plan. It was located between the outdoor playing fields and the Library, between the space of nature and its freedoms and the space of the mind and its discipline. Its humble materials, un-ceremonial entrance, meagre landscaping and general informality were representative of the institutional status of athletics and physical education within the University. In 1923, athletics, as opposed to military training, became an important attribute of student life when the Men's Athletic Association and Women's Athletic Association were formed and managed by the students themselves. The 1929 building, funded by the students, gave material form to that development.[48] By 1936 activities had augmented in number and kind and the University had begun to supervise, correct, prescribe, evaluate and otherwise systematize physical activity on campus.[49] With the outbreak of war in 1939, preoccupations with physical education largely reverted to the old model of male bodies fit for service, of drills and appropriately gauged manoeuvres. The growing appropriation of athletics by the University as it assumed greater supervisory prerogatives would be only temporarily delayed by the war effort, however. After the war the Physical Education programme, systematic but voluntary before the war, became mandatory and more particularly categorized. In 1947 incoming students were examined and their physical fitness assessed by the University Health Service.[50]

The new War Memorial Gymnasium was therefore designed during a period of renewed institutional change, shifting alliances and differing agendas among those involved in the commission and design of the facility.[51] The one thing that there seemed to be a consensus about was the inadequacy of the old gymnasium. It was judged incommensurate to the new role of athletics in size, participant amenity, spectator capacity and pedagogical service. This is borne out in the material form and representational spaces of its replacement. The new gym has the vocabulary of a sanatorium or hospital and the scale of an industrial installation. Unlike the old gym, the entry sequence is assertively expressed and unconventional, complex rather than straightforward; it is elevated and off axis. It rises above the disease-ridden earth to the health-giving sun. The spaces of the new gymnasium are complex, multilayered and discriminatingly subdivided and joined. Space is finely graded in its vertical dimension with double, triple and single height volumes; there are mezzanines and basements. Space is also articulated in its horizontal dimension so as to filter those who are and are not welcome. Unlike the simple distribution arrangement of the 1929 gym, its modern replacement is an elaborately graded system. The distribution of functions and hence people in space is directed via the placement of 'gates' – doors, stairs, corridors and balconies. Hence the cursory general public enters a shallow layer of space defined by the War Memorial Hall, a more athletically purposive public descends stairs to the bleachers, and pedagogical and institutional inhabitants follow a discrete system of corridors that rim the central space like a defensive and defining wall. Beneath are the spaces of preparation and transformation, of private and intimate actions – the spaces of showering, dressing, team bonding, the more intimate contact sports of boxing and wrestling and the corrective exercises and individual activities of the small apparatus gymnasium. Even further recessed, less publicly accessible, are the spaces of therapy. The War Memorial Gymnasium is a more complex spatial object than its predecessor, for with the resumption of peace in 1945, a new normality had been made operational.

Students recited the rhetoric of the time, perhaps anticipating greater leisure time or careers in the newly founded profession of physical education. The University anticipated enormous increases in enrolment and hence enhanced government funding. The Federal government advocated the growth in the humanities at universities to balance the technical emphases of the war years and to boost a post-war economy buoyed by the predicted growth in the leisure and recreation industry. Social commentators saw in sport places for social anchoring. Advertising exploited sport as a venue for marketing 'feminine' sporting attire and body moves that undercut any blurring of separate gender spheres or roles that had occurred because of the war effort: differences in gender could be marketed to profitable effect. Architects found an opportunity to make manifest the virtual gymnasium that had haunted their rhetoric of modern design as a restorative of the body and a cure for social ills.

The Body

The body was recruited to modern architecture's campaign to break with things learned by rote in the interest of instilling new behaviour and activating new memories. The photographs and advertising devised by the Bauhaus in the 1920s were intended to remind users how to fold their innovative chairs, and to instruct women on how to effortlessly use the new appliances in their labour-saving kitchens. While not memorial rituals in any conventional sense of the word, these quotidian manoeuvres produced modern bodies, which with every encounter adjusted their corporeal selves to the 'new spirit' of modern life – a lesson to be remembered if falling off the often precariously balanced tubular steel chairs of the period or other *faux pas* were to be avoided. Modernists called for a 'New Spirit' in buildings commensurate with the 'New Body' advocated by medical science, sport discourse, physiologists and even psychiatry.[52]

Clearly, as Henri Lefebvre and others have theorized, modern architecture and planning produced abstract, inhuman spaces. Yet the human body continued to occupy the spatial imagery of its architects. The human body, possibly diseased – tubercular, fatigued – occupying an urban scene, undoubtedly cancerous – airless, sunless, chaotic – marked the discourse of modern architecture.[53] Research into adequate spatial accommodation for public housing attempted not only to heal the disease-susceptible bodies of its prospective inhabitants but also to discipline working-class bodies to physical and perceptual norms determined by industrial production. Writing in the very years of the War Memorial Gym's design, Sigfried Giedion makes this point explicitly in *Mechanization Takes Command* (1948). 'The coming period must bring order to our minds, our production, our feelings, our economic and social development. It has to bridge the gap that, since the onset of mechanization, has split our mode of thinking from modes of feeling.'[54] Charting the changing relationship between bodies and machines – from harvesters and reapers to household appliances – Giedion outlines how all these modern machines reorganized tasks into patterns that are serial, continuous, regular, efficient, theoretically less fatiguing, and established by studies of movement and timed coordination. Giedion is also clearly sensitive to the fact that the machine and the human body exist in a certain state of tension. The hand, he points out, 'is an "organic tool", ill-fitted to work with mathematical precision, without pause ... Automation counters the organic movement of the hand, unable to sustain continuous rotation'. He also notes that 'the regularity with which the worker must follow the rhythm of the mechanical system is unnatural to man'.[55] His fascination with the time-lapse photos of Marey and Muybridge or photo-collage was not only due to an appreciation of their abstract graphic representation. It also involved a desire to ascertain what eludes the eye, with what might escape detection; an ambiguous realm as yet uncharted and un-colonized by mechanical production. Giedion's focus was movement – mechanical, 'natural', 'psychological' – across the land, within the household, of the body and in the subconscious – movement that gave order to space and time.[56] But were bodies to be like machines, given model numbers, tagged with 'best before' dates, used, periodically repaired, eventually discarded? Was modern architectural discourse not only concerned with the 'organic' and the 'natural', to use Giedion's 1948 terminology, with novel body experiences, with a new aesthetics of the body that developed in tandem or in tension with the new-fangled mechanized world?

That architectural theorists and practitioners should be concerned about the body, especially in the context of their unquestioning support of the body-alienating processes of industrialized mass production, suggests that architecture has some significant investment in the body. Hence this worried obsession that goes beyond a mere concern for ministering to corporeal health is provocative. It is not unprecedented, for architecture has an entrenched practice of finding analogies between itself and the body, be it of individual body parts as discrete form or of the building as an 'organic' whole. In architectural discourse the body could be a formal tool, providing and authorizing proportion, scale and dimension, or an anthropomorphic reference giving value to symmetry, hierarchy and compositional unity. It is not without significance, however, that the body in question has always been male. The foundational texts for Western architectural ideology, at least since Vitruvius (*c.*27AD), through the several Renaissance texts that continued his assumptions, to the modern movement, all fashion the normative male body as the basis for essential aesthetic criteria and syntactical rules. The body had more than an arcane significance – it also effected via sleights of metaphorical transformation a privileging of the male body as architectural lawgiver and thus to elaborate exclusions from and repressions within both the symbolic and practice sides of architecture. And that has meant, as Diane Agrest has argued, 'Woman not only has been displaced/replaced at a general social level throughout the history of architecture, but more specifically, at the level of body and architecture.'[57] While architectural treatises disposed architecture according to analogies, similes and references to the male body, architects distributed and secured bodies in space, be it the space of the office, the worksite or the building, according to this gender paradigm. Hence to lose sight of the body in architectural discourse would be to lose sight of its empowerments.

Consequently, this 'body talk' in the twentieth century, with its incorporation of diverse interests, was involved in revamping but also reinforcing established prerogatives. The body, in its dimensions and needs, was made normative and thus the basis from which the modern world of public housing and industrial complexes could be designed and optimized. Time and motion studies and the synchronizing of body to machine were borrowed from industry.[58] Bodies, specific body images, were integral parts of the world that modern architects imagined: the boxer who inhabited Le Corbusier's Citrohan house, the marble nude sculpture that articulated the enclosed space of Mies van der Rohe's Barcelona Pavilion, the figure of Lenin pasted onto Lissitsky's constructivist podium montage, photographs of women in modern attire demonstrating the use of unfamiliar Bauhaus furniture. The relationship between sport and both individual and social health was well documented by modern architectural theorists. Giedion plotted the history of sport's beneficial effect on individuals and societies as well as its contribution to the creation of the modern movement in architecture. Numerous views on sport were published in avant-garde architectural journals in the 1920s.[59] Nuances of meaning can be discerned in these images and texts. There are postulations about an athletic life as an antidote to moral degeneration and to the possible effeminate characteristics of white-collar jobs, and there are assumptions about gender and activity.[60] Each instance resonates with familiar presumptions about the ideal modern body as disciplined, athletic and able bodied for the tasks of modern life. These exemplify the modernist concern with the body as an instrument, a tool of industrial production, a repository for industrial consumption and as an idealization of discipline, moral rectitude and natural vigour.

But there is another body, less prominent but present nevertheless within modern architectural discourse. Giedion's history of 'mechanization taking command' also acknowledges the 'organic' movements of the body and a notion of what is 'natural' to it. He charts the introduction of efforts to balance mind and body through Rousseau-influenced exercise, replacing military compulsion with freedom and informality.[61] Chairs designed by modern architects could be therapeutic, with pivoting and moving parts made adjustable to predetermined 'natural positions', or orthopaedic, resiliently structured to hold the body firm.[62]

The relationship of modernism to the body was one of engagement and dissociation. Modern architects studied the most intimate movements of the wrist or foot in designing door handles and stair treads, but also reduced the body to a normative dimensioning device. Modern architecture was fascinated with the spaces created for the perfection of the body, as if these places held in concentrated form the proper, symbiotic relationship between modern architecture and the modern body. Both would be disciplined, hygienic and functional. Hence, Giedion's 1929 publication *Liberated Dwelling* devoted over half of its illustrations to hospitals and sport.[63] Although sanitaria, mountain lodges, seaside resorts and sports stadiums were illustrated, only the activities of gymnastics, swimming and tennis were included, not gymnasia. Gymnasia only appeared metonymically as equipment and open space inserted into or appended from modern houses, roof top gyms or bedroom exercise areas. They were private practices. 'Liberated dwellings', that is modern architecture, would be like gymnasia – optimal spaces for honing the body – of timing, comparing and measuring performance. The body was calibrated to modern space, fitted, like built-in kitchen cupboards, into the abstract object forms and volumes of industrial production. The gymnasium was the standard-bearer of the new body–environment paradigm.

There were experiments into enhancing, heightening or expanding the experience of the body, of making the body commensurate with the new percept of space and the novel experiences of the industrializing world. The body was essential to modernist architecture's self-representation, to the working out of the relationship of the individual and the collective to the new *machine age*. Adolf Loos erased convention and culture from Viennese bodies to more clearly write modernism upon them; his model was the athletic English yachtsman. Le Corbusier used images of male gymnasts and women in sporting attire to represent the new citizens of his ideal *Radiant City*. Bauhaus students flung their bodies onto projecting balconies and balanced precipitously on rooftops, their natural bodies augmented to enhance the expressive possibility of their gestures, dimensions and limbs.

Those arresting images of Bauhaus students dressed up in extravagant costumes that would allow their bodies to become sensing devices and eloquent mediums celebrated the unconventional. They were if not entirely unnatural, then at least uncanny. Kinetic bodies, modern day *flâneurs*, propelled by the trajectory of the Le Corbusier's architectural promenade, glimpsed fragments of form and space and were compelled to assemble from them a new space/time comprehension, part body memory and part cognitive processing. The viewing body became like a camera processing 24 frames per second, possessing vision commensurate with the new reality. As Giedion commented in a caption to the image of an active and athletic body, a golfer in full swing, in order to perceive modern space 'the eye must function as in the high-speed photographs of Edgerton'.[64] The mechanically reproduced image was a lesson in how to comprehend modern architecture. Learning this lesson, Giedion believed, would heal the rift between 'thinking and feeling'.

Others shared and even preceded Giedion's interest in exploring the relationship of body to implements, not all of them being interested in 'systems' and 'laws'. Many, however, were more attentive to flowing movement, rhythm and the uniting of body and soul. As Hillel Schwartz has perceptively chronicled, a new modern body was constructed from pioneering theorists of stage, dance and gymnastics, by kinaestheticians, graphologists, anthropologists and others endeavouring to release and build character via the rhythmic, 'natural' movements of the body.[65] They were assisted in their task by everyday experiences enjoined to mechanical invention. There were, Schwartz enumerates, the flowing penmanship facilitated by new implements, the playground jungle-gym, the pull of the zipper, the slide of the escalator, the glide of the bicycle, the roll of the roller coaster, the torque of the airplane and the cinematic close-up.[66] It was supposed that if the expressive self was revealed by movement, then movement could in turn shape the self. Freud himself had indicated the importance of gesture and bodily movements as a sign of deep subconscious processes, of repressed feelings needing outlets. Here we have a seminal idea of the avant-garde modernist – that the aesthetic sphere could repair the psyche via the calibration of the body to the objects of the industrial world, and hence heal 'the rift between thinking and feeling'.[67]

Hence, while the discipline of the body was a dominant rhetoric of the time and of modernist architects (for Giedion did after all complain about 'unscientific' sunbathing and 'unsystematic' exercise), there were also explorations offering some relief from that disciplinary pursuit. That release may have been a safety valve for creativity, a respite from the discipline of the State and rules of the game. While doubtlessly gender biased and class conscious, such interests in liberation from 'the invisible, insidious space of panoptic dominance and surveillance'[68] suggests that we look for traces of such an emancipatory ideology in the forms and spaces of any modern building. This is especially the case in a gymnasium where the rhetorical claims of freedom and discipline, leisure and work, national need and personal interest might embody simultaneously different spatial politics.

The War Memorial Gymnasium was initially proposed as a place of recreation, although it became a machine for competition and measured success – of time clocks and visibility, of things productive of the optimal body. Its glass basketball backboards, inverted truss roof, uninterrupted floor, specialized lighting and dedicated press box ensured the clear visibility needed to accurately measure distances, assess penalties and witness records broken. The time clock and centralized recording ensured precision of action and the correct length of play. Champions could be segregated from the mediocre; the systematic from the disorderly; natural 'free' exercise from the disciplined and manly; efforts could be ranked and groups classified, the imperfect and inefficient action admonished, the flawless and effective rewarded. It was a usefully ruled space, temporally, spatially and socially. No interruption to play would be caused by weather, unscheduled events or competing uses. Less regulated and visually engaging bodies would be submerged below, or transferred elsewhere.

The Architects

> Architects, designing in their own image, often centralise their own experiences of
> space and marginalise and negate the experiences of others. (Ruth Morrow)[69]

The question is: To what extent were the architects of the UBC gym the bearer of this architectural ideology or that of the now canonized modernists – Le Corbusier, Mies van der Rohe, Walter Gropius, or even Lasserre's mentor, Berthold Lubetkin?[70] Lasserre may have drafted some of Lubetkin's houses where bedrooms were combined with sleeping and exercise terraces, or his housing estates that were equipped with exercise spaces and healthful balconies.[71] Likewise, Ned Pratt conceived the extensive eaves-sheltered perimeter of his houses as space for healthy living and attached carports as play areas for children in inclement weather.[72] But to what extent are such ideals and pronouncements applicable to any discussion of the War Memorial Gymnasium?

Ned Pratt, as the architect of the War Memorial Gymnasium acknowledged by office protocol, archives and the popular press, may afford some insight into the workings of modernist architectural ideology in the gym.[73] Pratt was championed as a charismatic proponent of international modernism who made Le Corbusier indigenous.[74] Descriptions of his buildings celebrate their 'stripped-down modular', 'machine age' and 'high tech' currency. He is remembered as the quintessential modernist: war combatant, athlete, foe of entrenched attitudes and historicism. In photographs he assumes the archetypical pose of the modernist: he stands,

Figure 6.4   'The Elizabethan Ned Pratt, a modern architect with a zest for the past attacks life with gusto – like a knight on a charger.' (*Maclean's National Magazine,* 1958)

automobile at the ready, before his canonical modern building, his body marking the measure of the architecture, the image memorializing his authorship (see Figure 6.4).[75] Pratt, that 'knight on a charger' as *Maclean's Magazine* enthused, publicly remembered his protégé and colleague crusaders – all men, although at least one female architect worked extensively with him on a number of award-winning buildings.[76] Beyond espousing the salient tenets of modernism – simplicity, economy, efficiency and compliance with the modern formal determinants of volumes, planes and undecorated surfaces – he also worked with the more deeply foundational notions of plan, programme and technological prowess enhanced by delight, (Le Corbusier's 'forms which move the spirit'). Architecture was, Pratt asserted, an affair of 'areas, volumes, number of bodies', and the 'manipulation of space'.[77] He also shared in the modernist conviction that architecture had the power to 'change a frame of mind' and to affect the psychology of the user.[78] Pratt believed in progress, was critical of stylistic nostalgia, endorsed the conventions of office hierarchy and while he upheld the idea of architectural experimentation, it seems that when it came to the human body he preferred the rigours of a marching band. As to architecture as a custodian of memory – we know only that he is on record as saying that he 'would never have campaigned to save one of his old buildings'.[79] What Pratt thought about gymnasia, memorials or the body is far from clear: although he built much, he wrote little.

Lasserre, consultant architect on the project, might provide some further insight into this interpretive problem, as well as highlight attitudes to the body brought by architectural discourse to the design and execution of a modern gym. As the first opportunity to promulgate his concerns as the director of the newly formed School of Architecture, the War Memorial Gym functioned as his manifesto on modern architecture. What kind of modern architecture Lasserre intended with the War Memorial Gymnasium can be garnered from the curriculum he devised for that new school.

For Lasserre, modern architecture was that adumbrated in the international architectural press, *The Architectural Forum, Architectural Record* and *Progressive Architecture*.[80] It was a synthesis of engineering and the history of art and architecture, descriptive geometry and visual design, surveying and psychology, although it was more aligned with the fine arts than it was with engineering.[81] Modern architecture was practical and theoretical and concerned with a range of design problems from industrial design and prefabrication to town and regional planning. It was clearly scientific as opposed to formalistic, pragmatic rather than speculative.[82] It was, like the later Bauhaus, involved in the application of behavioural norms and industrial criteria to design and the prioritizing of sociological considerations over individual flights of fancy.

Lasserre was thoroughly steeped in modernism. He had a technical rather than a 'beaux arts' education.[83] His apprenticeship with Lubetkin at Tecton just before the war had placed him among practitioners enamoured of Le Corbusier, although after 1935 disenchanted with his politics. He followed the teaching of Walter Gropius at Harvard and especially Serge Chermeyeff in Chicago, making the latter his model for the School of Architecture.[84] Through them he also absorbed several features of the earlier Bauhaus programme: a balancing of *Formlehre* – fine arts, architectural theory, design fundamentals – with *Werklehre* – construction, and an involvement with industrial design, prefabrication and community planning. But there are also shifts from the earlier pedagogical model. There is a new emphasis on professional practice, less random experimentation or starting from scratch, learning by doing more confined to the conventions of the drafting board. Whereas the early Bauhaus pedagogy had incorporated theatre, dance and music, Lasserre reduced this broad array to the visual arts. Thus his modern architecture was international in extent, shaped by the aftermath of 1939 and concurred with that canonized in Giedion's 1941 *Space, Time and Architecture.*

If modernism had held within its ideology several attitudes to the body – as psychological register, sensing machine and industrial helpmeet – what were the attitudes to the body embedded within the War Memorial Gymnasium? We do know that Lasserre understood the disciplining effect of modern architecture. Whereas some early modernists had occasionally encouraged the notion of architecture as a stage for the unprogrammed exploration of bodily sensation, this does not seem to have been the idea retained by Lasserre. He complained: 'One of the small and very annoying by-products which we seem to be unable to combat is the general attitude that every part of the building is available to the students. They therefore use windows to get into the building when the building is closed.'[85] Obviously, the interpenetration of interior and exterior, the building as stage and the liberated body celebrated by some modernists were not the unqualified enthusiasm of the new director. He for one disapproved of any such unscheduled activity by students in the modest army huts that comprised the UBC School of Architecture. Lassserre asserted that student attitudes to built form were materially influenced by their contact with the environment. Constructions that were flimsy and temporary, structures vibrating with the weight of human footsteps, surfaces rough to the touch and details that were banal and unheeded were not the environment Lasserre had in mind. Alas, his opinion was the prevalent one at UBC. The new gymnasium would be monumental, permanent, its structure unmoving and unmoved by human presence, surfaces – apart from the functionally determined spring of the playing surface – would be smooth and unyielding, details precise, bodies disciplined.

Clearly, Lasserre shared the belief in the behaviour-shaping possibilities of built form. As he indicated, these possibilities were to be realized by quasi-scientific studies of the physiological and psychological aspects of design. As confirmed by the curriculum he set out, the body and psyche were translated into predictable sensation-generating mechanisms whose needs could be translated into and satisfied by abstractions of line, form, colour and texture.[86] The latter were the controls of the body and keys to the mind. This was a fairly standard line of reasoning in modern architecture: Le Corbusier talked about physio-psychological aspects of design in the 1920s, Gropius wrote about it in the 1940s. And it was given local prominence in the work of the Los Angeles modern architect Richard Neutra, who spoke at the University and in Vancouver in 1946. Neutra's signature building, much publicized at the time, was 'Dr Lovell's Physical Culture Center' of 1927. Dr Lovell popularized 'Care of the Body' in a column for the *Los Angeles Times*, where he made connections between physical culture and architecture.[87] This 'Health House', as it was also known, emphasized for Neutra the relationship between buildings and the psycho-physiological well-being of their occupants. This healthfulness was won by open space, glass walls admitting sun and air, access to the outdoors and, given its precipitous siting, projecting terraces and complex vertical planning – interesting to the eye and challenging to the limbs. It was a gymnasium of sorts, although what Lasserre thought of his athletic bioregionalism is left unrecorded.

According to Plan:
Remembering to Forget

SHERRY McKAY

The Plan and its Occupations

> If anything is described by an architectural plan, it is the nature of human
> relationships, since the elements whose trace it records – walls, doors, windows and
> stairs – are employed first to divide and then selectively to re-unite inhabited space.
> (Robin Evans, 1978)[1]

The plans of the War Memorial Gym show space divided according to
programmatic use and unified by a system of connecting passages; the
plans relate the building to its site and intimate its structure and
materiality. As Fred Lasserre confirms, 'walls, roofs, stairs, windows,
doors, floors' must be studied according to 'basic uses' and their 'essential
qualities'. He also asserts that 'the physiological needs of man' and 'social
forces' are 'basic elements of architectural study'.[2] The plan, as a
consequence, records something of how these physiological needs and
social forces are accommodated. But also implied in that conjunction of
physiology and society is an attention to behaviour and what Le Corbusier
among others called the 'physio-psychological', the emotive as well as
utilitarian aspect of architectural experience. The walls, stairs and other
prosaic elements by which the plan is parsed are also aesthetic elements,
'advancing and retreating planes … interpenetrating, hovering, often
transparent, without anything to fix them in realistic position', they
experience a 'flattening out so that the interior and exterior could be seen
simultaneously', and as such they might be understood as 'equivalent to
psychic responses'[3] (see Figure 7.1).

At first it may be difficult to discern in the now commonplace forms of
the modern gym anything but the dehumanizing forms of rationality and an
obvious derivation from uncompromised functionality. The building
appears so straightforward, so self-explanatory – a large unobstructed
interior volume, detached circulation spaces, an identifiable lobby, a proper
hierarchy of secondary spaces on the margins and in the basement. It seems
so obviously commonsensical, almost ordinary, as if it were the mere trace
of a straightforward response to the building brief. Its customary

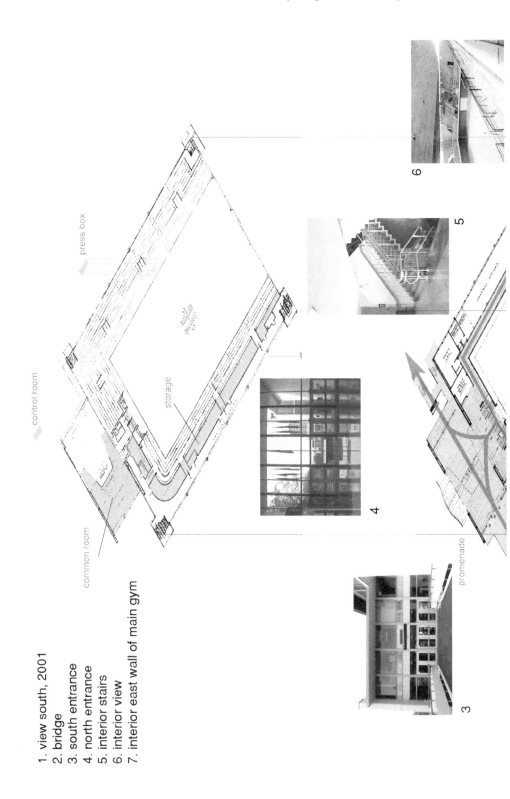

1. view south, 2001
2. bridge
3. south entrance
4. north entrance
5. interior stairs
6. interior view
7. interior east wall of main gym

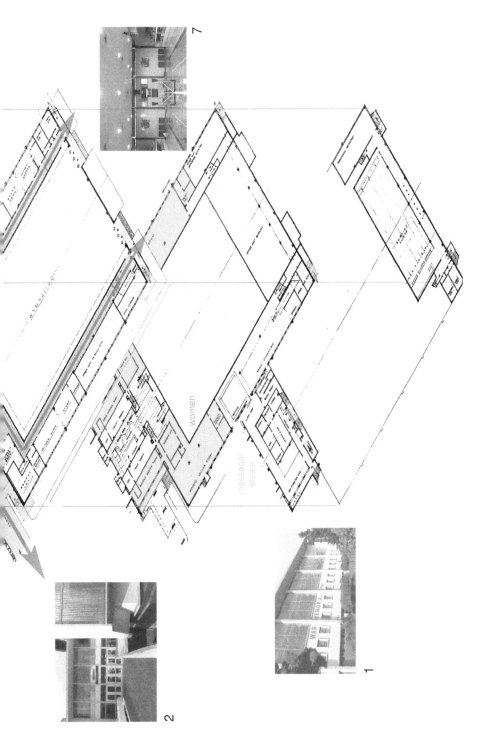

Figure 7.1   Plans of the War Memorial Gymnasium , All levels.

Figure 7.2   'Its up to You', The Bay College Shop, Hudson's Bay Co,
Advertisement. (*The Ubyssey*, 1946)

arrangement, however, dissimulates the power directed by its windows and
space-bridging mechanisms.

Although bodies (or what Evans quoted above would call 'human relationships') are clearly intended to occupy the War Memorial Gymnasium, they but
rarely appear in the representational spaces of its architectural design. In the
initial 'artist's conception' the few bodies inserted into the bird's-eye view of
the building are but emblematic figures, as conventional as the 'conception'
itself. In the slightly later plans by the architects, which record and reconcile the
habits and functions of individuals and of groups, figures appear not at all.
Therefore, to gain some purchase on how bodies were thought about
architecturally we must seek their representation elsewhere.

In an advertisement sponsored by the Hudson's Bay Company as part of the initial fund raising publicity, fashionably attired women float ethereally above an early model of the gymnasium (see Figure 7.2). The image prophetically, if perhaps inadvertently, reveals assumptions about women's roles as consumers and outsiders to the gymnasium's inner workings. Upon the gym's completion, newspaper photos capture individual athletes in mid-air, close-ups of extraordinary movement, success written on jubilant faces. Today, photographs of star athletes and noted alumni line the walls of the Memorial Hall. In these representations bodies are individualized, isolated by the camera lens, segregated, identified, displayed. These, of course, are partial and possible transcriptions of the accommodation of bodies discoverable in the plan. Bodies in locker or lecture rooms, in the corrective gym or the snack bar are apparently not for general viewing, and certainly without publicity value.

While the plan purports to give a representation of the whole, indicating how all the parts are coordinated – much like the rules of the game might describe basketball or boxing in its entirety – it is, like the rulebook, abstract and disembodied. The abstract space of the plan effects both dismember-ment and re-embodiment. It dismembers the building into different functions and diverse constituencies – students, faculty, spectators, janitors. The plan then reunifies these disparate elements by the circulation path – the architectural promenade that is so clearly re-embodied in the photographic record that publicized the building's modernity in the professional press.

Figure 7.3   War Memorial Gymnasium, view of the architectural promenade.

Such photographic records of bodies in the gymnasium suggest some ways in which we might consider the more representational intentions of the architectural plan. Like the photographic lens, the architecture frames bodies: according to the plan bodies are grouped and segregated, placed on pedestals or relegated to the background. The building's very use demands a physical response. To enter, every body is elevated above the plane of the earth; every body ascends a walkway (Figure 7.3), crosses a bridge, passes through a glass wall and enters the transparency of a single free-floating volume, then, more often than not, pivots 90 degrees to a bird's-eye view of the gymnasium floor. Hence, bodies are segregated, viewing bodies to the bleachers, participant bodies to the designated dressing rooms, administrators and instructors to their allocated offices. Or almost everyone. Not every body is so democratically admitted as the salient features of the plan might declare, there are doors hidden in the darkly painted, visually obscured basement of the building, doors through which other bodies pass, seemingly invisible; janitors, for example, might in this manner reach their closets, their labours unseen.

The insistent division of the building into salient fragments – walls, stairs, windows, doors – significantly distinguishes the new gymnasium from its 1929 predecessor, and is in fact the sign of its modernity.[4] Where once there was reassuring symmetry, the familiarity of a regularized fenestration pattern and the recognition of a customary 'collegiate gothic', the solidity of corner buttresses and the substantiality of walls firmly meeting the ground (although the buttresses were feigned and the walls of lath-and-plaster), now there was only asymmetry, unfamiliar glazing, and nothing of mass.[5]

In contrast to the old, the modern gymnasium configures a new athletic space, brings together more activities, distinguishes and specifies them more exactly, pulls itself more resolutely from the quotidian of the surrounding site. The gymnasium floor is larger, the number of spectators greater, its four levels of occupation more complex, its complement of activities more extensive. There are multiple washrooms and assorted stairs and ramps. Spaces are specifically dedicated for lectures and study, there is a space for bowling, and an array of spaces for offices and lounges, there is one space for individual activity and another for boxing, there are manifold storage stations, discretely positioned spaces for mechanical services and prominently positioned spaces for viewing. There is a dominant central gym and a minor peripheral one. There are team rooms and a boardroom. There is space for a business manager and an athletic director. Spaces are duplicated according to gender and status, student or faculty, and they are graduated in size according to the social relations, manager or secretary.

Deleted from the 1929 roster as categorically incompatible with the specialization of a modern gymnasium are the chess club and musical society. The dance studio and squash courts of the early plans are first banished to proposed appended pavilions and then omitted altogether. The swimming pool, while never realized as originally conceived, will be built, open air and architecturally mute. Rendered invisible by its apparent naturalness today, is the way in which categories were hardened, disciplinary boundaries firmed and functions spatialized. The modern gymnasium included body perfecting (massage, steam) and strategizing spaces (team, lecture and office) but not the space of dance or chorus. Compared with its pre-war predecessor it was also a more mechanically mediated and centralized space – a control point oversaw heat, ventilation, lighting, time keeping and recording. It was also more publicity-geared with its demonstrative display of spectatorship capabilities and planned press box.

The formal vocabulary of the modern gymnasium amalgamated industry-derived structures to the aesthetics of modern art forms that were self-referential, their psychological effect won from the relationship of colour, opaque and transparent surfaces. It was an architecture referencing the logic of construction and programme. The priority given to hovering volumes and dynamic planes suggests an aesthetic ambition. That suspicion is confirmed by the fact that originally the building was to be painted a dull green at the base and a light green stretching above it to the diaphanous glass walls of the north and south elevations, the intended perceptual effect of which was to disengage the wall from its foundations so that building mass would appear as if weightless, suspended above the earth.

The aim of this aesthetic resolve is revealed by the architectural promenade that engages the sentient body in movement through the discrete spaces of the building and hence with the independent forms that give space expression – cinematically. This architectural promenade begins with the entrance sequence. A ramp affords a long view of the south façade, a panning shot, then moves one closer to the luminous surface of the projecting stair tower, the close up, only to propel one past its translucent surfaces, to stride parallel to the opaque plane of its metamorphosis into a solid wall, a tracking shot. One sweeps past the threshold, touching it only discretely, a hand to the flat aluminum door handle set flush to the glass window wall, a foot gliding over the thin line of the door jamb, an initiation into a sequence of volumes marked by a series of viewing platforms, stair landing, floor, bleachers. Every seat is a viewing deck, every square inch of the centralized playing floor a reciprocating object of multiple lines of sight. Here in the major space of the gymnasium, vision is a priority. It is this unobstructed viewing space that is captured in the photographs published in the professional press. Surfaces are rendered smooth, flat, monochromatic, scarcely differentiated except for reasons of functional necessity. Forms have the allure of industrial production, each component predicable in quality, form and performance. The composition derives its logic, however, from more than the economies and practicalities of modern modularity and fabrication.

En route to their appointed places in the gym, anybody entering the building might notice the large glass expanse that forms the northern limit of the space. They might, as did others before them, wonder at the logic of such extensive glazing on a northern exposure, perhaps finding it regionally or locally inappropriate. Or they might, as did Fred Lasserre, approve of glass, even on the north wall, believing as he did that it 'increase[d] the feeling of well being, comfort and spaciousness', and used judiciously, was 'of greatest use and benefit' as 'a source of light and to bring views into the building'.

This 'large window to the north looking out on the view' was the embodiment of the 'memorial theme, the Memorial Window (see Figure 7.4).[6] But what can be remembered by looking at a transparent wall of glass, nicely proportioned though its support structure might be, as interesting as the views it proffers might appear? It bears no inscription, dedication, or narrative; without colour it is bereft of the spirituality attributed to glass by some modern architects in the years just before and after World War I. The Memorial Window was a banal unit of construction, an element of mass produced parts. It was also both a conceptually abstract space and an aperture on a place – the 'memorial window offering a view to Howe Sound and the Coastal Range', a 'window framing a view of the North Shore

Figure 7.4   View of the Memorial Window.

Mountains'.[7] The Memorial Window also framed the 'True North Strong and free', a reference to the nation as abstract and symbolic as a Lauren Harris painting of Northern Canada. If there is anything of an emotive nature here, it is occasioned by the spirituality of the view, an insubstantial gaze across an expanse to the enduring landscape beyond. In this space, before this view, the body, perhaps momentarily, casts a thought elsewhere. And then resumes the architectural path into more physical exertions.

Yet it is in such aesthetically manipulated and glimpsed fragments of mass-produced, anonymous hardware and industrial scale that Giedion had perceived the reunification of thinking and feeling. Giedion proposed that the individual, dispossessed by an industrial world, his or her psyche damaged by the alienation of mechanical reproduction, could be made whole in the compensatory plane of aesthetic experience. One would, in remembering the trajectory through space offered by the architectural promenade, reunify dispersed segments into a whole, an aesthetically contrived whole, as compensation for the division of thinking and feeling and the sense of alienation from one's labours or one's thoughts that was the modern condition. Whether it is a question of an alienation induced by the compartmentalization of specialized fields of knowledge, the separation of academic existence and social life, or in the more political understanding of alienation as the product of the division of labour and the disparities of the capitalist system, the gymnasium sought a new unity. The aesthetic of the building therefore purported to heal the psyche troubled by the experience of an alienating physical world.

In the decades of the gymnasium's construction, that the body–architecture relationship required some reinforcement was noted by no other than Le Corbusier. It was no doubt with some nostalgia that Le Corbusier looked back from the bleak war years to revive the human body from its near asphyxiation by modern technology and state building norms. The body formed the basis of Le Corbusier's *modulor*, whose genealogy includes a geometric scale superimposed on the figure of a male athlete from the 1930s and an English policeman.[8] The *modulor*, a system of measure linking the proportions of the human body to the abstract geometry of the golden section and offering a dimensioning scale able to coordinate the diverse measurements of modern construction, was initially formulated in 1943 and given its first public airing in 1948.[9] The *modulor* testifies to the continued interest among architects of maintaining a link, however tenuous, between bodies and architectural production, between the aesthetic reflex of the sensate human body and architectural forms optimized by industrial processes. It also continues the assumption that this modern world would take its measure from a male and preferably athletic body. This is not to say that such body anxieties explicitly called for the exclusion of the women's athletic programme or female athletes that eventually occurred during the design of the gym. But it does suggest how that exclusion might be considered natural, in the order of things. It corroborated assumptions about gender in the same seemingly innocent way that the Hudson's Bay advertisement did, or the debate over men's or women's rules of play in basketball.

However, the *modulor* is also a Janus figure, looking both forward and backward. It looks forward to the loss of references to the body, be it as a unit of measurement or, more generally, in structures of industrial production that find the rationale for their form and dimension elsewhere. It also looks back to the 'Vitruvian' figure of 2000 years of western architectural theory. The *modulor*, a hybrid body/measuring tool, still retains a human referent – albeit a male and athletic one, static save for the stretch of an arm, registering the mathematics of abstract conception, making it visible via a rhythmical gesture that is slightly more active, certainly more pragmatic than its Vitruvian predecessor, whose limbs were pinned down within the circumference of an ideal circle. Today, the 'modulor man' looks rather quaint next to the prosthetics-enhanced and steroid-altered bodies of today, the cyborgs and cinematic projections of impossible body moves. So too does the body-inscribed space the *modulor* meant to defend, the scale of the War Memorial Gym, for example, with its space configured by sight-lines and sporting dimensions based on the stretch of an arm, the height of a jump, the time of a return serve. Now the space of human vision is increasingly replaced by expanses predicated on the projection capabilities of huge video monitors, split screens and instant replays. Clocks of 24 seconds, the commercial breaks required of televised sport and the demands of the entertainment industry increasingly measure time and define the game.[10] It is the price of time in the expensive space of televised sport that dictates the specularized body's environment now. It had once, in those *modulor*-utopian days, been the belief that what related body to space were the laws of natural rhythm. Body and space were united by 'the rhythm of the heart beat and respiration', and, pertinently, 'the muscular mechanism of gesture, the origin of all creation of space by the traces of orientation which transform chaos into a place'.[11] That athletic male body that haunted Le Corbusier's spatial imagination also stalked the gymnasium.

It was this athletic body that was the subject of Giedion's *Liberated Dwelling* and among those hailed in his *Space, Time and Architecture*, and who would ideally follow the architectural promenade, subjectively discerning architectural elements along the way, reassembling those fragmented experiences into a sense of the whole building, the ideal work of art, complete and perfect unto itself.[12] Giedion and perhaps all those architects who took their cues from him, believed that such athletic subjects embodied an 'individual consciousness as a monadic and autonomous centre of activity able to maintain its stability against the plurality of divisive and corrosive effects of modernity'.[13] The modern aesthetics of the gymnasium aimed to bolster the individual against the dissolution caused by technological modernization, while at the same time celebrating unprecedented space/time simultaneity and the command of mechanization. But as K. Michael Hays admits: 'Of course, it must be recognized that actual individuals, by virtue of their complex and multiple historical and cultural affiliations, always exceed the subjectivities constructed by architecture.'[14]

And of course there were subjectivities exceeding the architecture of the War Memorial Gymnasium, those not made whole by the aesthetic palliative for the modern world, its geometry, proportions, and abstraction; the women who found no home there, the labourers who were de-skilled by its industrialized production. The humanist subject to be salvaged by the modernist aesthetic had been, after all, rhetorically, symbolically and ideologically male.

The War Memorial Gym – Living by Forgetting

> It is possible to live almost without memory ... but it is almost impossible to live without forgetting. (Nietzsche 1874)

If Nietzsche, that philosopher so influential for architectural modernists, was correct in asserting that it was impossible to live without forgetting, what forgetting made the War Memorial Gymnasium possible? Its modernist vocabulary might assist in forgetting the old gymnasium, with its informal and recreational uses or the Armoury building with its military functions. The location of the building, so much discussed, might serve to displace the memorial from the real spaces of war discoverable nearby. The military occupation, 'by way of trespass', was still in existence and influential in 1948.[15] The war had produced a very specific space, replete with its own markers and its own mementoes, along the northern edge of the campus and in places it had commandeered elsewhere within it. It was a space of precaution and surveillance – possible air raid shelters were scoured from university buildings; a Fort Camp of barracks arose, gun emplacements and wooden towers marked vigilant lookouts along the bluffs.[16] The occupation of the Point Grey Battery on the campus revamped the pastoral idyll of the University with road closures and re-routings. The diversion of Marine Drive to Main Mall by way of an inferior, perfunctory rather than ornamental roadway had 'threatened to destroy the unity of the original plan' and 'the front of the University grounds'.[17] These reminders of war gave physical form to the national fears that had served to justify the banishment of Japanese Canadians and their internment elsewhere. This space was no doubt felt best forgotten. And it is forgotten in the War Memorial Gymnasium, its site established instead to the south-east, along the 'civilian' edge of the campus, disengaged in its memorial function from the local memories of war.

Many of the original enthusiasms and some of the inclusiveness that had determined the initial building brief were also forgotten by the time of the building's completion. One of these now forgotten enthusiasms was the Dance Studio. All that remains of it now is the trace of its excision, its existence merely suggested in the oddly ample doors that open onto a banal lane and what was for decades a vacant space along the east façade. Dance was, however, a vibrant curricular activity with courses in Physical Education ranging from the 'Rhythmics' and Dancing that substituted for Boxing and Wrestling in the women's list of activities in 1941, to the addition of Folk and Ballroom dancing, first as separate activities for men and women and then as co-educational, to the wide range of options available by 1947.[18] Through the various amendments certain constancies obtained, however. While folk and ballroom dancing were deemed suitable for men and women, rhythmics and modern dance were consistently deemed women's activities. A gender thinking that can also be found in modern architecture.

Ostensibly deleted for financial reasons, the eviction of the Dance Studio is perhaps not entirely innocent, at least not without consequences. Dance was certainly not something eschewed by modernism. One, very prominent, trajectory of modernism was embodied in dance – the liberated, flowing, barefoot and loosely garbed dance of Isadora Duncan, or the unconventional, ironic movements of Josephine Baker. It had been at the forefront of a body revolution – literally and metaphorically. This was a dance that broke with the conventions of the academic and classic ballet body shackled by codified gestures and restricted movements, replacing it with the expressive body of fluid motion and natural transitions. Liberated from the impositions of civilization, and equated with the very rhythms of breath and blood flow, modern dance was understood as a vehicle for unmediated self-expression. It was a means by which to bring the deepest feelings to public view. And while men theorized about dance, and especially attempted to contain it within laws of rhythmic structure, it was women who were largely seen to be dancing, rhythmically if not lawfully.[19] Modern dance, it seems, could be the wellspring of catharsis and energy but it could also be the source of possible disorder and disruption. In its publicity at least, in the photos of dancers that accompanied the texts by Alain Jacques-Dalcroze or those published in avant-garde architecture and art journals it was the space of women. The War Memorial Gymnasium, it would seem, would not court such dangers and the Dance Studio, modern dance and the women who were its advocates were banished.

There is perhaps one other trace of architecture's liaison with dance deserving of recollection because it goes some way to explaining why a dance studio may have seemed less urgent, or its omission natural. Appearing in Le Corbusier's influential avant-garde journal *L'Esprit Nouveau*, and in more than one article, were discussions of the kinesthetic of dance that were obviously considered relevant to architectural modernism. It was a relevance based on a shared quest for rhythmic laws as the perceived goal of their respective aesthetics. 'Rhythm', wrote Albert Jeanneret, brother of Le Corbusier (né Charles-Edouard Jeanneret) and disciple of Jaques-Dalcroze (founder of the Ecole Française de Rythmique et d'Éducation Corporelle), 'is the basis of art as of life. The problems resolved by the machine create (font désirer) for this rhythmical machine which is the human body, or rather for this harmonization established between the body and the spirit, the desire for the same possibility of precision.'[20] Here, Jaques-Dalcroze's ideas of rhythm and corporeal education were merged with Le Corbusier's machine aesthetic. Jaques-Dalcroze in turn cited Le Corbusier's *Après le Cubisme* in his *Le Rythme, la musique et l'éducation* (1922).[21] What this theorist of the kinesthetic saw in Le Corbusier's Purist aesthetic was an affinity between the architect's search for a precise determination of laws of sensation and his own research into the invariants of rhythm.[22] Twenty years later, at the time of the War Memorial Gymnasium's design and construction, this rhythmic body responding to the invariants and laws of sensation will take the form of Le Corbusier's *modulor*, a more dependable legislator and replacement. There were limits to the emancipatory practices of body movement and more disciplinary objectives to achieve. The movements of liberated bodies, such as those of Isadora Duncan or Martha Graham, were chastised by the *modulor*. Similarly, architecture that embodied an accommodation of the body's every un-programmed whim with moveable, adjustable and convertible elements, such as that by Eileen Gray, was rebuked by Le Corbusier and erased from architectural memory.[23]

Once completed, the building could also begin to forget about its making. Its Massey Silver Medal for architectural excellence in the category of Recreational Buildings was awarded to Sharp, Thompson, Berwick & Pratt, Architects; even Fred Lasserre's consultant role is overlooked. Expunged from the photographic publicity of architecture are the labouring bodies, which made modernism physically manifest. Instead, the building traverses professional space emptied of bodies, pristine and unchanging in its photographic representation, disembodied and dislodged from the hurly-burly of the active life that is its ostensible function. Only on one rare occasion in the spaces of architectural publicity do we see this exemplary modern architecture occupied. In this instance it is two males, suited, one, the architect perhaps, arm extended, a *modulor* of sorts, who is framed by the structure, captured in the harsh light of the Memorial Window. This is what architecture wished to remember.

Whether the design of the War Memorial Gymnasium is attributed to Fred Lasserre, Ned Pratt, or Sharp, Thompson, Berwick & Pratt, it is men who are hailed. Whether it is seen as the expression of the pedagogical aspirations of the School of Architecture, or the professional office, it is men who are identified as their representatives. Architecture as a profession had been founded on its status as one of the liberal arts, on the distinction between 'idea building' and the 'mechanical arts'.[24] Coinciding with this theoretical position was another that proposed the distinction between spaces and practices for men (public and active) and spaces and practices for women (domestic and sequestered); architecture calibrated and distributed spaces and practices accordingly.[25] In the immediate post-war years the 'modulorized' virile athletic body re-enacts that regulatory function, an imaginary policeman keeping things and bodies in their proper place. As a learned, liberal and public occupation, architecture was still considered 'masculine territory'.[26] From the institution of physically demanding design assignments in academies of architecture to the conception of the war hero as the epitome of architectural value in the Bauhaus, this domain was bodily defended.[27] This, to some extent, was the experience of one of the architects associated with the design of the War Memorial Gymnasium.

Catherine Chard Wisnicki entered this 'masculine territory' in 1939 when McGill University admitted its first women, two, to its Architectural programme. This was partly the result of a new director and partly due to a reduced male enrolment as a consequence of the war. Hence the appearance of women in the profession of architecture here was perhaps philosophically motivated and certainly circumstantial. In 1943 Wisnicki was the first of these women to graduate; three years later she entered the firm of Sharp, Thompson, Berwick & Pratt and continued to be in their employ during the years of the War Memorial Gym's construction.

Wisnicki's entrance into the architectural profession can be attributed to the gradual and perhaps circumspect acceptance of modern architecture and pedagogy in North America. The Bauhaus curriculum of the 1920s had been revolutionary and gender inclusive, although by the 1930s women's enrolment had been restricted in number and limited to the craft shops while the identity of the architect rehearsed in the Bauhaus exploratory theatre had become ultimately masculine. As one historian of the Bauhaus recounts: 'Actors' assumed bodies that were 'mechanized, abstract, universalized – seemingly gender neutral yet representing those characteristics convention-ally associated with masculinity – control, self-mastery'.[28] When the Bauhaus arrived in North America in the form of an exhibition at the MOMA in New York women were not pictured among the faculty; by this time the former director of the Bauhaus, now resident in the United States, had reverted to conventional masculine apparel, the suit, and as Katerina Reudi Ray surmises, there would be 'no feminizing of the architectural profession'.[29]

Wisnicki was not overlooked because she was not a modernist; she was in fact an articulate spokesperson of modernist tenets. She believed the modern architect was a technician who must make 'the machine the instrument of the directing mind'. She was concerned with concise and economical solutions where 'structural functions [would] produce new forms, the product of social and technical conditions of our age'.[30] She, like other modernists, decried a lack of 'philosophy and clear conviction', and architecture's 'degeneration into sentimental aestheticism'. Wisnicki wrote on and designed for the things beloved of modernists – prefabrication, industry and urban planning. She was active internationally, participated in the Union Internationale des Femmes Architectes, and pursued urban studies in France.[31] However, despite the fact that Wisnicki's scholarly and professional interests strayed from the conventional assignation of 'women's work' to the home, she is not remembered for this but rather for her residential design. Later, when she assumed a teaching position in the School of Architecture in 1963, her former role as an ally in the building that was so important as a defining moment of modern architecture on the campus and as the flagship for the School was never publicized.[32] (And, although she was granted tenure after nine years in various positions in UBC's School of Architecture, it was without promotion.)[33] Clearly, architecture's professional practices, framing regimes and work expectations discouraged, if they did not preclude, women's participation.[34] Despite her obvious modernist sensibilities and the fact that she at least did not perceive architecture as 'male territory', clearly others did. Her presence was unrecognized in contemporary accounts of the War Memorial Gymnasium and, until recently, unnoticed in its attributions.[35]

Figure 7.5   'War Memorial Gym', text added to the gym.

Wisnicki's omission from the credits and accolades of the gymnasium is also in part because it was the protocol of practice within large firms in the 1950s to attribute work to the principals. As a designer at Sharp, Thompson, Berwick & Pratt, Wisnicki was embedded in a 'vertically' structured organization, meaning that all work was subsumed under the single identity of the firm. Office protocol then worked to assure that Ned Pratt, as a principal in the firm, was identified as the 'real' designer of the Gymnasium and to consequently suppress the collaborative reality of architectural practice. There must be star architects just as there must be star athletes. As one colleague remembers, Pratt was 'quite autocratic, [h]e collected around him a lot of partners, for a variety of reasons, but when push came to shove what Ned said would be done'.[36]

As Wisnicki remembered the design of the War Memorial Gymnasium some 50 years later, her role had been as an 'employee' of Sharp, Thompson, Berwick & Pratt during a very hectic period of office production.[37] She had been, in fact, a senior designer responsible for the working drawings.[38] She recollected that the architects' hopes for the gymnasium had been for a well-functioning and practical building, their intentions utilitarian rather than philosophical.[39] Wisnicki had once maintained that in architecture 'The problems are too complex for the individual. They must be faced by a sound body of workmen … [and] a technique of collective thinking to arrive at a system of collective action'.[40] Unfortunately, that collective action turned out to be quite exclusionary. Her envisioned profession where 'building unites manual and mental workers' did not occur here. It is therefore not so surprising that she should be overlooked as a participant architect of a gymnasium in the 1950s. Nor is it so surprising that the War Memorial Gymnasium would offer an opportunity to re-rehearse the body language and identities of its patriarchal line.

We can see and experience in the gymnasium the Cartesian mind at war with the Cartesian body. On the one hand, the gymnasium was rational, controlled and universalizing; it proclaimed disembodied action in the repetitive structural grid that announced the architect's mind at work. Yet the mind was in thrall to the body, its gait, attraction to light, its perception mechanisms, as can be experienced in ascending the stairs, traversing the bridge or apprehending the view. We can perhaps almost catch sight of the dream of liberation announced in that utilitarian objective paired with a memorial function that was the gymnasium.

Recently the words WAR MEMORIAL GYMNASIUM have been stencilled in large letters along the long, public south façade of the building, as if to stop this fact fading from memory (Figure 7.5). Clearly, there is less assurance that architecture can embody memory unassisted. In the end, memory did become unmoored from its architectural support, which had become a rather unresponsive harbour for the flotsam of recollections.

No Body/ies in the Gym

PATRICIA VERTINSKY, SHERRY MCKAY AND
STEPHEN PETRINA

> The stories we tell are constructed, and we know it … we tell stories in little
> spaces that necessarily force us to leave out much more than they allow us to
> include: but we do it because the alternative is to not tell stories at all.[1]

Places of memory inspire creative thinking and story-telling about the
historical past, reminding us of worlds we have lost in the broader pageant of
the past. When Walter Benjamin re-visioned history as a porous surface
whose holes provide windows into discarded memories he suggested that 'if
we look for them they will open to us like heliotropes meeting the gaze of the
sun'.[2] Throughout this book we have fixed our gaze – in very different ways
and from a variety of different disciplines and professional standpoints –
upon the porous surface of the history of the War Memorial Gymnasium – the
Memorial Window, the monumental entrances (and exits), the bleachers on
the basketball court, the bowling alley, and outwards along the old 'desire'
lines to the Women's gymnasium and Varsity Stadium. From it we have
looked across the campus to the Osborne Center, which never did, in fact,
replace the War Memorial Gym as the home of the School of Physical
Education. Within and around the gym we have sought to illuminate
meanings and memories of the past and to elicit new understandings about
the ideal modern body of architectural discourse and the education of the
athletic body in higher education in the years following World War II.

Fifty years on, the outside skin of the War Memorial Gym looks very
much as it always did. But from the moment it was conceived, through its
design, production, use and reconstructions in relation to changing use, the
inside of the gym has provided us with a narrative, a developing story, traces
of which are always present.[3] We have rendered its changing spaces into
places infused with human intention.[4] Within its walls, working spaces have
been re-apportioned, administrative structures changed, social relations reconfigured and patterns of activity transformed. Telling a world of stories
through photographic records are rows of fading pictures that have been
hung along the corridors. Infrequently looked at, they reflect the gendered
and racial compositions of graduating classes of years gone by and the
changing nature of the faculty and its leadership. Further illuminating the
past are some recently installed 'Down memory lane' exhibits in the

memorial lobby where faded pictures of star athletes and prominent alumni from earlier times are displayed to the casual passer-by.

Where once the men's changing rooms extended commodiously from north to south of the entire building and a male attendant was on duty to hand out freshly laundered white towels for the men's showers, a computer lab has now been inserted into a good portion of that 'uneasily disciplined' social and hygienic space – the locker room where corporeality cannot be avoided. The snack bar, a popular haunt for socializing faculty and students, has long since been closed down as a money-losing venture. Only the Coca-Cola machines replace it – witness to an exclusive and lucrative commercial agreement between university administrators and Coca-Cola Ltd rather than any particular effort to provide healthy refreshments for vigorously active students. A faculty and staff lounge now exists in the (still hotly contested) snack bar space that had been donated by the Legion, the lapping water and constant lively activity in the Empire Pool adjacent to it carefully screened by drapes and shutters.[5] Even the popular Empire Pool, built for the swimming and diving events of the British Empire and Commonwealth Games in 1954, is threatened by yet another campus redevelopment, which would jettison it for an expanded bus-loop – another potential triumph of machine over body, ousting the outdoor swimming activities of students and staff.[6] Like any machine the body is subject to occasional breakdown, and on the floor beneath the offices of Athletic Services one can now find rows of beds for injured and rehabilitating athletes in a physiotherapy-taping room replacing active routines in the original small apparatus gym for stunts, trampolining and formal gymnastics. Where once the six lanes of the bowling alley, manicured into the cellar of the gymnasium, were used to capacity, there is now a series of airless science laboratories and basement offices for the sport scientists on faculty at the School of Human Kinetics (for the name of the School changed in 1994 to represent more closely the academic mission of the unit and to invoke the cover of science for its survival).[7]

No longer a joint enterprise catering to the athletic needs of the students and professional training in physical education, the School was cut adrift from the Department of Athletic Services which now reports, not to an academic authority but to a newly created Vice-President for Students, and is expected to manage its own financial and administrative affairs as a business-like ancillary service.[8] 'We pay for our own water now, clean the ice, cut the grass, mark the fields, fix the roof', commented one of the Athletic Services team. With its offices squeezed down the west side of the gym and the School's administration and instructional units segregated on the eastern corridor, conversation which takes place between the two units is often limited to the apportioning of space and wrangles over how the utility bills for light and heat in the building should be divided. Intramurals has largely gone too, to a new student recreation building on the opposite side of McGinnes Field (effectively diminishing the open space available for play and further blocking the promised view of the mountains from the Memorial Window).

You might wonder if there are any 'modern' bodies left to educate in the War Memorial Gym and whether the sensory deprivation which seems to curse modernist buildings, the dullness, the monotony and tactile sterility of its spaces have dulled the quest for the study and celebration of the moving body. In many respects, within the gymnasium, technology has replaced the athletic body in motion, and the recreational body (already cut off from the School's academic programme of study in the early 1980s)[9] has long since fled to a dedicated new building where fees, and taxes on fees, are charged for students to hone their bodies in the fitness facilities.[10] Physical activity instruction courses once provided as an integral component of the undergraduate degree programme have also hit the dust to be replaced by performance analysis and more theoretical observation. The task of providing compulsory physical education as a service to all first and second year students, which had been considered so essential in the years before and after World War II, was gradually abandoned as the School focused – not upon the student's body, or the student body – but upon developing its research agenda and academic and graduate programmes. One of the main objectives (and indeed requirements) of Bob Osborne's successor in the 1980s was to rid the curriculum of the active body – to separate the coaches from the academics, and to bring the study of physical education into line with other scientific disciplines in higher education.[11] Having a physical activity instructional programme within an academic unit was increasingly seen as incompatible with the mission of a research university, and the new Director worked assiduously to elevate the status of the School by using applied science research to drive curricular reforms.[12]

The contested spaces above the memorial lobby where Mr Vincent used to teach compulsory ballroom dancing to the physical education students in the early years of the gym are now the sedentary cubicles of graduate students – an arrangement hotly contested by Athletic Services, who believe the space should be theirs to accommodate a Hall of Fame dedicated to the past athletic glories of UBC and memorable events in the War Memorial Gymnasium. Training for school physical educators has left too – to be found now in a small and beleaguered unit in the Scarfe Building of the Faculty of Education.[13]

Indeed, training for school physical education has not fared well in recent decades, especially since the 1950s and 1960s when Bob Osborne claimed that 'physical education programme development in the schools was almost sensational … There has been as much progress in physical education in the schools as there has been in automobiles', in an interview with a former student in 1966.[14] Continued growth seemed assured to Osborne at the time, for he wrote 'the goals of physical education will probably remain the same for generations to come … and suggestions to change the name of physical education to kinesiology may receive only temporary support'.[15] The residents of the Women's gymnasium would have applauded such sentiments at the time. However, the early dedication of women physical educators such as Marian Henderson to the exemplary training of female physical education teachers and the physical and character development of girls and women in sports and gymnastics would be supplanted over the years by female (or mostly male) athletic coaches on yearly contracts who can be fired after three years if they do not produce winning teams.

The pressures for change in the War Memorial Gym came from within and without and were withstood or accommodated on a variety of levels and with a broad range of short- and long-term consequences. But it was the moving body that suffered as the Cartesian divide maintained and intensified its hold upon the academic enterprise. Changes in approach to physical education began in earnest in the late 1960s as physical education leaders in North America were called upon to defend its place in higher education. Bob Osborne's enthusiasm for the health of physical education, especially in the schools, might perhaps have been tempered by a growing concern among the public that physical education in the cold war was not proving to be a guarantor of physical fitness and healthy youth.[16] And there was increasing questioning among North American academics about the lack of a carefully defined domain of content in physical education. The enthusiastic and social reformist claims of an emerging profession in the 1890s – 'there are few scientific fields which offer opportunities for the study of problems of greater value to the human race'[17] – had surely come unstuck.

In an indictment of what he saw as the physical education profession's inability to identify and support a clearly focused mission, Franklin Henry, a professor at the University of California, Berkeley, called in 1964 for a much needed renewal through the development of an academic discipline of physical education.[18] He was no doubt influenced by James Bryant Conant's comments that physical education represented the worst of what was wrong with graduate programmes in American universities. Conant, former president of Harvard University, said:

> I am far from impressed by what I have heard and read about graduate work in the field of physical education. If I wished to portray the education of teachers in the worst terms I should quote from the descriptions of some graduate courses in physical education. To my mind, a university should cancel graduate programs in this area. If the physical education teacher wishes to enter into a research career in the field of physiology of exercise and related subjects he should use the graduate years to build on his natural science background a knowledge

of the physiological sciences that will enable him to stand on an equal
footing with the undergraduate major in these sciences.[19]

Though his plan led to a concerted and partly successful effort by academics
to build a systematic body of knowledge about the fundamental process of
human movement in all its forms, physical education in the schools
remained tied to such broadly defined educational goals that they became
almost impossible to achieve.[20]

At UBC the distance between the gym teachers and the sport scientists
would steadily grow and eventually lead to complete separation as teacher
training moved out of the War Memorial Gym altogether. Had the schism
occurred earlier, the University administration may have thought more
carefully about its decision to move the School of Physical Education under
the administrative control of the Faculty of Education in 1963 – a year
before Henry's influential clarion call to change academic direction from the
'professional years' of the 1950s. For Henry, physical education was
technical and professional, the academic discipline (later called kinesiology)
was theoretical and scholarly. From this perspective, physical education
belonged in a School or College of Education but kinesiology did not and
should find its home in a Faculty of Arts and Science.[21] As it turned out, the
administrative change would not prove to be propitious for either the
profession or the discipline.[22]

After the 1970s, the study of human movement in higher education was
slowly reconstructed as a discipline-based field concerned with human (and
animal) movement, sport, exercise and leisure.[23] Many academics
internalized the belief that 'disciplines provide dreams and models, both of
reality and learning … [creating] modes of knowledge that seem to the
participants uniquely real'.[24] In rushing to legitimate their own, albeit partial,
knowledge about the body, they felt they were on the verge of an exciting
development, though few could have realized the extent to which the field
would be reconfigured and in some cases obliterated from the higher
education scene.[25] The debates raged for the next two decades or more,
symptomatic of a discipline/profession in transition, and the emergent sub-
disciplinary emphases as well as the changing programmes, foci and
department names were often bitterly contested.[26] And as productive as some
of the sub-disciplines that flourished became in achieving a greater depth of
understanding about human movement, a pervasive limitation remained in
the inability of the field to capture the intricacy and comprehensiveness of
the human mover. Locked into a pattern of highly specialized, technical and
narrow sub-disciplinary fragmentation, physical education, human
movement sciences, kinesiology or human kinetics, as it became known at
UBC, became unable – or unwilling – to integrate knowledge about the
exercising body and act upon those embodied connections.[27]

Decisions about the curriculum, career paths, priorities for faculty hiring, the selection of leaders and the criteria for faculty rewards further polarized faculty identities and group affiliations.[28] Human Kinetics faculty came to inhabit 'small and different worlds' focused increasingly upon applied science and the technical management of sport.[29] In their quest for institutional (ego) centrality to the mission of the university they sought grants, research projects, complex laboratories, and organized specialized journals, international connections and enlarged graduate programmes. Sport science's technological emphasis on the 'virtual' body moved faculty members further down the Cartesian corridor[30] – quantitatively reducing the phenomena of movement from a distance and objectifying the moving subject. The hegemonic image in human kinetics remained a reductionist one of the body-as-machine.[31]

Given the fact that the debate was controlled largely by white males committed to a traditional view of science and employed at elite research universities, this was hardly surprising.[32] And given the Canadian government's decisions in these decades to foster research nationally on elite sporting performance, it followed that a host of opportunities opened for mostly male scientists working on the scientific aspects of sporting performance, such as exercise physiology and biomechanics.[33] A natural corollary to these impulses was the growth of sport management to provide technical experts to professionally manage the Canadian sport system. The preoccupation of these groups with technique and commodification in sport, especially high performance sport, pitted them against the traditional physical educators and others who shared a concern with the role of physical activity in the total development of the person.[34] But it lent credence to Rorty's observation at the time that much of what gets defined as knowledge in a society can be recognized as those beliefs and modes of practice that are successful in helping official groups in that society do what they want to do.[35]

There were also dangers lurking in this approach. Similar situations elsewhere in North America caused Franklin Henry to articulate new concerns. In 1978, he noted that:

> When a physical education department demonstrates that many of its courses and the research of its students and faculty are, in fact, possible within the various traditional disciplines, it also signals the university administration that it can be phased out ...[36]

Other leaders were concerned that a potential fragmentation of the field was imminent. 'I worry', said Shirl Hoffman:

> about the academic character of some of the PhDs we are graduating, exceptionally narrow people – technicians almost – who lack a

scholar's understanding of how their discipline relates to the broader field of physical education and academic life, and who studiously avoid anything that looks, or sounds too philosophical.[37]

Clearly the evolution from physical education to sport science was not immune to controversy. As Swanson and Massengale have pointed out, the drive to develop an academic discipline out of what had been considered a profession brought with it the difficult task of creating and organizing a 'usable' body of knowledge and an intense commitment to research that drove the creation of other specializations.[38] Accompanied by the acceleration of the women's movement, the drive for civil rights and a dawning recognition that science did not hold all the answers to society's ills, the sport sciences were pressed to engage in some self-reflection.

In the decade leading up to the end of the millennium, and as part of a generalized trend toward affirmative action and the need for gender-sensitive university policies, administrators were encouraged to hire more women to the faculty in the School of Human Kinetics. But the War Memorial Gym remained, in the minds of some at least, the bastion of 'the basement boys', the male scientists who still took up most of the working space there.[39] 'My biggest disappointment', said one female faculty member who had been assigned office space in a building far removed from the main gym, 'was that we seemed unable to work as a team in building this new human kinetics. I think it is part of the building,' she said, 'for sure it's the nature of the discipline … they don't want to play ball with us, they don't even want us on their team'.[40]

In the large gymnasium, surrounded by new sets of bleachers, however, men and women are playing ball regularly – basketball, volleyball and even tossing balls in rhythmic gymnastics in the early dawn hours – for the floor, even though it has had to be replaced due to overuse by the ceremonies office at graduation time, is still valued for its pliancy and forgiving nature.[41] Men's and women's varsity basketball teams (as well as the volleyball teams) both visibly now share the playing space and practice times, and it is widely accepted that games such as basketball are good for developing physical mastery and group coordination for women, just as they are for men.[42]

Basketball is still the game of choice in the War Memorial Gymnasium, and basketball playing students, once the embodiment of modernity and the character-building ethos of sport in higher education, can now use their sport and their trained bodies to pay for their education through athletic scholarships.[43] Yet despite the new world of commodified and globalized sport the playing and organization of varsity basketball games easily provoke reminders of gender/ed attitudes and policies of years gone by. The women's intercollegiate basketball games are still scheduled in the 6.15 p.m.

time slot, 'the opening act' to the prime time men's basketball games at 8.00 p.m. just as they were in earlier years when it was argued that it was only the men's sports that could bring in honour, prestige and revenues to the University. But then spectators of either gender seem less and less interested in watching any of the games, and revenues can no longer be counted on to bolster athletic services for students – if they ever could. Although there are no more co-ed Beauty Queens to 'throw the ball in' at the commencement of important basketball competitions, the women continue to play different basketball rules (International Basketball Federation) from the men who play National Collegiate Athletic Association (NCAA) rules.[44] Presumably, their rules allow the men to showcase their greater expertise, talent and speed to a much larger crowd, a condition which apparently requires the addition of three more men to oversee the event (as against the two assigned to organize the women's game). And, in the headquarters of the Department of Athletics and Sport Services down the west side of the building, the office space is largely taken up with male coaches. Of the 22 Head Coaches for intercollegiate athletic teams, only the women's basketball coach is currently a female. The lion's share of the athletic budget still flows to the men's sports.

So when we ask whether the modernist architecture of the gymnasium freed the body from its architectural 'corsets' as students had imagined in their 1940s campaign, it is difficult to find the active, moving body at all on one side of the gym – in the disciplined spaces of the School of Human Kinetics – and the student body has long since ceased to have any control over the working or the playing spaces of the gym. And when we ask whether the gym became the symbol of fun that David Brock spoke of in his attempt to persuade President Mackenzie that this was no place for a memorial of wars or men who die in them, we find that the gym, first proposed as a place of recreation, has become a machine for competition and measured success, for therapy and muscle mending, and in the academic arena, a repository for sophisticated equipment and reductionist experiments rather than the enlightened education of bodies.

What, then is the 'truth' of the modern gymnasium – a place for memories, a place for bodies, a 'palace of sweat'? Is it true, as McKay has pointed out in an earlier chapter, that every modernist project was a gymnasium of sorts – a space that was measured and regulated according to the dictates of the architectural game and whose social arrangements were organized for the delineated activities of the modern body?

The architects of the War Memorial Gymnasium eschewed the monument with its associations of time stopped and space stilled, of temporal stasis and the immobility of mass. They jettisoned the use of familiar precedents and the requisite conventions of assured meaning. Instead, memory was to be evoked by space that was abstract and cool, literally and phenomenally transparent, prosaic and chastened. Memory would not be pinned down to any specificity by the architecture: that would require the added 'ornamental' flourishes of texts and photographs, plaques and ceremonies. But the War Memorial Gymnasium was not immune to the solicitations of memory.

In the 1950s the architectural public of the War Memorial Gymnasium had garnered their architectural values from two texts that were considered obligatory reading: Siegfried Giedion's *Space, Time and Architecture* and Sir Bannister Fletcher's *History of Architecture on a Comparative Method*. From Giedion's 'Space, Time' readers learned to think about the body and architecture as both enhanced and disciplined by the new technologies of space production. Here space was a social production only in as much as it was a technologically mediated one. From Sir Bannister's 'Comparative Method' they learned to think of the history of architecture as the embodiment of cultural values, where the comparison of buildings served to reveal superior ('Western') and inferior ('Other') architectural solutions.[45] Such evaluation was measured, of course, by Eurocentric assumptions about the superiority of structure over ornament, permanent over impermanent materials, innovation over convention. Together, these texts allowed buildings to be positioned culturally as they were evaluated aesthetically. The War Memorial Gymnasium registered, via its emphasis on structure, modern materials and technology-derived proportions and scale, the (Eurocentric) cultural assumptions that had been attributed to such characteristics so explicitly in Sir Bannister's text. After the rhetoric of the war, a much larger audience would be sensitive to this message.[46] This is perhaps the deep memory of the War Memorial Gymnasium. This 'living memorial' is the register of a cultural memory that is tethered to progress and hence committed to the exclusion of 'other' memories that have been so exactingly erased by the abstraction of the Gymnasium's production and the purported 'disinterestedness' of its forms.

Despite modernism's aversion to monuments, each 11 November the Remembrance Day Service transforms the War Memorial Hall into a monumental space. Once a year, bodies file in, present arms, stand at attention, bow heads; bodies take up symbolic positions as stand-ins for the armed forces, citizens, the fallen and the absent (see Figure 8.1). Their ritual performance gives social and political significance to lives that were and times gone by. The space of memorial is a space of consensus and exaltation, where differences are, albeit temporarily, overcome if not resolved. Philosopher Henri Lefebvre speaks of the exchange that transpires between these symbolic bodies and their corporeal counterparts, and he underlines the significance of their architectural support. The anxiety of death and of time passing that is summoned by memorials is, Lefebvre contends, repressed by architecture's permanence. Here, momentarily, can

Figure 8.1   War Memorial Service, War Memorial Gymnasium.

'the space of death be negated, transfigured into a living space which is an extension of the body'.[47] When 'basketballing' students resume play in the quotidian space of the adjacent recreation centre gym another exchange between symbolic and virile codes takes place within the durable structures of architecture and the repetition of the game. It is perhaps not so strange, therefore, that a memorial is paired with a gymnasium where on other days of the year a similar play of metaphor and substitution occurs.

Lefebvre identifies a revolutionary potential in monuments, which might, if only for a moment, 'evoke a fleeting euphoric sensation … a point of rupture which reveals the totality of possibilities of daily experience'.[48] There is little evidence that the architects of the War Memorial Gym envisioned any such euphoric sensation breaking through the defining structural grids of their construction. Spatial volumes intentionally elevated and windows made blind by interior structure rendered events within inscrutable to, and aloof from, the daily experience that swirled around them. The curricular preoccupations and legitimacy claims of professional sports education were similarly attuned to the creation of a more exclusive space than the milieu in which it was sited. And the concern of both architects and educators with appropriate form, building and human respectively, and with the efficient deployment of space and time, would undermine any revolutionary potential of the monument as festival. To transform the distanced and disengaged into lived experience, to affect a dialectical transcendence, calls for a different relationship of the body to space and to time than that proposed by the modernism of the gym.[49]

Now in the opening decade of the twenty-first century, the relationship of architecture to the human body is fraught with controversy, indecision and revised opinion. Alternatively, some seek a quite different body, one that is 'mobile, multiple and mutable', rather than static, internally consistent and composed of an idealized and hierarchal set of relationships.[50] They seek a body re-conceptualized as assemblage, fusion, mutation, evolution and fluidity, a human body more in keeping with the architecture of a digitized world. In this world 'the formulation of alien bodies is often the vehicle for speculating on models of possible advanced terrestrial life forms.[51] Others find in prosthetic-enhanced cyborgs a possible liberation from gender assumptions associated with the conventions of the physical 'natural' body.[52] Architecture continues to produce the bodies its theory requires, as it did during the modern era. Hybrid, or fluid and mutable, contemporary thinking about the body and architecture would seem to find little solace in durable form and little investment in memory. Perhaps it is due to this negation that some return to the unified, static modernist body as a model of proportion, hierarchy and measure, as a source of visual perception,[53] or a more haptic responsiveness,[54] is still proposed. The resuscitated human body remains a measure of and analogy for an architecture threatened by obsolescence.

These current conceptualizations of monuments and bodies serve to highlight the 'unnaturalness' of the War Memorial Gymnasium's embodiment of an idealized and timeless body, both literally and metaphorically, and the ideological functions which this embodiment served. They also provide an update of the conflicted relationship between the body and architecture, between memory and monument. Modernism's idealized body and contemporary theory's mutable body share one consequence: they both absent familiar corporeal selves from architecture's abstract and conceptual space, and without that body there can be no 'fleeting, intensely euphoric sensation', no monument such as Lefebvre describes.

Today, the view offered from the Memorial Window is of another gymnasium – the UBC Student Recreation Centre (see Figure 8.2).[55] The new gym stands as an uncanny echo of the old. It has the same three basketball courts, weight and exercise rooms, but also the dance hall 'forgotten' by its predecessor. It nominally at least has the same function, except that it serves recreation rather than pedagogical discipline, students rather than faculties. And where the old gym pulled bodies into its idealized space, the new recreation centre turns bodies to the outside, propelling them out of multiple doors along viewing promontories and balconies that overlook the playing field. Although it serves no official memorial function, the recreation centre is the work of an architect preoccupied with an aleatory memory filtered through an artistic temperament, unmoored.[56] The building defines place rather than illustrates spatial abstractions. It situates itself within a recreational precinct adjacent to a field, edging a pedestrian mall, bordering the Student Union Building, rather than withdrawing as an object raised above and aloof from the surrounding campus, as an object-building upon a plane of abstract space. The interior concourse facilitates views and movement to the playing field, a memory landscape recalling the origins of recreation perhaps, or the old and much loved Varsity Stadium? And on the east façade the strange canted mass of a concrete plane evokes the memory of the climbing wall eliminated due to the imposition of a conception of the body as liability and of the space of recreation as the space of litigation. The new gymnasium cannot recall the grand narratives of war, but neither can it muster bodies to the decorum and propriety demanded of monuments and the histories they script. It can, however, free bodies from the burden of their symbolic representation and free-up space for those chance memories of unofficial, everyday life.

As we conclude our book about the War Memorial Gymnasium we are confronted with the very question of how memory, monument and modernity are constructed in war. We are told, post-September 11, that the world is once again a dangerous place. Only now, the enemy is terror or, more literally, terrorism – at once invisible yet photogenic. Bombs, bullets and propaganda are finding their targets and the consequences are far from

Figure 8.2   Student Recreation Centre. Henriques & Partners with IBI Group, 1995.

clear. The authors of this war on terror, be they soldiers, journalists, academics or evening news viewers, find themselves looking over their shoulders while watching their mouths. On the home front, wherever that is today, the war on terror is celebrated and concentrated, contested and protested. The same will be true when it is time to commemorate and monumentalize the tragedies.

Immediately following the atomic bombing of Hiroshima and Nagasaki, countries allied with the United States went to work on establishing the form that war memorials would take. Canada was no exception, and its universities were among the first institutions to debate the merits of traditional cenotaphs versus the new notions of 'functional living memorials'. University students, for the most part, preferred 'useful', living structures. A student union building at the University of Saskatchewan, a memorial football stadium at St Francis Xavier University and a memorial skating rink at the University of New Brunswick were favoured over the static cenotaphs popularized after World War I.[57]

While the War Memorial Gymnasium at UBC, by its very existence, gave voice to the celebrants of World War II, it animated a particular body or image of war. The Gymnasium failed (and fails) to memorialize the voices of dissent in World War II. Perhaps this is the only way it could have been, for the memorial symbolized the subject of war. Yet it was no less, figuratively speaking, an object of dissent. Somewhere between amnesia and memory, dissent was forced beneath the surfaces of the memorial. After all, this was the 1940s and 1950s, not the 1960s, and who dared be against a useful monument to fallen soldiers and war? Who could have questioned the recollection and re-enactment of the wins and losses on the battleground?

As momentum gathered around the construction of the War Memorial Gymnasium in the mid to late 1940s, dissenting opinion formed in its opposition. For example, in late 1946, letters flowed into the student newspaper, *The Ubyssey*, as proceeds for the gymnasium rolled in from raffles, rummage sales and beauty contests. One critic questioned the commemoration of war, and noted that 'memorials were neither necessary nor desirable'. 'At best', he continued, 'they keep alive a spirit of nationalism; faith in the strength of arms; the glories of war, and hatred for another nation because their grandfathers had fought our grandfathers'. War memorials were handy political 'devices for obtaining things we have always wanted, but could not expect to obtain very soon by straightforward methods'. By using this tactic at UBC, Mr Peers concluded, 'we have cheapened the sacrifices of war to the status of an excuse for building a luxurious playground for schoolboys'. Similarly, Ms Effie Smallwood questioned the idea of building a memorial to benefit less than one per cent of the province's population. 'Spending half a million dollars on the luxury of a gymnasium', she wrote, 'is a vulgarity at this time when veterans' families are forced to live in attics, cellars, and chicken coops'. Other critics accepted the notion of a memorial and encouraged a realistic portrayal of war or a more reverent symbolism. 'By no means let us hush up war', John Randall argued:

> Let us instead flood the press with scenes of ravaged farm lands, cities of rubble, lifeless corpses, and disembowelled women. Let us go to Europe and make films of the homeless refugees and hunger-crazed children who wander aimlessly from one pile of bricks to the next. These are the fruits of war! This is what happens when mighty man girds himself in shining armour and marches to conquer the foe. Were a War Memorial to be lined with scenes such as these, some useful purpose might be achieved.

Advocating spiritualism, another wrote, 'the only alternative to Christian significance is an empty sterile "naturalism" which is simply paganism'. 'While it might memorialize the "hollow men" ... who callously invited the second [World War] by their cynicism, selfishness and apathy ... it certainly would not express the very real faith of anything' but war. He feared that the War Memorial Gymnasium was bound to become an idol to 'the goddesses of architectural or natural beauty', or worse, 'a pagan temple to the glory of the human body'.[58]

Memory was and remains a source of conflict. What and how we choose to commemorate or remember is the result of struggles between individual and collective consciences, or between interests. Even today, it is not clear whether it is in our best interest to nourish the civic memory with static and living monuments, to leave memory to the cultivation of historians, or to leave the past alone to individual minds. When we choose to commemorate, it is unclear whether we ought to abstract a sterile form of memory from history or whether we ought to provide as realistic a portrayal as possible. Herein lies a subtle yet important truth of UBC's War Memorial Gymnasium. Neither timeless nor frozen in time, the gymnasium continues to stir memories in the private and public body. As this book attests, the power of memory does not rest in the gymnasium; rather, power and memory are in need of political upkeep. Not every memorial helps people to remember things, or ensure that future generations will remember things as precisely as the present one does. It is as if once we assign monumental form to memory we have to some degree divested ourselves of the obligation to remember.[59] But a good memorial, says Svetlana Bohn, 'doesn't clean up history. It leaves part of the mess, part of the argument'.[60] Hence, it was not our intention merely to document the history of the War Memorial Gymnasium. Instead, our effort is aimed at politicizing this history. After all, we presume, a living memorial ought to be treated with living memories.

Notes on Contributors

Editors

Patricia Vertinsky is a Professor of Human Kinetics at the University of British Columbia. Her research focuses on the social and cultural history of the body, exercise and physical culture. She is the author of *The Eternally Wounded Woman: Women, Doctors and Exercise in the late 19th Century* (1994), co-author with Sandy O'Brien Cousins of *Physical Activity, Aging and Stereotypes* (1996), and with John Bale of *Sites of Sport: Space, Place and Experience* (2003). She is past-President of the North American Society for Sport History, Vice-President of the International Society for the History of Sport and Physical Education and is on the editorial boards of the *Journal of Sport History*, the *International Journal of the History of Sport*, *International Sport Studies*, *The Sports Historian* and *Sporting Traditions*.

Sherry McKay is an Associate Professor of Architectural History and Theory at the University of British Columbia School of Architecture. Her research brings feminist and cultural theory to the investigation of architectural and urban production and consumption. Her recent publications include 'Dream Homes', *Dream Home, work by Renée van Halm* (2002); 'Architectural Negotiations of the Pacific Rim: Vancouver, Canada', *Bulletin de l'Institut Pierre Renouvin* (2000); 'Unveiled Borders: Le Corbusier and Algiers', *l'Image* (2000); 'Mediterraneanism: The Politics of Architectural Production in Algiers in the 1930s', *City and Society* (2000); and 'Housing Race and Gender in 1930s Algiers', *Politics and the City* (ACSA, 1998). Forthcoming is her book *Design and Dissent: Algiers, Le Corbusier, Henri Prost and Others*.

Contributors

Erin Bentley is an MA candidate in Sociology at the University of British Columbia. Her research interests include critical studies in the sociology of sexualities, feminist and anti-racist social theory, qualitative methodologies, and social histories of sex education and nation-building in Canada's inter-war period. Her MA research is an institutional ethnographic study of gay homeless youth and is entitled '(No)Where to Go? Female Sexual Minority Youth and Relations of Ruling'. She began her competitive athletic career at the age of seven with the Prince George Track and Field Club, became an award-winning point guard, and coached basketball, volleyball and swimming over a 12-year period.

Stephen Petrina is Associate Professor of Curriculum Studies at the University of British Columbia. His work is generally situated in Science and Technology Studies and Cultural and Media Studies. He has written on the history of automation in education and psychology, and is currently researching the politics of alternative medicine and medical freedom.

Becki Ross is jointly appointed in Sociology and Women's Studies at the University of British Columbia. She teaches in the areas of feminist and anti-racist theory, qualitative methods, queer studies and the sociology of sexualities. She has published in the *Journal of the History of Sexuality*, *Atlantis: A Journal of Women's Studies*, *Labour/le travail: Journal of Canadian Labour Studies*, *Journal of Canadian Studies* and *Feminist Review*. Her current book project in progress is entitled *Oiling the Economy: Vansterdam's Striptease Past*. She is a past varsity curling champion, Queen's University, 1983.

Notes

Series Editor's Foreword

1. Pierre Rigouslost quoted in Anne Applebaum, *Gulag. A History of the Soviet Camps* (London: Allen Lane, 2003), p. 5.
2. Patricia Vertinsky and Sherry McKay (eds), *Disciplining Bodies in the Gymnasium: Memory, Monument, Modernism* (London: Frank Cass, 2004), p. 7.
3. Ibid., p. 1.
4. Noel Dyck and Eduardo P. Archetti (eds), *Sport, Dance and Embodies Identities* (Oxford: Berg, 2003),p. 1.
5. Ibid., p. 2.
6. Ibid., p. 18.
7. Ibid., p. 7.
8. Quoted in Dyck and Archetti, *Sport, Dance and Embodied Identities*, p. 8.
9. Vertinsky and McKay, *Disciplining Bodies in the Gymnasium*, p. 157.
10. Ibid.
11. Ibid., p 162.
12. Ibid., p. 164.
13. Ibid., p. 168.
14. Ibid., p.171.

Introduction

1. To Faculties of Education, Faculties of Applied Health Sciences, Sports Science Departments, Cultural Studies groups, and so on.
2. Among them, kinesiology, human movement sciences, sport and exercise sciences, and human kinetics.
3. David Kirk, 'Schooling Bodies in New Times', in Juan-Miguel Fernandez-Balboa (ed.), *Critical Postmodernism in Human Movement, Physical Education and Sport* (Albany, NY: Suny Press, 1997), p. 61.
4. Sandra Harding, 'After Absolute Neutrality: Expanding Science', in Maralee Mayberry, Banu Subramaniam and Lisa H. Weasel (eds), *Feminist Science Studies. A New Generation* (London: Routledge, 2001), p. 292.
5. See for example, George W. Fitz, who was a founding member of the degree programme and research laboratory for physical education, 'A Bachelor of Science in Anatomy, Physiology and Physical Training at Harvard', in Ellen W. Gerber, *Innovators and Institutions in Physical Education* (Philadelphia, PA: Lea and Febiger, 1971), p. 304.
6. Robert Brustad, 'A Critical Postmodern Perspective on Knowledge Development in Human Movement', in Balboa, *Critical Postmodernism in Physical Education*, p. 88.
7. Ibid., p. 92.
8. Chris Shilling, *The Body and Social Theory* (London: Sage, 1993).
9. Kirk, 'Schooling Bodies in New Times', p. 62.
10. Henning Eichberg, 'The Enclosure of the Body – On the Historical Relativity of "Health",

"Nature", and the Environment of Sport', *Journal of Contemporary History*, 21 (1986), p. 101.

11.   Michel Foucault, *Discipline and Punish* (Harmondsworth Penguin, 1975).

12.   Larry Owens, 'Pure and Sound Government. Laboratories, Playing Fields, and Gymnasia in the Nineteenth-Century Search for Order', *ISIS*, 76 (1985), pp. 189–90.

13.   Edmund J. Welch, *Edward Hitchcock, MD, Founder of Physical Education in the College Curriculum* (North Carolina: the author, 1966).

14.   Gerber, *Innovators and Institutions*, p. 279.

15.   Edward Hitchcock, 'Athletics in American Colleges', *Journal of Social Sciences*, XX (July 1885), Saratoga Papers of 1884, p. II, pp. 27–44.

16.   Isabel C. Barrows (reported and edited), 'Physical Training: A Full Report of the Papers and Discussion of the Conference held in Boston in November, 1889' (Boston).

17.   Owens, 'Pure and Sound Government', pp. 189–90.

18.   'Editorial Note and Comment', *American Physical Education Review*, IX (June 1904), pp. 151–2.

19.   A.K.P. Harmon, 'Letter of A.K.P Harmon to Board of Regents' (University of California, Berkely, Archives, 1879), 380g P18 V.1 – pamphlets.

20.   Academic Senate, 'Regents' Records, 1887–89, CU–1:6–2.

21.   Roberta Park, 'For Pleasure? or Profit? or Personal Health?: College Gymnasia as Contested Terrain', in Patricia Vertinsky and John Bale (eds), *Sites of Sport: Space, Place and Experience* (London and Portland, OR: Frank Cass, 2003).

22.   James Russell calls it 'Harvard's most welcoming recent building with the studied generosity of its programmatic and architectural elements', in 'A Gym Shapes Up', *Architectural Record* (May 1990), p. 83.

23.   Park, 'For Pleasure?'.

24.   Neil Smith and Cindi Katz, 'Grounding Metaphor. Towards a Spatialized Politics', in Michael Keith and Steve Pile (eds), *Place and the Politics of Identity* (New York: Routledge, 1993), p. 67.

25.   Raphael Samuel, *Theatres of Memory in Past and Present Contemporary Culture*, Vol. 1 (London: Verso, 1994), p. 27.

26.   Leslie Roman, Opening Remarks, The University As/In Contested Space, UBC Conference, (Vancouver, 1 May 1998).

27.   Robert Rhodes James (ed.), *Winston S. Churchill, His Complete Speeches, 1876–1963* (London: Chelsea House, 1974), pp. 68–9.

28.   Elizabeth Grosz, 'Bodies–Cities', in Beatriz Colomina (ed.), *Sexuality and Space* (Princeton, NJ: Princeton University Press, 1992), p. 242.

29.   Kent C. Bloomer and Charles W. Moore, *Body, Memory and Architecture* (New Haven, CT, and London: Yale University Press, 1977), p. 59. Similarly, they note buildings can encourage a choreography of dynamic relationships among the persons moving within their domains.

30.   Elspeth Probyn, *Sexing the Self: Gendered Positions in Cultural Studies* (London: Routledge, 1993).

31.   Rosa Ainsley (ed.), *New Frontiers of Space, Bodies and Gender* (London: Routledge, 1998), p. 64.

32.   Henning Eichberg, 'Race-Track and Labyrinth: The Space of Physical Culture in Berlin', *Journal of Sport History*, 17, 2 (1990), p. 246.

Chapter 1

1.   Quoted in Harry T. Logan, *Tuum Est. A History of the University of British Columbia* (Vancouver, BC: Mitchell Press, 1958), p. 173.

2.   Two years later, at the 2001 War Memorial Service, attendance was up dramatically – a response not so much to memories of long ago wars as to the terrible events of 11 September and new global threats of terrorism and war. Threats of war have increasingly recharged the public's enthusiasm for collective demonstrations of the need to 'go to war for peace'.

3.   Letter from J.J. Sutherland, AMS President, to Sharp, Thompson, Berwick and Pratt, Architects, 21 July 1949. AMS Box 17, file 8. Despite such sentiments, provincial franchise

extensions were only provided to Canadians of Chinese and East Indian descent in 1947, and it was 1949 before Japanese Canadians could vote and were once again allowed freedom of movement on the west coast.

4. In James Young, *The Texture of Memory. Holocaust, Memorials and Meaning* (New Haven, CT, and London: Yale University Press, 1997), p. 116.

5. Earle Birney, Foreword to the *Record of Service in the Second World War. A* Supplement to the University of British Columbia's War Memorial Transcript Record (Vancouver, 1955), p. 23.

6. Andrea Bear Nicholas, 'Citizenship Education and Aboriginal People: The Humanitarian Art of Cultural Genocide', *Canadian and International Education*, 25, 2 (1996), p. 78.

7. John Macrae from Guelph, Ontario, wrote 'In Flanders Fields'. He was serving as a medical officer with the Canadian army when his poem was published anonymously in *Punch* in 1915 and became used as a highly successful recruitment device in World War I. see Jonathan Vance, *Death so Noble. Memory, Meaning and the First World War* (Vancouver, BC: University of British Columbia Press, 1997), p. 201.

8. Fraser Bell, 'Propaganda lies in Flanders Fields', *Globe and Mail*, 9 Nov. 1998, A15.

9. Sheila Myoshi Jager, 'Monumental Histories: Manliness, the Military and the War Memorial', *Public Culture*, 14, 2 (2002), p. 388.

10. Ludmilla Jordanova, *History in Practice* (New York: Oxford University Press, 2000), p. 149.

11. Vance, *Death So Noble*, pp. 3, 9.

12. And, of course, what is 'usable' changes over time.

13. James Young, 'Memory and Counter Memory', *Harvard Design Magazine* (Fall 1999), p. 13.

14. Young, *The Texture of Memory*, p. 1.

15. Kirk Savage, 'The Past in the Present', *Harvard Design Magazine* (Fall 1999), p. 14. This is not to deny that there are memorials across Canada and elsewhere for those killed on both sides of the same conflict, and for those who served in the Papal Guard and the American Civil War, and so on.

16. Young, *The Texture of Memory*.

17. Patricia Molloy, 'Lest We Remember – War, History and the Commemorative Practice as a Form of Forgetting', *Krieg/War* (Vienna: Wilhelm Fink Verlag, 1999), p. 2.

18. Billie Melman, 'Gender, History and Memory: The Invention of Women's Past in the Nineteenth and Early Twentieth Centuries', *History and Memory*, 5, 1 (Spring/Summer 1993), p. 9.

19. Nancy Wood, 'Memory's Remains/Les Lieux de Mémoire', *History and Memory*, 6, 1 (Spring/Summer 1994), p. 31.

20. Quoted in Vance, *Death So Noble*, pp. 3, 9.

21. Thomas W. Laqueur, 'Names, Bodies and the Anxiety of Erasure', in Theodore R. Schatzki and Wolfgang Natter, *The Social and Political Body* (London: The Guildford Press, 1996), p. 132.

22. Wordsworth, *The Character of the Happy Warrior*, 1807. See John A. Hayden (ed.), *William Wordsworth. Selected Prose* (Harmondsworth: Penguin Classics,1988).

23. Vance, *Death So Noble*, p. 210.

24. Jay Winter, 'The Generation of Memory: Reflections on the "Memory Boom" in Contemporary Historical Studies', *GHI Bulletin*, 27 (Fall 2000), p. 71.

25. John R. Gillis (ed.), *Commemoration. The Politics of National Identity* (Princeton, NJ: Princeton University Press,1995), p. 5.

26. Alan Sears, 'Something Different to Everyone: Conceptions of Citizenship and Citizenship Education', *Canadian and International Education*, 25, 2 (1996), p. 20.

27. Roger A. Simon, Sharon Rosenberg and Claudia Eppert (eds), *Between Hope and Despair: Pedagogy and the Remembrance of Historical Trauma* (New York: Rowman and Littlefield, 2000), p. 3.

28. Mike Filey, *Toronto Sketches: 'The Way We Were'* (Toronto, ON: Dundurn Press, 1992), pp. 32–3.

29. Logan, *Tuum Est*, p. 106; *The Ubyssey*, 11 Nov. 1926, p. 1.

30. Undated manuscript in the possession of Mrs S. Lett; in Reginald Roy, *Sherwood Lett. His Life and Times* (Vancouver: UBC Alumni Association, 1991), p. 86.

31. 'War being simply sport on a grand scale and the individual qualities exercised in both being to some extent synonymous, any attempt to justify sports' appropriateness for soldiers is superfluous.' Ex-Non-Com, 'The Soldier in Relation to Regimental Sport', *The United Services Magazine*, IX (1919–20), p. 35.

32. Jager, 'Monumental Histories', p. 389.
33. David Leverenz, *Manhood and the American Renaissance* (Ithaca, NY: Cornell University Press, 1989), p. 73.
34. Ralph Connor, *The Sky Pilot in No Man's Land* (New York: George H. Doran, 1919), p. 275.
35. J.D. Campbell, 'Training for Sport is Training for War. Sport and the Transformation of the British Army, 1860–1914', *The International Journal of the History of Sport*, 17, 4 (2000), pp. 21–58.
36. C. Veitch, 'Play Up, Play Up, and Win the War: Football and the First World War, 1914–1915', *Journal of Contemporary History*, 20 (1985), p. 363.
37. *UBC Calendar* (1915–19), p. 97.
38. Minutes of meeting of UBC Senate, 32, 15 Dec. 1948, p. 1461.
39. *UBC Calendar* (1941–42), p. 336.
40. Logan, *Tuum Est*, p. 104.
41. Roy, *Sherwood Lett*, p. 87.
42. *UBC Calendar* (1931–32), p. 38.
43. There were 1,103 males and 734 female students on campus at the time.
44. Logan, *Tuum Est*, p. 135.
45. Maury Van Vliet was the male physical education instructor and Gertrud Moore the instructor for the female division. Maury Van Vliet died in 2001 at the age of 87. In his obituary, Fred Hume noted that during the 10 years he was at UBC he was the inspiration and force behind the intramural programmes and UBC's new emphasis on physical education. In addition he was an outstanding coach of basketball, football, track and boxing. He moved from UBC to become Dean of Physical Education at the University of Alberta, where he began a degree programme in physical education. He was inducted into the Hall of Fame at UBC in 1993.
46. *UBC Calendar* (1936–37), p. 26.
47. Fred Hume, Hall of Fame notes on Gordon Shrum.
48. Logan, *Tuum Est*, p. 132.
49. Filey, *The Way We Were*, p. 21.
50. Lee Stewart, *It's up to You: Women at UBC in the Early Years* (Vancouver, BC: University of British Columbia Press, 1990), p. 111.
51. Logan, *Tuum Est*, p. 134.
52. Birney, *Record of Service*.
53. This was 939 in the officer training group and 802 in the basic training group.
54. Stewart, *Its up to You*, p. 110.
55. Logan, *Tuum Est*, p. 143.
56. *The Province*, 6 Oct. 1941.
57. Though denied the vote, Canadians of Japanese descent were bound by the obligations of Canadian citizenship, including military service. At the time of the Boer War, Japanese Canadians had offered to raise and equip their own fighting unit but had been turned down by the Laurier government. Of the 196 Japanese Canadians who had fought in World War I, those who returned were granted the franchise.
58. Elaine Bernard, 'A University at War: Japanese Canadians at UBC during WW2', *B.C. Studies*, 35 (Aug. 1977), p. 38.
59. President Klinck, quoted in *Vancouver News Herald*, 7 Jan. 1942, p. 1.
60. Bernard, 'A University at War', pp. 50–1.
61. Margaret A. Ormsby, *B.C. A History* (Toronto, ON: Macmillan, 1958), p. 448.
62. 'Gym Building Date to be Decided Soon', *The Ubyssey*, 25 Sept. 1947, p. 1.
63. Birney, *Record of Service*, p. 30.
64. UBC publications featured sections on the activities of male war vets, but not on those of women. Stewart, *Its up To You*, p. 85.
65. *The Ubyssey*, 26 Jan. 1946, p. 2.
66. *News of the School*, newsletter of the Margaret Eaton School and the University of Toronto (Nov. 1946), p. 8.
67. Letter to Provincial Government, Premier John Hart from Norman Mackenzie (2 March 1945).
68. *Vancouver Sun*, 15 Aug. 1945, p. 14.
69. 'Buildings as Memorials Preferred', *The Daily Colonist*, 11 Jan. 1945, p. 2.

70.   'Gyms favoured as Memorials Provided by the Forces', *The Daily Colonist* (Victoria), 11 Jan. 1945, p. 2.
71.   'Peaceful Universities', *The Daily Colonist* (Victoria), 17 Sept. 1944, p. 4.
72.   'A Fitting Memorial', *Vancouver News Herald*, 1 Feb. 1945, p. 1.
73.   'War Memorials Dedicated', *Victoria Daily Times*, 19 Dec. 1951, pp. 1, 7; 'Kitsilano Plans Centre as Memorial', *Vancouver Sun*, 31 Jan. 1945, p. 2.
74.   'Proposed Arena to be Memorial', *Victoria Daily Times*, 10 Nov. 1944, p. 16.
75.   'At Odds Over Memorial', *Vancouver News Herald*, 6 Feb. 1946, p. 2.
76.   [Article title], *The Daily Colonist*, [day] Nov. 1945, p.[?].
77   'UBC Students Plan New Building as Memorial to Soldier-Scholars', *Vancouver News Herald*, 24 Nov. 1945, p. 7.
78.   George Pringle's article in *The Point*, 2 Feb. 1946, p. 9.
79.   'Governors Approve Campus Memorial', *Vancouver News Herald*, 31 Jan. 1946, p. 2.
80.   'Hall of Heroes for 'U' Memorial', *Vancouver News Herald*, 4 Feb. 1946, p. 3.

Chapter 2

1.   Fred Hume – Million Dollar Gym, *Totem*, 1951, p. 5. 4. box 17, file 8.
2.   The Massey medals were established in 1950 by the soon to become Governor General Vincent Massey at the urging of the editor of the JRAIC. Juries made their decisions from submitted photographs which were exhibited across the country. 'Recreation Buildings', *RAIC Journal*, serial 329, 30, 1 (1953), pp. 24–7.
3.   'Best Rec Building', *The Ubyssey*, 15 Jan. 1953, p. 3.
4.   'UBC Now Has One of the Finest College Gyms on the Continent', *UBC Alumni Chronicle*, Dec. 1950, p. 8.
5.   *UBC Alumni Chronicle*, Dec. 1950, p. 9.
6.   The story goes that Lieutenant Robert Hampton Gray led an attack on a Japanese destroyer on 9 Aug. 1945 and was shot down by anti-aircraft fire, but with his aircraft in flames he pressed home his attack and sank the destroyer.
7.   'Students Pledge $100,000 for Memorial Gym at UBC', *The Vancouver Daily Province*, 2 Feb. 1946, p. 3.
8.   *The Ubyssey*, 5 Nov. 1946, p. 3.
9.   Fred Hume, *The Point*, 1997; Buzz Moore, personal communication.
10.   'Gym Building Date to be Decided Soon', *The Ubyssey*, 130, 2 (1947), p. 1.
11.   'Rally Set for Noon Today', *The Ubyssey*, 12 Feb. 1946, p. 2.
12.   'Rallies, Dances Aid Gym Drive', *The Ubyssey*, 5 Nov. 1946, p. 3.
13.   'Five Basketballers Caught Near Scene of Huge Fire', *The Ubyssey*, 29 March 1946, p. 5.
14.   'Legion Sponsored Buses to Nowhere', *The Ubyssey*, 133, 31 (1950), p. 5.
15.   'Plans Go Ahead on Gym Funds Scheme', *The Ubyssey*, 19 Oct. 1950, p. 3.
16.   'War Memorial Gym for All UBC Sports', *Vancouver Sun*, 2 Feb. 1946, p. 13.
17.   The War Memorial Gymnasium Committee included representatives from the student body, the Alumni Association, the Legion, the Physical Education Department, the University administration and the general public.
18.   Letter from Howard Travers, American Consul General, Department of State, Washington, DC, to Grant Livingstone, 12 Sept. 1947.
189. Letter from Grant Livingstone, Chair of War Memorial Committee to members of general committee, 5 Aug. 1947.
20.   Minutes of the War Memorial Gym Committee, 2 Dec. 1947; see also letter to contributors to the fund from David Brousson, Chair of the War Memorial Gym Committee, 8 Nov. 1948.
21.   *UBC Alumni Chronicle*, Dec. 1950, p. 20.
22.   'Snack Bar to Begin Operation', *The Ubyssey*, 6 Feb. 1951, p. 1.
23.   Letter from Marian Henderson in Toronto to Fred Lasserre, 12 July 1947.
24.   Letter from Bob Osborne to Ned Pratt, 3 Aug. 1949. Department of Physical Education and Athletics.

25.   Letter from Marian Henderson to Ned Pratt, 6 Aug. 1949.
26.   Letter from J.J. Sutherland, President of AMS to architects Sharp, Thompson, Berwick & Pratt.
27.   Ormonde J. Hall, 'Speaking Editorially', *Graduate Chronicle*, 2 (3 Oct. 1948), p. 34.
28.   Kent C. Bloomer and Charles W. Moore, *Body, Memory and Architecture* (New Haven, CT, and London: Yale University Press, 1977), p. 59.
29.   J. Carsten and S. Hugh Jones (eds), *About the House: Levi Strauss and Beyond* (Cambridge: Cambridge University Press, 1995), p. 2.
30.   Hall, 'Speaking Editorially', *Graduate Chronicle*, 2 (3 Oct. 1948), pp. 34–6.
31.   David Harvey, *The Condition of Postmodernity* (Oxford: Blackwell, 1990), p. 32.
32.   Rhodri Windsor-Liscombe, *The New Spirit: Modern Architecture in Vancouver, 1938–1963* (Vancouver: Canadian Centre for Architecture, Douglas and McIntyre, 1997), p. 179.
33.   Windsor-Liscome, *The New Spirit*, p. 122.
34.   William J.R. Curtis, *Le Corbusier: Ideas and Forms* (London: Phaidon Press, 1986), p. 162.
35.   *The Ubyssey*, 15 Jan. 1953, p. 3.
36.   Interestingly, just as students had promoted a Department of Physical Education, it was the undergraduate pre-architecture students who mobilized the support of local architects and the university administration to form a Department of Architecture. See Windsor-Liscombe, *The New Spirit*, p. 32.
37.   Audio-tape of memorial service, UBC Archives.
38.   Windsor-Liscombe, *The New Spirit*, p. 84.
39.   Letter from Charles Thompson to Fred Lasserre, 3 Dec. 1946.
40.   Letter from Fred Lasserre to Charles Thompson, 4 Dec. 1946.
41.   Letter from Fred Lasserre to President Mackenzie, 28 Oct. 1949.
42.   Letter from Secretary of Senate to Charles Thompson, 29 July 1949.
43.   John Napier-Hemy, 'Building Program Viewed by Ubyssey', *The Ubyssey*, 133, 53 (1951), p. 1.
44.   Charles Joseph Thompson left his job as assistant architect with the CPR to join George Lister Thornton Sharp in 1908 and form the firm of Sharp and Thompson. Both men were born and educated in England but played an important role in the development of the built environment of Vancouver. In 1912, Sharp and Thompson won the competition for the contract to design the Point Gray Campus for UBC. The firm built the first four original campus buildings and became the official architectural firm to the University until the late 1950s. In 1945 Berwick and Pratt joined the firm as partners. Jane Bellyk, *The Firm that Built Vancouver: An Administrative History of Thompson, Berwick, Pratt and Partners*, History paper 545, Department of History, UBC (14 April 1989). In 1950 Thompson told President Mackenzie that he was leaving for a six-month vacation and that Ned Pratt would be in charge of the War Memorial Gym, letter to Mackenzie, 21 June 1953.
45.   OISE (Ontario Institute of Education) costs at the same time were 70 cents a cubic foot. Letter to architects STB&P from Marani and Madris, Toronto, 17 Feb. 1950.
46.   Windsor-Liscombe, *The New Spirit*, pp. 86–7.
47.   Lasserre quoted in Windsor-Liscombe, *The New Spirit*, p. 75.
48.   Arthur Erickson also came from McGill and worked briefly with Sharpe, Thompson, Berwick and Pratt – he would later design Simon Fraser University and demonstrate his affinity for monumental presence and classical mien, open to sky and sun. His characteristic line was the horizontal. Windsor-Liscombe, *The New Spirit*, p. 26.
49.   Windsor-Liscombe, *The New Spirit*, p. 86.
50.   R. Samuel, *Theatres of Memory in Past and Present Contemporary Culture*, Vol. 1 (London: Verso, 1994), p. 59.
51.   John Napier-Hemy, 'Focus Now on Gym, Girls Dormitories', *The Ubyssey*, 2 March 1951, p. 1.
52.   Sherry McKay, 'Modernism on Campus', in *UBC Reports*, 15 Dec. 1997.
53.   D. Harvey, *Spaces of Hope* (Berkely, CA: University of California press, 2000)p. 237.
54.   Edward Relph, 'Modernity and the Reclamation of Place', in David Seaman (ed.), *Dwelling, Seeing and Designing* (New York: Suny Press, 1993), p. 26.
55.   Beatriz Colomina, *Privacy and Publicity: Modern Architecture as Mass Media* (Cambridge, MA: MIT Press, 1994), p. 8.
56.   Lewis Mumford, 'The Case Against Modern Architecture', in *The History and the City* (New York, 1965), p. 34.

57. Arthur Erickson quoted in Windsor-Liscombe, *The New Spirit*, pp. 36–7.

58. C. Jencks, *Le Corbusier and the Tragic View of Architecture* (London: Penguin Books, 1987), p. 112; Witold Rybcznski, 'Le Corbusier', *Time*, 51, 22 (8 June 1998), pp. 56–7.

59. Le Corbusier, *The Decorative Art of Today* (trans. James I. Dunnett), (London, 1987 [1928]) p. 142. Le Corbusier was a tireless proselytizer, addressing the public in manifestos, pamphlets, exhibitions, dozens of books and his own magazine.

60. Le Corbusier, *When the Cathedrals Were White: The City of tomorrow and its Planning* (trans. from *Urbanisme* by F. Etchells) (New York, Dover Publications, 1987), p. 23: (London: Routledge, 1925), p. 35; Marius Kwint, Christopher Breward and Jeremy Aynsley (eds), *Material Memories* (New York: Berg, 1999), p. 93.

61. In his mission to join classical principles of measurement and order to new systems of utilitarian building he composed a Domino skeleton of concrete and steel rectangular blocks that would become an icon of modern architecture. See Curtis, *Le Corbusier: Ideas and Forms*, p. 43.

62. Jane Jacobs, *The Death and Life of Great American Cities* (New York: Vintage Books, 1992), p. 343.

63. C.A. Poole, 'Theoretical and Poetical Ideas in Le Corbusier's Une Maison – Un Palais', *The Journal of Architecture*, 3 (Spring 1998), p. 4.

64. Le Corbusier, *Vers une Architecture*, [1927] (trans. Frederick Etchells) (New York: Dover, 1986), p. 53. 'In geometry the proofs of the will are to be found: power. Priests and tyrants demonstrating their strength, established architecture on geometry.' Le Corbusier, *The City of Tomorrow and its Planning* (trans. from *Urbanisme* by F. Etchells) (New York, Dover Publications, 1987), p, 23. 'I am a mathematician at heart', he said … 'I have an implacable sense of rigor that leads me toward proportion, you see … proportion is the appreciation of relations'. From the last recorded interview in Ivan Zacnic, *Le Corbusier: The Final Testament of Père Corbu* (New Haven, CT, and London: Yale University Press, 1997), p. 119.

65. Le Corbusier, *When the Cathedrals Were White*, p. 47. Adrian Forty illustrates how form, as it has been used by most modernists, is male, a masculine ideal. She highlights Vincent Scully's description of Le Corbusier's building at Chandigarth: 'The high court is a great hollowed out concrete mass, its glass skin … pushes upward and out with threatening power. Up through this projection … rise the great piers as purely upwardly thrusting forces. Between these, men enter, and ramps of almost Piranesian violence rise behind them. Their physical power can be grasped … as the confident human body assuming a position in a place, as Le Corbusier demands.' Adrian Forty, 'Masculine, Feminine or Neuter', in Katerina Ruedi, Sarah Wigglesworth and Duncan McCorquodale (eds), *Desiring Practices, Architecture, Gender and the Interdisciplinary* (New York: Black Dog, 1996), p. 152.

66. Le Corbusier, *Urbanisme*, pp. 23, 27.

67. Eichberg's post 1980 views on sport, space and place are discussed in John Bale and Chris Philo (eds), *Body Culture. Essays on Sport, Space and Identity – Henning Eichberg* (London: Routledge, 1997).

68. Henning Eichberg, 'New Spatial Configurations of Sport? Experiences from Danish Alternative Planning', *International Review of Sociology of Sport*, 28, 2/3 (1993). p. 246.

69. Le Corbusier, *When the Cathedrals Were White*; Hening Eichberg, 'Race-Track and Labyrinth: The Space of Physical Culture in Berlin', *Journal of Sport History*, 17, 2 (1990), p. 245.

70. Le Corbusier, *City of Tomorrow*, p. 22.

71. For a discussion of Fascist body aesthetics see George L. Mosse, 'Fascist Aesthetics and Society: Some Considerations', *Journal of Contemporary History* 31, 2 (1996), pp. 245–52.

72. Harvey, *The Condition of Postmodernity*, p. 33.

73. Le Corbusier, *When the Cathedrals Were White*, p. 141. In the same discussion he described Vassar College as a joyous convent – paradise to begin with and hell afterwards!

74. Michel Foucault, *Discipline and Punish* (Harmondsworth: Penguin, 1975); see Hening Eichberg, 'The Enclosure of the Body – on the Historical Relativity of "health", "Nature" and the Environment of Sport', *Journal of Contemporary History*, 21 (1986), p. 115.

75. Samuel, *Theatres of Memory*, p. 57.

76. Le Corbusier, quoted in Curtis, *Le Corbusier: Ideas and Forms*, p. 223.

77. Colomina, *Privacy and Publicity*, p. 136.

78. Le Corbusier, *When the Cathedrals Were White*, p. 76.

79. The Parthenon and the great cathedrals served as examples of supreme mathematics and he compared their rigorous discipline to that of the machine. Machinery was the result of geometry, thus the machine became a generating element in Le Corbusier's architecture.

80. Le Corbusier, *Vers une Architecture*, p. 89.

81. Curtis, *Le Corbusier: Ideas and Forms*, p. 43.

82. Zacnic, *Le Corbusier: The Final Testament*, p. 117.

83. Aaron Betsky, *Building Sex: Men, Women, Architecture and the Construction of Sexuality* (New York: William Morrow and Co., 1995), Ch. 1.

84. Richard Sennett, *Flesh and Stone: The Body and the City in Western Civilization* (New York: W.W. Norton and Co., 1994), p. 49. What Le Corbusier did not seem to consider, however, in his reverence for Greek form was that the Greeks worked hard to counterbalance extremes of rigidity and training of the body with education in music and more well-rounded activities. Shigehisa Kuriyama, *The Expressiveness of the Body and the Divergence of Greek and Chinese Medicine* (New York: Zone Books, 1999), p. 139.

85. Rob Imrie, 'The Body, Disability and Le Corbusier's Conception of the Radiant Environment', in Ruth Butler and Hester Parr (eds), *Mind and Body Spaces. Geographies of Illness, Impairment and Disability* (New York: Routledge, 1999), p. 35. Le Corbusier did not ask the question that Hanns Sachs did as to why the ancient world did not discover machines as it did mathematics. Sachs concludes that the Greeks saw machines which replaced human bodies as 'uncanny' because of the threatened breaking of ego boundaries presented by the animate–inanimate. 'In peoples whose narcissism was more strongly developed than ours, and more strongly related to body-ego there is a shrinking from the mechanical.' In modern man, Sachs implied, the desire for narcissistic satisfaction had taken another route, violating bodily integrity in achieving a wider dispersal of libidinal energies. Hanns Sachs, 'The Delay of the Machine Age', *The Psychoanalytic Quarterly*, 2 (1933), pp. 404–24.

86. Luis E. Carranza, 'Le Corbusier and the Problems of Representation', *Journal of Architectural Education*, 48, 2 (1994), pp. 70–81.

87. Last recorded interview, Zacnic, *Le Corbusier: The Final Testament*, p. 120.

88. Jean Jenger, *Le Corbusier: Architect, Painter, Poet* (New York: Harry N. Abrams, 1993), p. 94; Curtis, *Le Corbusier: Ideas and Forms*, p. 164.

89. Curtis, *Le Corbusier: Ideas and Forms*, p. 164.

90. Henri Lefebvre, *The Production of Space* (Oxford: Oxford University Press, 1992), p. 303.

91. Beatriz Colomina, 'The Split Wall. Domestic Voyeurism', in Colomina (ed.), *Sexuality and Space*, p. 104.

92. Le Corbusier, quoted in Colomina, 'The Split Wall', p. 113.

93. Colomina, 'The Split Wall', pp. 114–15.

94. Eichberg, 'New Spatial Configurations', pp. 248, 253.

95. John Bale, *Landscapes of Modern Sport* (Leicester: Leicester University Press, 1994), p. 12.

96. Brian Pronger, 'Outta My End Zone. The Territorial Anus', *Journal of Sport and Social Issues*, 23, 4 (1999), pp. 373–89.

97. That is, except for Catherine Chard Wisnicki, a female architect who worked as an employee for Sharp, Thompson, Berwick and Pratt between 1946 and 1953. Attempting to recapture the forgotten work of female architects, The Women in Architectures Exhibits Committee published the profiles of five early women architects in British Columbia in 1996. In the chapter on Wisnicki, who became an assistant professor of architecture in 1969, mention is made of her participation in designing some of the first examples of modernist architecture in Canada, including the War Memorial Gymnasium. There is, of course, no mention in the archives about Wisnicki's assistance to Pratt in designing the gymnasium and although she herself remembers being an employee of the firm, it appears that Ned Pratt demanded control over all aspects of the design. There was perhaps as little space for women in the architectural team as there would be in the gymnasium. 'Constructing Careers', Vancouver, Architectural Institute of BC, 1996. For more on Wisnicki see Mckay in Chapters 6 and 7.

Chapter 3

1.   Doreen Massey, *Space, Place and Gender* (Minneapolis, MN: University of Minnesota Press, 1994), p. 154.
2.   David Harvey, *Spaces of Hope* (Berkeley, CA: University of California Press, 2000), p. 39.
3.   David Harvey, 'Cosmopolitanism and the Banality of Geographical Evils', *Public Culture*, 12, 2 (2000).
4.   Beatriz Colomina (ed.), *Sexuality and Space* (Princeton, NJ: Princeton University Press, 1992); Harvey, *Spaces of Hope*, p. 140. See also Rhodri Windsor-Liscombe, *The New Spirit: Modern Architecture in Vancouver, 1938–1963* (Douglas and McIntyre, Vancouver, BC: Canadian Center for Architecture, 1997), p. 2.
5.   Henning Eichberg, 'Race-track and Labyrinth: The Space of Physical Culture in Berlin', *Journal of Sport History*, 17, 2 (1990), p. 249.
6.   He once proposed replacing the centre of Paris with 18 60-storey towers. Witold Rybczynski, 'Le Corbusier', *Time*, 51, 22 (8 June 1988), pp. 56–7.
7.   Frederic Lasserre, JRAIC 29, 4 (April 1952), p. 83. See Windsor-Liscombe, *The New Spirit*, p. 78.
8.   All, of course, was not lost for modernism in Vancouver, for in 1963 Arthur Erickson won the competition to build the new Simon Fraser University in modernist style, though one which advanced beyond the austere directness of post-war modernism and provided symbolic and functional spaces of monumental and historical forms. However, if the spirit of modernism lives on, its physical legacy has proved less durable, for most modernist buildings in Vancouver have been demolished. Windsor-Liscombe, *The New Spirit*, p. 78.
9.   'Ineffective Education', *The Ubyssey*, 13 Jan. 1953, p. 2.
10. Le Corbusier, *The City of Tomorrow and its Planning* (trans. from *Urbanisme* (1925) by Frederick Etchells) (New York: Dover, 1987), p. 22.
11. Harry T. Logan, *Tuum Est: A History of the University of British Columbia* (Vancouver, BC: Mitchell Press, 1958), p. 230.
12. President Norman Mackenzie apparently used to sit with his dogs in the stands at the old gymnasium and in the Varsity stadium watching the basketball and other sports teams practise in the evenings and at weekends.
13. In 1965, Ivor Wynne, Director of the School of Physical Education at McMaster University and former faculty member at UBC, underscored how the development of many sports in Canada was a result of the enthusiasm and opportunities of a relatively privileged class of men in the late nineteenth and early twentieth centuries. 'They reached an organized or codified form under the leadership of men from the military or the universities, i.e. men who had time and money.' In Maurice L. Van Vliet (ed.), *Physical Education in Canada* (Scarborough, ON: Prentice Hall, 1965), p. 178.
14. 'Femme Version of Sepia Wizardry to Meet Chiefs', *The Ubyssey*, 23 Feb. 1946.
15. See Clifford Geertz, *The Interpretation of Cultures* (New York: Basic Books, 1973) for a discussion of stories that cultures tell themselves about themselves. We are talking here, of course, about those who did not have long commutes to campus on public transport and were not able to participate in the gym's activities.
16. Edward Relph, *Place and Placelessness* (Pion: London, 1976), p. 36.
17. Hayden reminds us that restricting access to space has been one of the most consistent ways to limit the economic and political rights of groups. Dolores Hayden, T*he Power of Place: Urban Landscapes as Public History* (Cambridge, MA: MIT Press, 1995), p. 22.
18. Karl Raitz, *The Theatre of Sport* (Baltimore, MD: The Johns Hopkins University Press, 1995), p. vi.
19. Eichberg, 'Race-track and Labyrinth', p. 245.
20. Linda McDowell, *Gender, Identity and Place: Understanding Feminist Geographies* (Minneapolis, MN: University of Minnesota Press, 1999), pp. 4–5.
21. Heidi Nast and Steve Pile (eds.), *Places Through the Body* (London and New York: Routledge, 1998), p. 4.
22. Don Mitchell, *Cultural Geography: A Critical Introduction* (Oxford: Blackwell, 2000), p. xviii.

23. Massey, *Space, Place and Gender*, p. 149.

24. Mitchell, *Cultural Geography*, p. xxi.

25. Douglas Booth and Colin Tatz, 'Reply to the Reviewers of One-Eyed', *Sporting Traditions*, 17, 11 (2000), p. 125.

26. Fred Hume, *The Point*, 2001.

27. Elizabeth Grosz, 'Bodies–Cities', in Colomina (ed.), *Sexuality and Space*, pp. 241–52. Luce Irigary's conception of woman as commodity – the object of physical and metaphorical exchange among men – is critical to understanding the gendering of space. In terms of ownership, men own space and women as property, whereas women are owned as property, confined as and in space. In patriarchal relations of exchange men move through space as subjects of exchange, whereas women are moved through space between men as sexual commodities – as objects of exchange. Jos Boys, quoted in Louise Durning and Richard Wrigley (eds), *Gender and Architecture* (Chichester: Wiley, 2000), p. 143; see also Mitchell, *Cultural Geography*, p. 216.

28. For discipline to do its work it is important to enclose space, and in doing so specify it as different from other spaces. Partitioning is a procedure aimed at knowing and seeing. see Michel Foucault, *Discipline and Punish* (New York: Vintage Press, 1979), p. 147 and Henning Eichberg, 'The Enclosure of the Body: On the Historical Relativity of "Health", "Nature", and the Environment of Sport', *Journal of Contemporary History*, 21 (1986), p. 101. For a more detailed discussion of Foucault's disciplining procedures see Nikolas Rose, *Inventing Ourselves. Psychology, Power and Personhood* (Cambridge: Cambridge University Press, 1996).

29. Larry Owens, 'Pure and Sound Government: Laboratories, Playing Fields, and Gymnasia in the 19th Century Search for Order', *ISIS*, 76 (1985), pp. 182–94.

30. See Helen Gurney, *Girls' Sports. A Century of Progress in Ontario High Schools* (Don Mills, ON: OFSAA Publications, 1979), p. 24, for a discussion of early collegiate gymnasia in eastern Canada.

31. Martha H. Verbrugge, 'Recreating the Body: Women's Physical Education and the Science of Sex Differences in America 1900–1940', *Bulletin of the History of Medicine*, 71, 2 (1997), p. 275.

32. Patricia Vertinsky, 'Reclaiming Space, Revisioning the Body: The Quest for Gender-Sensitive Physical Education', *Quest*, 44 (1992), p. 372.

33. Verbrugge, 'Recreating the Body', p. 278.

34. Quoted in Anne Collier Rehill, 'Where Women Played', *The Penn Stater*, 85, 6 (July/Aug. 1998), pp. 54–5.

35. Quoted in Rehill, 'Where Women Played', p. 54.

36. Paul Rabinow (ed.), *The Foucault Reader* (New York: Pantheon, 1984).

37. 'The Co-ed Sport Corner: The Girls are Interested', *The Ubyssey*, 5 Nov. 1946, p. 6.

38. Joan Fraser, 'Girls Can Have Athletic Lethargy', *The Ubyssey*, 21 Nov. 1950.

39. Lee Stewart, *It's up to You. Women at UBC in the Early Years* (Vancouver, BC: UBC Press, 1990), p. 91.

40. Sharp and Thompson's architectural plans for the UBC campus in 1912, which envisioned a separate women's gym and athletic field as well as women's residences had certainly not materialized.

41. *The Ubyssey*, 20 Feb. 1947.

42. Stewart, *It's up to You*, p. 92.

43. 'Girls and Sport', *Province Newspaper*, 25 Sept. 1932.

44. Stewart, *It's up to You*, p. 117.

45. 'Girls and Sport', p. 15. See also Patricia Vertinsky, *The Eternally Wounded Woman: Women, Doctors and Exercise in the Late 19th Century* (Urbana and Chicago, IL: University of Illinois Press, 1994), and Helen Lenskyj, *Out of Bounds. Women, Sport and Sexuality* (Toronto, ON: Women's Press, 1986).

46. Andy Lytle, 'Girls Shouldn't Do It', *Chatelaine* (May 1932), pp. 21–3. Lytle, the sports writer for the *Vancouver Sun*, is quoted by Ann Hall in 'Alexandrine Gibb: In No Man's Land', in J.A. Mangan and Fan Hong, *Freeing The Female Body: Inspirational Icons* (London: Frank Cass, 2001), pp. 149–72.

47. Stewart, *It's up to You*, p. 119.

48. The reasons for this invitation were complex. The Edmonton Grads, the best team in Canada, were unable to go, and in the United States women physical educators objected to the Women's Games in principle and no team was sent. Because the officials of the World Games wanted the Canadians to play in the final, the UBC team played and won only one game to become the victors. Their trophy can be found today in the War Memorial Gym. Louisa Zerbe, 'The 1930 UBC Women's Basketball Team: Those Other World Champions', in Reet Howell (ed.), *Her Story in Sport: A Historical Anthology of Women in Sports* (New York: Leisure Press, 1982), p. 550.

49. Margaret Bell, MD, 'Why, From the Health Point of View we Urge Girls' Rules for Girls', in Eline von Borries (ed.), *A Handbook of Basketball for Women* (Baltimore, MD: Sutherland, 1929), p. 14. Marjorie Bateman, 'Health Aspects of Girls' Basketball', *Mind and Body*, 42 (April 1935), p. 22.

50. M.W. Barnard, J.B. Amberson and M.F. Loew, 'Tuberculosis in Adolescents', *American Review of Tuberculosis*, 3 (April/June 1933), discussed in Roy B. Moore, 'An Analytic Study of Sex Differences as they Affect the Program of Physical Education', *Research Quarterly* (12 Oct. 1941), p. 601.

51. Nancy Cole Dosch, 'The Sacrifice of the Maidens, or Healthy Sportswomen? The Medical Debate over Women's Basketball', in Joan Hult and Mariane Trekell, *A Century of Women's Basketball. From Frailty to Final Four* (Reston, VA: National Association for Girls and Women in Sport, AAPHERD, 1991), pp. 125–36.

52. Frances Kidd, 'Is Basketball a Girls' Game?' *Hygeia*, 13 (Sept. 1935), p. 834.

53. Marjorie Phillips, Katharine Fox and Olive Young, 'Sports Activities for Girls', *Journal of Health, Physical Education and Recreation* (30 Dec. 1959), pp. 25, 54.

54. Genevieve Rail, 'Physical Contest in Women's Basketball: A First Interpretation', *International Review for the Sociology of Sport*, 25 (1992), p. 746.

55. Stevada Chepko, 'The Domestication of Basketball', in Hult and Trekell, *A Century of Women's Basketball*, p. 118.

56. Chepko, 'The Domestication of Basketball', p. 114.

57. Verbrugge, 'Recreating the Body', p. 304.

58. She divided the court into three equal sections and required players (anywhere between five and ten on a team) to play only in their particular section. If the game was played with six players, as it often was, the two forwards, two centres and two guards each were limited to one third of the court. The guards defended the forwards and passed the ball to one of the centres whose sole purpose was to pass the ball to the forwards, the only ones allowed to shoot. Players could not steal or bat the ball from another's hands, they could not hold the ball more than three seconds, and they could not bounce or dribble the ball more than three times. Nor were they allowed to play for more than 30 minutes at a time, or more than twice a week. Preface in Senda Berenson Abbott (ed.), *Spalding's Official Basketball Guide for Women* (New York: American Sports, 1912), p. 5.

59. Quoted in Joan S. Hult, 'The Saga of Competition. Basketball Battles and Governance Wars', in Hult and Trekell, *A Century of Women's Basketball*, p. 25.

60. Quoted in Miriam Gray, 'Why Play Girls' Rules in Basketball?', in Marie D. Hartwig (ed.), *Official Basketball and Officials Rating Guide for Women and Girls, 1947–8* (New York: A.S. Barnes, 1947), p. 34.

61. The Guides were originally a collaboration between the Spalding Company and the Women's Committees of the American Physical Education Association. They included official rules for various sports as well as articles by leading physical educators.

62. Thomas J. Baerwald, 'Basketball', in Raitz (ed.), *The Theatre of Sport*, p. 178.

63. Pamela Dean, 'Dear Sisters and Hated Rivals: Athletics and Gender at Two New South Women's Colleges, 1893–1920', *Journal of Sport History*, 24, 3 (Fall 1997), p. 352.

64. Quoted in Hult, 'The Saga of Competition. Basketball Battles and Governance Wars', p. 229. 'Women's rules have been developed for women by women. Women and girls all over the country have participated in rule changes making the game better suited for girls. Ever since the first rule change … the three court game … women have been making the rules more adaptable and more suitable for women and girls. Women's basketball is a women's game. It is their own game; they made it and developed it for themselves.' Joanna Davenport, 'The Tides

of Change in Women's Basketball Rules', in Hult and Trekell, *A Century of women's Basketball*, p. 103. Davenport also offers a full discussion of the rules.

65. Interview with Miss Cleary, in Gurney, *Girls' Sports*, pp. 21–3.
66. Gurney, *Girls' Sports*, p. 49.
67. Ibid., p. 24.
68. Bruce Kidd, *The Struggle for Canadian Sport* (Toronto, ON: University of Toronto Press, 1996).
69. The Edmonton Commercial Graduate Club, most often referred to as the Edmonton Grads, was founded and coached by J. Percy Page for 25 years. They established a record and an image between 1915 and 1940 that is unparalleled in basketball history. John Dewar, 'The Edmonton Grads. The Team and Its Social Significance from 1915 to 1940', in Howell, *Her Story in Sport*, p. 541.
70. Where each player was permitted to play the whole court instead of being restricted to two thirds of it and there were five instead of six players on a team. Winona E. Wood, 'Physical Education and Recreation for Girls and Women', in Van Vliet, *Physical Education in Canada*, p. 164. By 1941 a national survey indicated that the numbers playing women's basketball using men's and women's rules were about even. See Kidd, *The Struggle for Canadian Sport*.
71. See Gurney, *Girl's Sports*, pp. 35–7, for the actual platform and list of girls rules.
72. *Physical Education and Recreation*, p. 164. Interestingly, notes Gurney (*Women's Sports*, p. 35), the concern for the negative effects of basketball (and track and field) on women and girls that passed from US women physical educators to Canada did not seem to apply to tennis, swimming or other sports that women had begun to play.
73. Alice Frymer, *Basketball for Women* (New York: A.S. Barnes, 1930).
74. For example, Jesse Herriott of McGill was an American who had studied at Columbia University in New York, as had Helen Bryans, Director of Women's Physical Education at the Ontario College of Education in Toronto. See Florence Somers, *Principles of Women's Athletics* (New York: A.S. Barnes, 1930).
75. Marian Henderson, 'Development in Canada of Basketball for Women in the Spaldings Women's Basketball Guide', *Basketball: Athletic Activities for Women and Girls* (New York: American Sports, 1935–36), pp. 59–60.
76. Kidd, *The Struggle for Canadian Sport*, p. 123.
77. Helen Bryans, 'Secondary School Curriculum for Girls', in Van Vliet, *Physical Education in Canada*, pp. 124–39.
78. My thanks to Ann Hall for sharing her interview notes with me in this interview with Marian Henderson Penney (Victoria, BC, 5 Dec. 1998).
79. Ibid.
80. Eleanor Metheny, *Vital Issues* (American Alliance for Health, Physical Education and Recreation, 1977), p. 14.
81. It is not clear just why Gordon Shrum had such power over hiring practices in the School of Physical Education. Appointed in 1925, Shrum was Head of Physics, played a major role during the war as officer in charge of the COTC, and then was in a critical period of the University's growth. But Shrum was always there when coaches were being hired. Jack Pomfret remembers having to report to Shrum's house early one morning for an interview when he was being recruited for the School of Physical Education in 1946. 'Do you play Badminton', he said, 'and do you think you could beat me?' 'Any day', said Pomfret. 'Then you are hired, kid', said Shrum. Interview with Jack Pomfret, Vancouver, 2001.
82. 'Bird Hoopman Prepping', *The Ubyssey*, 5 Nov. 1946, p. 7.
83. Whilst high school authorities in Vancouver had initially frowned on basketball for girls, permission had been granted for a girl's team at Lord Robert's School as early as 1903. Coached by Harry Godfrey, crack player of the Vancouver men's basketball team, it went on to beat teams from Seattle and the University of Washington. The BC Pro-Rec movement during the 1930s had also promoted women's basketball alongside the hugely popular men's game, which had been particularly cultivated through the auspices of the YMCA. Barry E. Mitchelson, 'The YMCA Brings Basketball to Canada, 1892–1914', in *Proceedings of the 1st Canadian Symposium on the History of Sport and Physical Education* (Edmonton: University of Edmonton, Alberta, May 1970).

84.   Interview with Barbara Schrodt, Vancouver, 2001. The Alma Mater Society actually set up a one-man commission led by future prime minister John (Chick) Turner to neutralize the considerable influence exerted by Marian Henderson in the Women's Athletic Directorate, who was said to use it as a 'special preserve for female physical education majors'. Chick Turner, Report of the Investigating Commission on the Position of the Women's Athletic Directorate, delivered to the Student's Council, 28 Feb. 1949.

85.   Interview with May Brown, former lecturer in the School of Physical Education, Vancouver, 2001.

86.   M. Ann Hall, *The Girl and the Game. A History of Women's Sport in Canada* (Peterborough, ON: The Broadview Press, 2002), p. 71.

87.   John D. Eaton, 'Dr A.S. Lamb: His Influence on Canadian Sport', in *Proceedings of the 1st Canadian Symposium*, pp. 417–30.

88.   There was a crucial difference, however, in the nature of the professional relationship between Ethel Cartwright and Arthur Lamb and between Marian Henderson and Bob Osborne. Ethel Cartwright's views on physical education and athletics for girls represented an extremely conservative 'maternal feminist' current in women's sport in the inter-war years. Accepting the prevailing medical view that females were not physiologically and temperamentally as strong as males they argued that women's sport must be closely supervised and carefully restricted. I first learned from Carty, said one of her students, 'that being female meant that I was different and somewhat inferior'. (Kidd, *Struggle for Canadian Sport*, p. 121.) Indeed, the McGill faction led the way in trying to impose girls' rules nationally. Arthur Lamb, who had studied at Springfield College in the USA – a bastion of traditional training of male physical educators – believed that women were biologically and emotionally unsuited for strenuous physical activity. On the basis of his views, Lamb voted against women's participation in the Olympics and opposed all forms of sports competition for women. Arthur S. Lamb, 'Physical Education for Girls' in *Proceedings of the 62nd Annual Conference of the Ontario Educational Association* (Toronto, ON: Clarkson W. James, 1923), p. 288. Bob Osborne, unadulterated by specialist training in physical education or US educational links, seemed unafraid to promote women's competitive instincts, especially in basketball.

89.   May Brown interview, Vancouver, 2001.

90.   Inge Andreen and Ann Tilley interviews, Vancouver, 2001.

91.   Eleanor Metheny, 'Will We Lose Our Tennis Courts?', *Vital Issues*, pp.78, 80, 81.

92.   May Brown, interview, Vancouver, 2001.

93.   Inge Andreen interview, Vancouver, 2001.

94.   Ibid.

95.   Barbara Schrodt interview, Vancouver, 2001.

96.   Elizabeth Grosz, *Space, Time and Perversion* (London and New York: Routledge, 1995), p. 135.

97.   'I went on leave for a few months to have the baby and was quite expecting to come back. Marian was banking on me going back. She had the schedule ready. Then the university said, "She can come back but she can't be an instructor or an assistant professor – she's got to be a lecturer (a temporary position)." And there I remained year after year as a lecturer, no benefits whatsoever, each year having to wait for a reappointment.' Interview with May Brown, Vancouver, 2001.

98.   The old Varsity stadium was torn down in 1967 to make way for a student union building. It was replaced by the Thunderbird stadium at a cost of more than a million dollars. The new stadium, far from the centre of campus, accommodated 3,000 spectators under cover of a roof suspended by cables and supported by 12 concrete columns topped with huge concrete Thunderbirds (*UBC Calendar*, 1968–69, A74). The building contained several dressing rooms, press and TV facilities, a fully equipped training room, offices and a wrestling room. It was financed by the Board of Governors. The stadium was later reconfigured in 1994–95 to handle festivals of up to 30,000 people.

99.   President's Committee on Facilities for Physical Education and Recreation. Report to the President, 8 Dec. 1964.

100.   Delegation from Women's Athletic Committee (Dec. 1969) to Board of Governors. The Men's Athletic Committee also wrote to the President to convey their annoyance about the demolition since 'several of our men's athletic teams currently use the women's gym and we would like

absolute assurance that the women's gym will be adequately replaced before demolition begins'.

101. *UBC Calendar* (1968–69), A74.
102. *UBC Reports*, 13, 1 (Jan. 1967), p. 7. With the stadium included, the campus total was 125 acres for the use of athletics and the School of Physical Education.
103. The new profession that Luther Halsey Gulick had claimed in 1890 would become one of the most important studies of the twentieth century and underwent huge changes during the 1960s as demands for a new scientific approach to physical education focused the field upon disciplinary knowledge about human movement and separated professional concerns from its main thrust. Roberta J. Park, 'The Second 100 Years: Or, can Physical Education become the Renaissance Field of the 21st Century', *Quest*, 41 (1988), p. 1.
104. Kidd, *The Struggle for Canadian Sport*, p. 144.
105. Evalyn Gendel, 'Women and the Medical Aspects of Sport', *Journal of School Health*, 37 (1967), p. 430.
106. Vertinsky, 'Reclaiming Space', p. 377.
107. Wood, *Physical Education and Recreation*, p. 174.
108. Hall, 'Creators of the Lost and Perfect Game', p. 252; Gurney, *Girl's Sports*, p. 49.
109. H. Eckert, 'Women and Competitive Basketball', *Journal of CAHPER*, 26, 6 (1960), pp. 5–8.
110. Women's Athletic Association, President's Report, (Oct. 1960).
111. Mary E. Keyes, 'The Administration of the Canadian Women's Intercollegiate Athletic Union', *CAHPER Journal*, 40, 6 (1974), pp. 21–3, 32–3. The first national championships were in gymnastics, volleyball and swimming and diving, followed soon after by basketball. Sue Hilton, 'National Intercollegiate Competition for Women', *CAPHER Journal*, 33, 6, p. 4. Interview with Marilyn (Russell) Pomfret (1967). Vancouver, 2001.
112. 'Sport Talk', *The Ubyssey*, 20 March 1970.
113. 'Women Athletes Eligible', *The Ubyssey*, 5 Feb. 1971. The first referendum for men's athletics was in 1952, when students paid $2.00. In 1957 this was increased to $4.20. For women, the allocation in 1961 was 65 cents increased to 80 cents in 1966. In 1970 a referendum for a $5 increase overall failed to pass. The average athletic fee across Canada was $16, with 82 per cent going to men's athletics and 18 per cent to women's. 'More money needed', *The Ubyssey*, 20 Feb. 1973.
114. 'AMS Support Intramurals', *The Ubyssey*, 17 Sept. 1971.
115. Women's Athletic Association, Special Report of the President (Feb. 1967), AMS box folder 15, 14. Women's Athletic Association meeting minutes, 1 April 1969.
116. Board of Governors (4 Nov. 1969); Letter to the President from Chair of Men's Athletics, 21 Oct. 1969.
117. Men's Athletics Committee Minutes, Deficit of $11,784 wiped out by Board of Governors, 22 June 1966. AMS report on financial situation of Men's Athletics Committee (9 Nov. 1964).
118. 'Fie on the Jock fee raise', *The Ubyssey*, 18 March 1969, p. 6.
119. Title IX, passed in 1972, was designed to require equal opportunity and funding for men and women in all publicly funded educational institutions in the United States. *Report of the Royal Commission on the Status of Women* (Ottawa: Information Canada, 1970). From 1970 to 1975 UBC women's teams won three intercollegiate championships in basketball, two in volleyball; the swimming team took the national title once, and finished second or third on all other occasions. Individually, women trained for national and international sporting events, winning honours both for themselves and UBC in track and field, curling and skiing. Despite the outstanding successes of the women's athletic programme, the university's attitude towards funding women in sports had not altered substantially. Nancy Horsman, 'The Good Sports. Do they have a Sporting Chance?' *UBC Reports*, 5 Nov. 1975, p. 129.
120. 'Physical Recreational Facilities for Women Students at the University of British Columbia', A Brief prepared by the Women's Athletics Committee for presentation to the President and Board of Governors (Dec. 1969), pp. 10–11.
121. Phase 2 was completed in 1972 and contained two gyms, locker rooms, offices and a classroom lounge. It cost just over half a million dollars and was financed by the Board of Governors. Unit 1 had been completed in 1970 and contained two large gyms, locker rooms and two classrooms. It cost $900,000. The whole centre was renamed the Osborne Center when Bob Osborne retired in 1978.

122. Interview with Barbara Schrodt, Vancouver, 2001.
123. Interview with Marilyn Pomfret, Vancouver, 2001.

Chapter 4

1.   'Extension to Brock Building', 28 Dec. 1955, p. 2, Roll 435, 'Bowling Alleys', President's
     Office Fonds, University of British Columbia Archives (UBC Archives). Among recent
     scholarly work on bowling is Andrew Hurley, *Diners, Bowling Alleys and Trailer Parks:
     Chasing the America Dream in Postwar Consumer Culture* (New York: Basic Books, 2001).
     See also Robert Putnam, *Bowling Alone: The Collapse and Revival of American Community*
     (New York: Simon & Schuster, 2000).
2.   On leisure and recreation studies, see, Michael Argyle, *The Social Psychology of Leisure* (New
     York: Penguin, 1996); Chris Rojek, *Decentring Leisure: Rethinking Leisure Theory* (London:
     Sage, 1995); Chris Rojek, *Leisure and Culture* (London: Macmillan Press, 2000); Shirley
     Tillotson, *The Public at Play: Gender and the Politics of Recreation in Postwar Ontario*
     (Toronto, ON: University of Toronto Press, 2000); Betsy Wearing, *Leisure and Feminist Theory*
     (London: Sage, 1998); Derek Wynne, *Leisure, Lifestyle and the New Middle Class* (New York:
     Routledge, 1998). On the body and sport, see: Tim Armstrong (ed.), *American Bodies: Cultural
     Histories of the Physique* (New York: New York University Press, 1996); Andrew Blake, *The
     Body Language: The Meaning of Modern Sport* (London: Lawrence and Wishart, 1996);
     Kenneth R. Dutton, *The Perfectible Body: The Western Ideal of Physical Development*
     (London: Cassell, 1995); Sue Scott and David Morgan (eds), *Body Matters: Essays on the
     Sociology of the Body* (London: The Falmer Press, 1993); Patricia Vertinsky, 'Aging Bodies,
     Aging Sport Historians, and the Choreographing of Sport History', *Sport History Review*, 29
     (1998), pp. 18–29.
3.   On the revival of bowling, see: Gideon Bowker and Bianca Lencek-Bowker, *Bowled Over: A
     Roll Down Memory Lane* (San Francisco, CA: Chronicle Books, 2002); Leanne Delap,
     'Bowling Alleys Strike it Rich with Nightclub Gimmicks', *Globe and Mail*, 24 (Jan. 1998), c1;
     Amanda Smith, 'Bowling – The New Glamour Sport?', in 'Radio National: The Sports Factor',
     (2 Feb. 2002) accessed at http://www.abc.net.au/rn/talks/8.30/sportsf/stories/s635097.htm.
4.   'Council Squashes Innocent Bid for Pool Room', *The Ubyssey*, 16 Feb. 1949, p. 1; 'Side-
     Pocket Politics', *The Ubyssey*, 16 Feb. 1949, p. 2; Ray Baines, 'Out of Nowhere', *The Ubyssey*,
     17 Feb. 1949, p. 2.
5.   Dawn Hanna, 'Memory Lanes', *Vancouver Sun*, 22 Jan. 1994, Greater Vancouver 5-Pin
     Bowling Association, BC 5-Pin Bowler's Guide (Vancouver, BC: Author, 1949); National
     Council on Physical Fitness, *National Survey of Recreation in Canadian Communities* (Ottawa:
     Author, 1951).
6.   Frederick Bell, 'What's Behind this Bowling Business', *Canadian Business*, 25 (Feb. 1952),
     pp. 24–6, 102–3; Hurley, *Diners, Bowling Alleys.*
7.   '$30 Billion for Fun', *Fortune*, 49 (June 1954), pp. 115–20, 226–32; Charles K. Brightbill and
     Harold Meyer, *Recreation: Texts and Readings* (New York: Prentice-Hall, 1953); James
     Charlesworth (ed.), *Leisure in America: Blessing or Curse?* (Philadelphia, PA: American
     Academy of Political and Social Science, 1964); Fred Coalter (ed.), *Freedom and Constraint:
     The Paradoxes of Leisure* (New York: Routledge, 1989); Foster R. Dulles, *America Learns to
     Play* (New York: Appleton-Century, 1940), pp. 365–73; Kathryn Grover (ed.), *Hard at Play:
     Leisure in America, 1840–1940* (Amherst, MA: University of Massachusetts Press, 1992);
     Theodore Johannes and C. Neil Bull (eds), *Sociology of Leisure* (Beverly Hills, CA: Sage,
     1971); Max Kaplan, *Leisure in America: A Social Inquiry* (New York: Wiley, 1960); Pauline
     Madow, *Recreation in America* (New York: H.W. Wilson, 1960); Anthony Wylson, *Design for
     Leisure Entertainment* (Boston, MA: Newnes-Butterworths, 1980).
8.   Dewey quoted in Viola Kleindienst and Arthur Weston, *Intramural and Recreation Programs
     for Schools and Colleges* (New York: Appleton-Century-Crofts, 1964), p. 10; Catherine
     Callahan, 'Down the Alley', *Journal of Health and Physical Education*, 11 (Feb. 1940), pp.
     90–2; A.E. Florio, 'Bowling as Part of the Curriculum', *Journal of Health and Physical*

Education, 11 (April 1940), pp. 232–4; Robert F. Osborne, 'Origins of Physical Education in British Columbia', in *Proceedings of the First Canadian Symposium on the History of Sport and Physical Education* (Ottawa: Department of National Health and Welfare, 1970), pp. 363–93; Milton Raymer, 'Bowling A Recreation of Youth', *Journal of Health and Physical Education*, 22 (Sept. 1951), pp. 11–12; Phyllis Schrodt, 'A History of Pro-Rec: The British Columbia Provincial Recreation Programme, 1934–53' (Ph.D. dissertation, University of Alberta, 1979); Cor Westland, *Fitness and Amateur Sport in Canada: An Historical Perspective*, (Ottawa: Recreation Canada, 1979).

9. Kathro Kidwell, 'Bowling Instruction in Colleges and Universities' (Ph.D. dissertation, Teachers College, Columbia University, 1954); Marjorie Phillips and Dean Summers, 'Bowling Norms and Learning Curves for College Women', *The Research Quarterly*, 21 (1950), pp. 377–85.

10. 'Letters to the Editor', *The Ubyssey*, 12 Nov. 1946, p. 2; Livingstone to Haar, 13 June 1950, p. 3, Box 66, Folder 16, Alma Mater Society (AMS) Fonds, UBC Archives; UBC War Memorial Gymnasium, 1950, Box 66, Folder 15, AMS Fonds, UBC Archives; Sharp, Thompson, Berwick & Pratt to Livingstone, 5 Nov. 1947, p. 1, Box 17, Folder 8, Thompson, Berwick & Pratt Fonds, UBC Archives; Burges to Sharp, Thompson, Berwick & Pratt, 27 Sept. 1950, p. 2, Box 65, Folder 2, AMS Fonds, UBC Archives.

11. 'Bowling for PE Option', *The Ubyssey*, 9 Nov. 1951, p. 3; 'Bowling Alleys may be in Gym by Fall: Student Approval Asked', *The Ubyssey*, 9 Nov. 1951, p. 1; 'Vote Favors Status Quo, Gives Go Ahead to Alley', *The Ubyssey*, 15 Nov. 1951, p. 1; 'AMS gets Rolling on Alleys', *The Ubyssey*, 16 Nov. 1951, p. 1.

12. 'Bowling for PE Option', *The Ubyssey*, 9 Nov. 1951, p. 3.

13. Tracey to Duclos, p. 1, Box 65, Folder 4, AMS Fonds, UBC Archives; 'Brunswick-Balke-Collender Co. of Canada Specifications for Centennial Regulation Bowling Alleys', Box 65, Folder 4, AMS Fonds, UBC Archives.

14. One year after the Sharp, Thompson, Berwick & Pratt estimate, a general contractor, the Wilson Construction Company, submitted the figure of $13,769 to complete what the architectural firm had left. Burges to Sharp, Thompson, Berwick & Pratt, 27 Sept. 1950, p. 2, Box 65, Folder 2, AMS Fonds, UBC Archives; Burges to Sharp, Thompson, Berwick & Pratt, 29 Sept. 1950, Box 65, Folder 2, AMS Fonds, UBC Archives; Wilson to Duclos, 4 Nov. 1952, Box 65, Folder 4, AMS Fonds, UBC Archives.

15. Lyon to MacKenzie, 23 Nov. 1951, Roll 43, 'War Memorial Gym', President's Office Fonds, UBC Archives; 'Board of Governors meeting minutes', 26 Nov. 1951, Roll 43, 'War Memorial Gym', President's Office Fonds, UBC Archives; MacKenzie to Lyon, 28 Nov. 1951, Roll 43, 'War Memorial Gym', President's Office Fonds, UBC Archives; Duclos to Wilson, 13 Dec. 1951, Box 65, Folder 4, AMS Fonds, UBC Archives; 'BEG Pool History Outlined', *The Ubyssey*, 14 Jan. 1955, p. 1; MacPhee to MacKenzie, 20 Dec. 1954, Roll 412, 'BEG Pool', President's Office Fonds, UBC Archives; 'BEG Operating Costs', 3 Jan. 1955, Roll 412, 'BEG Pool', President's Office Fonds, UBC Archives.

16. 'Alley Bowling', *Canadian Business*, 30 (Oct., 1957), pp. 20–21; Vince Lunny, 'Here's One Business That Just Can't Lose', *Financial Post*, 20 (Dec. 1958), p. 50; Hurley, *Bowling Alleys, Diners*.

17. President's Committee on Athletics, 'Athletics', 20 May 1952, Roll 381, 'President's Committee on Athletics', President's Office Fonds, UBC Archives; 'Recommendations of the UBC Alumni Special Committee on Athletics', 13 April 1953, Roll 381, 'President's Committee on Athletics', President's Office Fonds, UBC Archives; 'Student Committee on Extramural Athletics', 18 March 1957, pp. 5–8, 11, 18, Box 15, Folder 3, AMS Fonds, UBC Archives; 'AMS Fee Increase Proposed by Council for Athletics, Pub', *The Ubyssey*, 5 March 1957, p. 1; Hank Hawthorn, 'More to Athletics? Fee Increase Mooted', *The Ubyssey*, 12 March 1957, p. 1; George Morfitt, 'AMS Largesse reaches $157,100', *The Ubyssey*, 11 Oct. 1957, p. 3.

18. Allan Fotheringham, 'UBC Program in Bad Shape', V*ancouver Sun*, 6 March 1957, p. 16; Allan Fotheringham, 'UBC Problem: Two Attitudes', *Vancouver Sun*, 7 March 1957, pp. 18–19; Allan Fotheringham, 'High Schools on Their Own', *Vancouver Sun*, 8 March 1957, p. 18; Allan Fotheringham, 'Give Children an Early Start', *Vancouver Sun*, 9 March 1957, p. 10;

Men's Athletic Committee, 'Expenditures 1953–54 to 1963–64', 9 Nov. 1964, Box 15, Folder 3, AMS Fonds, UBC Archives.

19.   Bray to MacKenzie, 28 Nov. 1955, Roll 435, 'Bowling Alleys', President's Office Fonds, UBC Archives; MacKenzie to Bray, 2 Dec. 1955, Roll 435, 'Bowling Alleys', President's Office Fonds, UBC Archives; Osborne to MacKenzie, 15 Dec. 1955, Roll 435, 'Bowling Alleys', President's Office Fonds, UBC Archives; 'Extension to Brock Building', 28 Dec. 1955, p. 2, Roll 435, 'Bowling Alleys', President's Office Fonds, UBC Archives; MacKenzie to Bray, 3 Jan. 1956, Roll 435, 'Bowling Alleys', President's Office Fonds, UBC Archives.

20.   'Students say No to Bowling Alley', *The Ubyssey*, 2 Dec. 1955, p. 8; 'Bray Explains Alleys in Brock', *The Ubyssey*, 2 Dec. 1955, p. 9; 'Investment Analysis', 2 Dec. 1955, Roll 435, 'Bowling Alleys', President's Office Fonds, UBC Archives; 'Board of Governors Meeting', 27 Aug. 1956, Roll 435, 'Bowling Alleys', President's Office Fonds, UBC Archives; MacKenzie to Bonner, 26 Sept. 1956, Roll 435, 'Bowling Alleys', President's Office Fonds, UBC Archives; Bonner to MacKenzie, 29 Oct. 1956, Roll 435, 'Bowling Alleys', President's Office Fonds, UBC Archives; 'Board of Governors Meeting', 29 Oct. 1956, Roll 435, 'Bowling Alleys', President's Office Fonds, UBC Archives.

21.   'Bowling to be Installed in Memorial Gym at Year's End', *The Ubyssey*, 22 Feb. 1957, p. 1; Thomas to Student Union Officers, n.d., Box 51, Folder 26, AMS Fonds, UBC Archives; Sutherland to Osborne, 17 Aug. 1956, Roll 435, 'Bowling Alleys', President's Office Fonds, UBC Archives; 'Bowling Alleys- Subcommittee', 12 Feb. 1957, Roll 435, 'Bowling Alleys', President's Office Fonds, UBC Archives.

22.   Lasserre to Hughes, 22 May 1957, Roll 435, 'Bowling Alleys', President's Office Fonds, UBC Archives; MacKenzie to Hughes, 30 Oct. 1957, Roll 435, 'Bowling Alleys', President's Office Fonds, UBC Archives.

23.   'The UBC Bowling Alleys', 13 April 1957, Roll 435, 'Bowling Alleys', President's Office Fonds, UBC Archives; 'Schedule of Priority and Rates for Bowling Alleys, 1957–58', 6 May 1957, Roll 435, 'Bowling Alleys', President's Office Fonds, UBC Archives; 'Schedule of Rates for Bowling Alleys', 30 Dec. 1957, Roll 435, 'Bowling Alleys', President's Office Fonds, UBC Archives.

24.   Hughes to MacKenzie, 14 Nov. 1957, Roll 435, 'Bowling Alleys', President's Office Fonds, UBC Archives; Callahan, 'Down the Alley'; Kidwell, 'Bowling Instruction in Colleges', pp. 13–69; Joe Falcaro and Murray Goodman, *Bowling for All* (New York: Ronald Press, 1957); Charlotte Fosburg, 'Hints on Bowling Organization', *Journal of Health and Physical Education*, 18 (Feb. 1947), pp. 96–7; Gus Lombardi, 'How to Teach Bowling', *Athletic Journal*, 43 (Oct. 1962), pp. 34–5, 72–8; Lloyd F. Owens, *So You Want to Bowl: Techniques of 5 pin Bowling* (Vancouver: Copp Clark, 1959); Milton Raymer, *Curriculum for the Teaching of Class Room Bowling for Junior and Senior High Schools and Colleges and Universities* (Chicago, IL: American Junior Bowling Congress, 1958); Paul Shebby, 'Strikes and Spares in Physical Education Class', *Journal of Health and Physical Education*, 34 (March 1959), pp. 34–5; Jow Wilman, *Better Bowling* (New York: A.S. Barnes, 1953).

25.   'Philips Makes Strike With Automatic Pinsetter', *Financial Post*, 31 Jan. 1959, p. 1; David Francis, 'Canada Converts U.K. to Five-Pin Bowling', *Financial Post*, 10 Sept. 1960, p. 20; Hal Higdon, 'Five-Pin Bowling: The Canadian Version', *Popular Mechanics* (May 1960), pp. 106–7; Jane Becker, 'Culture Note: Ten-Pins Anybody?' *MacLean's Magazine*, 74 (1961), p. 74; Vera Fidler, 'Something on Bowling', *The Canadian Banker*, 69 (Autumn 1962), pp. 103–10.

26.   'Minutes of the Committee on Revenue Producing Facilities', 9 Oct. 1957, Roll 206, 'President's Committee on Recreation', President's Office Fonds, UBC Archives; Hurley, *Diners, Bowling Alleys*, pp. 130–49; 'Boys in Demand', *Business Week* 25 (Dec. 1943), pp. 44–6; Kate Clugston, 'When Pin-Setters are Children', *Survey*, 81 (1945), pp. 9–10; US Department of Labor, *The Boy Behind the Pins, US Department of Labor Bulletin* 170 (Washington, DC: Author, 1953); Clara Beyer, 'A Break for Pinboys', *Children* (Sept. 1954), pp. 185–8.

27.   'Intramural Program', 1957, Roll 355, 'Physical Education', President's Office Fonds, UBC Archives; 'Financial Considerations for the SUB Games Area', (1963), Box 51, Folder 3, AMS Fonds, UBC Archives; Kleindienst and Weston, *Intramural and Recreation Programs*.

28. Hurley, *Diners, Bowling Alleys*, pp.150–76; Kidwell, 'Bowling Instruction in Colleges', pp. 7–12; William B. Furlong, 'Big Strike – From "Alley" to "Supermarket"', *The New York Times Magazine* 29 (Nov. 1959), pp. 42, 47–8, 50; 'The Social Whirl of Ladies Bowling', *Life*, 49, (12 Dec. 1960), pp. 99–107; Kurt T. Dunn, 'Why the Ladies love to Bowl', *Today's Health*, 39 (March 1961), pp. 36–9, 72–3; Russell Lynes, 'Bowling Goes Bourgeois', *Horizon*, 5 (March 1963), pp. 89–95; Carole A. Oglesby, 'Bowling and Women' in *Encyclopedia of Women and Sport in America* (Phoenix: Oryx Press, 1998), pp. 34–6; Women's Athletic Association, 'Special Report to the President', Box 51, Folder 3, AMS Fonds, UBC Archives.

29. UBC, *Totem* (Vancouver: UBC, 1961), p. 270; UBC, *Totem* (Vancouver, BC: UBC, 1962), p. 262; UBC, *Totem* (Vancouver: UBC, 1963), p. 264; UBC, *Totem* (Vancouver, BC: UBC, 1964), p. 264.

30. Frank Raymond, 'Bowling in Canada is Now Big Business', *Saturday Night*, 77 (Nov. 1962), pp. 27–8; Lynes, 'Bowling Goes Bourgeois', p. 89; MacPhee to MacDonald, 14 Feb. 1963, Roll 435, 'Bowling Alleys', President's Office Fonds, UBC Archives; Davies to MacPhee, 4 March 1963, Roll 435, 'Bowling Alleys', President's Office Fonds, UBC Archives; Osborne to White, 16 July 1964, Roll 435, 'Bowling Alleys', President's Office Fonds, UBC Archives; 'Board of Governors Meeting', 28 July 1964, Roll 435, 'Bowling Alleys', President's Office Fonds, UBC Archives; 'Brunswick Bowling Operator's Guide' (1958), p. 15, Box 51, Folder 3, AMS Fonds, UBC Archives.

31. MacPhee to MacDonald, 14 Feb. 1963, Roll 435, 'Bowling Alleys', President's Office Fonds, UBC Archives; Osborne to White, 16 July 1964, Roll 435, 'Bowling Alleys', President's Office Fonds, UBC Archives; 'Proposal from National Bowling & Billiards, Ltd.', 17 July 1964, Roll 435, 'Bowling Alleys', President's Office Fonds, UBC Archives; Clifford Brownell and Roy Moore (eds), *Recreational Sports* (Mankato, MN: Creative Recreational Society, 1961), pp. 59–88.

32. Bill Redmond, 'Report to the SUB Planning Committee: Outlook for Bowling Lanes in the Union', 22 Jan. 1963, pp. 1–5, Box 51, Folder 3, AMS Fonds, UBC Archives.

33. 'Report to the SUB Planning Committee: Student Survey', 22 Jan. 1963, pp. 11, 42–6, 83–8, Box 51, Folder 3, AMS Fonds, UBC Archives; 'Bowling Lanes in the SUB', 24 Aug. 1966, Box 51, Folder 3, AMS Fonds, UBC Archives; Cooper to Assaly, 17 Feb. 1967, Box 51, Folder 3, AMS Fonds, UBC Archives; AMS President to Students' Council, 3 Nov. 1967, Box 51, Folder 3, AMS Fonds, UBC Archives.

34. 'Spare Us', *The Ubyssey*, 5 Oct. 1967, p. 4; 'Pool Sinks SUB Lanes', *The Ubyssey*, 12 Oct. 1967, p. 3; Jon Strom, 'Bowling Urgent', *The Ubyssey*, 20 Oct. 1967, p. 4; 'SUB Gets Lanes', *The Ubyssey*, 7 Nov. 1967, p. 3; Irene Wasilewski, 'SUB Official Opening Today but Most Doors Remain Locked', *The Ubyssey*, 26 Sept. 1968, p. 1; Lynes, 'Bowling Goes Bourgeois', p. 89.

35. Osborne to Vance, 20 Sept. 1965, Box 66, Folder 16, AMS Fonds, UBC Archives; 'To the Staff of the SUB Games Area', 1969, 3, Box 51, Folder 3, AMS Fonds, UBC Archives; 'Brunswick Bowling Operator's Guide', 1958, p. 11, Box 51, Folder 3, AMS Fonds, UBC Archives.

36. McBride to Boyd, 22 Jan. 1969, Box 51, Folder 26, AMS Fonds, UBC Archives; 'Building Usage Evaluation After One year's Operation', 27 Oct. 1969, p. 6, Box 51, Folder 25, AMS Fonds, UBC Archives; Redden to Nikolic, 17 Feb. 1986, Box 10, Folder 3, AMS Fonds, UBC Archives; Redden to Hi Tech, 1 Oct. 1986, Box 100, AMS Fonds, UBC Archives; Redden to Tomlinson, 4 March 1987, Box 10, Folder 3, AMS Fonds, UBC Archives; Redden to Nevraumont, 26 Jan. 1988, Box 10, Folder 3, AMS Fonds, UBC Archives; Putnam, *Bowling Alone*.

37. Statistics Canada, *Culture Statistics: Recreational Activities* (Ottawa: Author, 1976), pp. 16, 27–9, 36; Brian G. Milton, *Social Status and Leisure Time Activities: National Survey Finding for Adult Canadians* (Montreal: Canadian Sociology and Anthropology Association, 1975), pp. 35–40; Eric Broom, *Leisure Services in British Columbia* (Victoria: Ministry of Travel Industry, 1974); Wilder Penfield, 'The Age of Leisure', in *Proceedings of the Canadian Symposium of Recreation* (Montreal, PQ: Canadian Symposium of Recreation, 1967), p. 12.

38. Bryan Turner, *The Body and Society* (New York: Basil Blackwell, 1996); Rojek, *Leisure and Culture*, pp. 8–25; Wearing, *Leisure and Feminist Theory*, pp. 103–26.

Chapter 5

1.   Rebecca Grant, 'The Cold War and the Feminine Mystique', in P.R. Beckman and F. D'Amico (eds), *Women, Gender, and World Politics: Perspectives, Policies, and Prospects* (London: Bergin and Garvey, 1994), p. 119.

2.   Pat Armstrong, 'The Welfare State As History', in Raymond Blake et al. (eds), *The Welfare State in Canada: Past, Present, and Future* (Toronto, ON: Irwin Publishing, 1997), p. 52.

3.   Dionne Brand, '"We weren't allowed to go into factory work until Hitler started the war": The 1920s to the 1940s', in Peggy Bristow et al. (eds), *We're Rooted Here and They Can't Pull Us Up: African Canadian Women's History* (Toronto, ON: University of Toronto Press, 1994), p. 189.

4.   Gary Kinsman, 'Constructing Gay Men and Lesbians as National Security Risks', in G. Kinsman et al. (eds), W*hose National Security? Canadian State Surveillance and the Creation of Enemies* (Toronto, ON: Between the Lines, 2000), p. 144.

5.   Franca Iacovetta, 'Recipes for Democracy? Gender, Family, and Making Female Citizens in Cold War Canada', *Canadian Woman Studies Journal*, 20, 2 (Summer 2000), p. 13.

6.   Doug Owram, *Born at the Right Time: A History of the Baby-Boom Generation* (Toronto, BC: University of Toronto Press, 1996), p. 18.

7.   Ibid., p. 17.

8.   See David Welky, 'Viking Girls, Mermaids, and Little Brown Men: U.S. Journalism and the 1932 Olympics', *Journal of Sport History*, 24, 1 (1997), p. 42, and Samantha King, 'Consuming Compassion: AIDS, Figure Skating, and Canadian Identity', *Journal of Sport and Social Issues*, 24, 2 (2000), p. 148.

9.   Welky, 'Viking Girls, Mermaids, and Little Brown Men', p. 28.

10.   In a letter by sports reporter Sheila Kearns in *The Ubyssey* (1951), she notes that 'in the States most colleges forbid any women's athletic competition on the university level', p. 8.

11.   Lee Stewart, *It's up to You: Women at UBC in the Early Years* (Vancouver: University of British Columbia Press, 1990), p. 122.

12.   That UBC did not have a women's track and field team until the early 1960s, is evidence of deep-rooted gender discrimination. This absence is especially perplexing given the shining Olympic successes of Canadian female track and field stars, Myrtle Cook, Florence Bell, Bobbie Rosenfeld and Ethyl Catherwood during the 1920s and 1930s. (However, after the collapse of some female runners at the end of the 800 metre race at the 1928 Olympics, this event would not be reinstated until the 1960 Olympics in Rome.) Female students at UBC who participated in competitive track and field often chose to train with Vancouver's Hudson's Bay track team.

13.   Betty Stuart, 'Chalk Talk', *The Ubyssey*, 29, 18 (5 Nov. 1946), p. 4.

14.   Jackie Shearman, 'Letter', *The Ubyssey*, 29, 50 (20 Feb.1947), p. 4.

15.   Chick Turner is John Turner, former Prime Minister of Canada. In 1984, he publicly patted the buttocks of liberal colleague Iona Campagnolo, a move which was widely denounced by feminist critics across the country as a demeaning, chauvinist act.

16.   Chick Turner, 'Chalk Talk', *The Ubyssey*, 29, 50, 20 Feb. 1947, p. 4.

17.   Chick Turner, 'Report of the Investigating Commission on the Position of the Women's Athletic Directorate', 28 Feb. 1949, p. 3.

18.   See: Patricia Vertinsky, *The Eternally Wounded Woman: Women, Doctors and Exercise in the late Nineteenth Century* (Manchester and New York: Manchester Univesity Press, 1990); Helen Lenskyj, *Out of Bounds: Women, Sport and Sexuality* (Toronto: Women's Press, 1986); Gregory Stanley, *The Rise and Fall of the Sportswoman: Women's Health, Fitness and Athletics, 1860–1940* (New York: Peter Lang, 1996).

19.   Stewart, *It's up to You*, p. 74.

20.   Maryrose Reeves Allen, 'The Development of Beauty in College Women Through Healthy Physical Education', archived in M.R. Allen Papers, Box 160–4 (folder 4), (Maryland-Sprinarm Research Center, Howard University, Washington, DC, 1938), p. 1.

21.   Women's magazines, and campus sororities' newsletters and handbooks throughout the 1950s, especially in the USA, detailed college women's dream of getting both an education and 'a man'.

22. Turner, 'Report of the Investigating Commission', p. 2.

23. Cited in Susan Cahn, *Coming On Strong: Gender and Sexuality in Twentieth Century Women's Sport* (New York: The Free Press, 1994), p. 83.

24. Joan MacArther, president of the Women's Athletic Directorate at UBC and coach of the women's basketball team, was a 'member of the famed Edmonton Gradettes basketball team, lead up club to the Edmonton Grads who were world champions for so many years', J. Crafter, 'Women's Sport', *The Ubyssey*, 34, 12 (19 Oct. 1951), p. 4. For valuable historical documenting of the Edmonton Grads, access www.womensbasketballmuseum.com. Also see the National Film Board docu-drama, 'Shooting Stars' (1987).

25. Anon., 'Powell River Gives Varsity A Loss', *The Ubyssey*, 33, 38 (19 Jan. 1951a), p. 4.

26. Future interviews with former female (and male) athletes at UBC, 1945–55, are essential, and would supply a richer, more complicated picture of conformity and resistance.

27. Anon., 'War Memorial Gym Bonds Show Large Profit in Sales and Interest – Profits Go to Gymnasium Fund', *The Ubyssey*, 32, 33 (6 Jan. 1950a), p. 1.

28. Interview with Jennifer (a pseudonym), conducted by Patricia Vertinsky, 2001.

29. J.D. McLeod, 'Build a better British Columbia. Support UBC's War Memorial', *Facts and Figures for Organizers, Speakers and Canvassers for the UBC War Memorial Gymnasium Campaign* (Vancouver, BC, 1946), p. 19.

30. Ibid., p. 3.

31. Anon., 'Students Show Apathy at MAD, WAA Elections', *The Ubyssey*, 31, 6 (16 Feb. 1949), p. 4.

32. Anon., 'Marshall Announces Plan to Increase Enthusiasm', *The Ubyssey*, 33, 13 (24 Oct. 1950), p. 1.

33. Anon., 'Budget Outline for AMS, 1951/2', *The Ubyssey*, 34, 3 (28 Sept. 1951), p. 3.

34. In an AMS special edition of the *The Ubyssey* (1 Oct. 1953), the MAD expense report stated that salaries in the MAD budget totalled $8,800, which was more than four times the money allocated for the Women's Athletic Directorate's entire budget (p. 1). We suspect that female coaches and sports administrators either volunteered their time and expertise or were paid small honoraria.

35. Sheila Kearns, 'Women's Sport', *The Ubyssey*, 33, 65 (29 March 1951), p. 8.

36. Anon., 'The University of British Columbia: The War Memorial Gymnasium', 15 July 1950. Special Collections, UBC, Box no. 1.

37. It hardly seems an accident that both Frederic Lasserre and Ned Pratt – architects who shaped the new, modernist and masculinist Gym – were both accomplished athletes.

38. A. McClintock, *Imperial Leather: Race, Gender, and Sexuality in the Colonial Conquest* (New York and London: Routledge, 1995), p. 72.

39. Anon., 'Let's Not Quit Now', *The Ubyssey*, 33, 53 (27 Feb. 1951), p. 2.

40. Anon., 'Games to be Televised', *The Ubyssey*, 37, 8 (5 Oct. 1954), p. 4.

41. Douglas How, 'Blonde on Blades', *Maclean's* (15 February 1947), pp. 45–6.

42. See A. Lumpkin and L. Williams, 'An Analysis of Sports Illustrated Feature Articles, 1954–87', *Sociology of Sport Journal*, 8 (1991), pp. 16–32, and L. Davis, *The Swimsuit Issue and Sport: Hegemonic Masculinity in Sports Illustrated* (Albany, NY: State University of New York Press, 1997), pp. 2–18.

43. Anon., 'Thunderbird Cage Gals Face Choc Co-Eds Tuesday', *The Ubyssey*, 32, 53 (24 Feb. 1950), p. 4.

44. On the sexist, racist stereotyping of black women's bodies, see Evelynn Hammonds, 'Towards a Genealogy of Black Female Sexuality: The Problematic of Silence', in M. Jacqui Alexander and Chandra Mohanty (eds), *Feminist Genealogies, Colonial Legacies, and Democratic Futures* (New York: Routledge, 1997), pp. 170–82.

45. For more about the history of efforts to inculcate African American female athletes with 'feminine' behaviours, see Patricia Vertinsky and Gwendolyn Captain, 'More Myth Than History: American Culture and Representations of the Black Female's Athletic Ability', *Journal of Sport History*, 25, 3 (Fall 1998), pp. 540–1.

46. For examples of racist commentary in *The Ubyssey*, 1945/55; see 'Chief Billy Scow of the Qwi-qua-su-tiniuk Indian Tribe', 31, 17 (20 Oct. 1948), p. 1; and on the discriminatory practices of female sororities at UBC, see 'Colored Girls Eliminated From Pan-Helenic

Invitation Listings – Not Invited to Join Sororities,' *The Ubyssey*, 37, 10 (8 Oct. 1954), p. 1.

47.   Anon., 'Lethargic Football Fans Will Be Drawn to Games by New Lure', *The Ubyssey*, 32, 13 (20 Oct. 1949), p. 1.

48.   Anon., '400 Mums and Orchids Bribe Gals to Come', *The Ubyssey*, 31, 14 (14 Oct. 1948), p. 3.

49.   S. Kearns, 'Female Hockey Players Seek 200 Blind Dates – Pacific Northwest Grass Hockey Finals Hosts Thirteen Entrants', *The Ubyssey*, 33, 17 (2 Nov. 1950), p. 4.

50.   B. Bailey, *From Front Porch to Back Seat: Courtship in Twentieth Century America* (Baltimore, MD, and London: Johns Hopkins University Press, 1988), pp. 57–76.

51.   J. Crafter, 'Varsity Girls Off to PNW Grass Hockey Tourney', *The Ubyssey*, 34, 18 (2 Nov. 1951), p. 4.

52.   See Walter Gage, 'Letter to Donald Jabour', UBC Special Collections, Box 9–13. Athletics, Women, Misc. 1949/60, 18 March 1957, for details of the Dean's decree to mandate chaperones for sportswomen, as described to AMS president, Donald Jabour, 1.

53.   Stewart, *It's up to You*, p. 80.

54.   In '"We Were Ladies, We Just Played Basketball Like Boys": African American Womanhood and Competitive Basketball at Bennett College, 1928–1942', Rita Liberti notes that particular pressure was placed on black female athletes in the American South to conform to middle-class standards of propriety in light of the legacy of stereotypes of African Americans as immoral and uncivilized. It would appear that there were no African Canadian female competitive athletes enrolled at UBC during 1945–55. *Journal of Sport History*, 26, 3 (Fall 1999), pp. 567–84.

55.   What is perhaps most interesting is that neither elite female athletes nor professional strippers 'fit' the image of the (white) marriageable madonna with whom every male student was, eventually, supposed to 'settle down'. Female elite athletes in 'non-traditional sports' challenged, even defied, the prescriptions for proper womanhood in the 1950s; female strippers garnered undivided male attention, and yet were stigmatized as unmarriageable, damaged whores.

56.   In a one-time spoof of beauty contests, all seven female candidates for the 'Plebian Queen of the Mardi Gras' were crowned, and they were all dressed in workers' uniforms appropriate to their individual trade union sponsors (see Anon., 'Democracy Wins: Plebs Elect Seven Queens', *The Ubyssey*, 32, 42 (31 Jan. 1950), p. 1.

57.   F. McNeil, 'Negligee, Swim Suit Capture Men's Eyes', *The Ubyssey*, 35, 54 (27 Feb. 1953), p. 1. The Women's Undergraduate Society also hosted a speakers' series in 1948–49, and included the Manager of Woodward's (a downtown department store) to lecture on chinaware, Miss Pope from Spencer's drugstore to speak on cosmetics and Mrs Henderson from the Province Kitchen to speak on food.

58.   Anon., 'Understanding Wives Helps Veterans on Campus', *The Ubyssey*, 31, 37 (25 Nov. 1948), p. 1.

59.   J. Manfredi, 'Peptalk: The History of Cheerleading', *Seventeen*, 42 (1983), p. 94. On the paradoxical spectacle of female cheerleaders cheering female athletes, see Laurel Davis, 'A Postmodern Paradox?: Cheerleaders at Women's Sporting Events', *Arena Review*, 13, 2 (1989), pp. 124–33, reprinted in Susan Birrell and Cheryl Cole (eds.), *Women, Sport and Culture*, (Chamaign, IL: Human Kinetics, 1994), pp. 149–58.

60.   Anon., 'Revived Drum Majorettes Show First At Homecoming', *The Ubyssey*, 33, 16 (31 Oct. 1950), p. 1.

61.   Anon., 'Beauty Queens and Cheer-leaders for Game Sunday', *The Ubyssey*, 31, 18 (21 Oct. 1948), p. 4.

62.   See Patrizia *Gentile*, '"Government Girls" and "Ottawa Men": Cold War Management of Gender Relations in the Civil Service', in Gary Kinsman et al. (eds), *Whose National Security? Canadian State Surveillance and the Creation of Enemies* (Toronto, ON: Between the Lines, 2000), pp. 131–41. According to Gentile, the ideal 'Miss Civil Service' was white, single with no children, heterosexual, well-groomed, tall, thin, 'beautiful', with shiny hair (p. 135). Also see Candace Savage, *Beauty Queens: A Playful History* (Vancouver: Greystone Books, 1999).

63.   Anon., Editorial: 'Totem Queen, Jan Olsen, Editorial', *The Ubyssey*, 31, 51 (20 Jan. 1949), p. 4.

64.   Anon., 'Sex to Spark Lunch Time Basketball Fixture', *The Ubyssey*, 31, 56 (28 Jan. 1949), p. 4.

65.   The beauty queens were also applauded by many gay men who, in their own worlds, appreciated the campy elements of the contests.

66. V. Burstyn, *The Rites of Men: Manhood, Politics, and the Culture of Sport* (Toronto, ON: University of Toronto Press, 1999), pp. 163–8.

67. Ibid., p. 74.

68. On the paradox of homoeroticism in men's sports, see Brian Pronger, *The Arena of Masculinity: Sports, Homosexuality, and the Meaning of Sex* (New York: St Martin's Press, 1990), pp. 177–214.

69. Anon., 'Fashion Briefing', *The Ubyssey*, 32, 41 (27 Jan. 1950), p. 3.

70. For more on gender norms and disavowals, see Judith Butler, *Bodies That Matter: On the Discursive Limits of 'Sex'* (New York: Routledge, 1993), pp. 1–23.

71. Not only were many men indifferent to women's sporting successes, some were convinced that women had no place at all on university campuses. In *The Ubyssey*, Allan Fotheringham wrote: 'The gals might be nice for decoration but they have never been accused of inspiring anyone to cop off a Nobel prize. You see, women are like booze or a weekend show, they're entertainment, an added attraction after a week of slugging it out with Chem problems ... Since they are the cherry on top of the sundae, they shouldn't be available all the time but just brought out for special occasions. You can have females around a university if you want, but keep them off in one corner of the botanical gardens ... They should be shut in with pots and pans in the home ec. building ... They are as about as conducive to studying as is a Lili St. Cyr TV programme.' See his article, 'Freshettes, Femmes, and Rhododendrons', *The Ubyssey*, 36, 35 (2 Feb. 1954), p. 2.

72. Stewart, *It's up to You*, p. 118.

73. M. Keyes, 'Women and Sport', in D. Morrow, M. Keyes, W. Simpson, F. Cosentino and R. Lappage (eds), *A Concise History of Sport in Canada* (Toronto, ON: Oxford University Press, 1989), p. 233. In 1927, Miss Jean Gilley, President of the Women's Athletic Association at UBC, received a letter from A.E. Marie Parkes, Women's Athletic Association, University of Toronto and secretary of the Women's Amateur Athletic Federation of Canada (headquarters: Toronto). Parkes advised Gilley to support the ban on long-distance racing for women due to the 'great physical strain' female runners incurred. UBC Special Collections.

74. Marian Penny (née Henderson), was interviewed by M. Ann Hall in December 1998 in her home outside Victoria, BC, at the age of 90. I am grateful to Professor Hall for access to the transcript of her interview. For a detailed discussion of women's basketball rules, see Vertinsky, this volume.

75. Keyes, 'Women and Sport', p. 233.

76. J. Leiper, 'Women's Sport', *The Ubyssey*, 34, 4 (2 Oct. 1951), p. 4.

77. Synchronized swimming was also known as 'ornamental swimming' or 'fancy swimming'.

78. The practice of women hosting social events for visiting teams has a long history. Historian Robin Bell Markels notes that the women's basketball team at Ohio State University organized after-game receptions for their rivals in 1904. It was during the receptions that the female athletes were expected to re-enter the world of decorum, where conviviality, social graces, hospitality and decorum trumped athletic accomplishment. See 'Bloomer Basketball and Its Suspender Suppression: Women's Intercollegiate Competition at Ohio State, 1904–1907', *Journal of Sport History*, 27, 1 (Spring 2000), p. 36.

79. Rita Liberti notes that by 1942 support for black women's intercollegiate basketball at Bennett College (and elsewhere) in the USA had been withdrawn. After two decades of successful women's basketball which emphasized competition, travel and winning, the focus shifted to intramurals and play-days. See Liberti, 'We Were Ladies', p. 578. In white-dominated schools, bans on women's basketball were invoked much earlier, such as the 1907 ban at Ohio State.

80. See Lenskyj, *Out of Bounds* and H. Lenskyj, 'No Fear? Lesbians in Sport and Physical Education', *Women in Sport and Physical Activity Journal*, 6, 2 (1997), pp. 7–22; Cahn, *Coming on Strong*; P. Griffen, *Strong Women, Deep Closets: Lesbians and Homophobia in Sport* (Champaign, IL, Il: Human Kinetics, 1998); H. Sykes, 'Lesbian and Heterosexual P.E. Teachers', (Ph.D. thesis, Department of Educational Studies, University of British Columbia, 1998).

81. Richard Von Krafft-Ebing, *Psychopathia Sexualis with Especial Reference to the Antipathic Sexual Instincts*, trans. F.J. Rebman (Brooklyn: Physicians and Surgeons Book Co., 1908), p. 333.

82. Ibid., pp. 140–1.

83. L. Browne, *Girls of Summer: In Their Own League* (Toronto, ON: Harper Collins, 1992), p. 6.

84.   Cahn, *Coming on Strong*, p. 202.
85.   Ibid., p. 187.
86.   Stewart, in *It's Up to You*, notes that the three residences were named to honour Isabel MacInnes, Mary Louise Bollert and Anne Wesbrook, all of whom contributed to the lives of women's students in the early years (p. 88).
87.   See Anon., 'Kinsey Called Defense Threat Sending Mom to Pub for Sex', *The Ubyssey*, 36, 25 (8 Jan. 1954), p. 1 and Anon., 'Minister's Son Does His Part to Crush Kinseyism', *The Ubyssey*, 36, 29 (19 Jan. 1954), p. 1.
88.   See Jennifer Terry, *An American Obsession: Science, Medicine, and Homosexuality in Modern Society* (Chicago, IL, and London: University of Chicago Press, 1999), pp. 297–314, for analysis of the mid century medicalization of homosexuality. Gary Kinsman, *Regulation of Desire: Homo and Hetero Sexualities*, 2nd edn (Montreal, Quebec: Black Rose, 1996), pp. 213–87., for an account of homosexual behaviour as criminal behaviour.
89.   Kinsman, 'Constructing Gay Men and Lesbians', p. 143.
90.   See Vanessa Cosco, '"Obviously Then I'm Not Homosexual"': Lesbian Identities, Discretion, and Communities' (Unpublished MA thesis, Department of History, University of British Columbia, 1996), and Karen Duder, cited in Elisa Kukla, 'Suburban Parties: The Real History of Lesbian Butch and Femme', *Xtra! West* (21 Sept. 2000), p. 12.
91.   See Jaye Zimet, *Strange Sisters: The Art of Lesbian Pulp Fiction 1949–1969* (New York: Penguin Books, 1999), pp. 17–24.
92.   On the obscenity case, see Mary Louise Adams, *The Trouble With Normal: Post-war Youth and the Making of Heterosexuality* (Toronto, ON: University of Toronto Press, 1997), p. 158.
93.   David Bianco, 'The Heyday of Lesbian Pulp Novels', *Planet Out*, p. 1. http://www.planetout.com/pno/news/history/archive/07191999.html: 2001.
94.   M.J. Kane and H. Lenskyj, 'Media Treatment of Female Athletes: Issues of Gender and Sexualities', in Lawrence A. Wenner (ed.), *Media Sport* (New York: Routledge, 1998), p. 200.
95.   Sarah Banet-Weiser, *The Most Beautiful Girl in the World: Beauty Pageants and National Identity* (Berkeley, CA: University of California Press, 1999), pp. 10–12.
96.   Jayne Caudwell notes how perceptions of butch lesbian identity generate tensions and homophobic distancing among some female football players. See J. Caudwell, 'Women's Football in the United Kingdom: Theorizing Gender and Unpacking the Butch Lesbian Image', *Journal of Sport and Social Issues*, 23, 4 (Nov. 1999), pp. 390–402.
97.   See Sarah Banet-Weiser, 'Hoop Dreams: Professional Basketball and the Politics of Race and Gender', *Journal of Sport and Social Issues*, 23, 4 (Nov. 1999), p. 404.

Chapter 6

1.   Michel de Certeau, *The Practices of Everyday Life* (Berkeley, CA: University of California Press, 1984), p. 86.
2.   Of course, this easy slippage between history and memory would be censored by contemporary theorists who argue that history (as a discipline and usurper of memory) and memory are not the same thing, and, in fact, are opposite in their working, aims and coercive power. The current discourse on memory and architecture is pervasive, as witnessed in the recent Harvard Design review dedicated to the subject. Key texts include Pierre Nora, *Les Lieux de mémoire* (Paris: Gallimard, 1984), Frances Yates, *The Art of Memory* (London: Pimlico, 1966), and the seminal text, Maurice Halbwachs, *La Mémoire collective* (Paris: Michel, 1997).
3.   Charles D. Maginnis, 'Living Memorials', *Architectural Forum*, 81 (Sept. 1944), pp. 106–10.
4.   Adrian Forty, 'Memory', in *Words and Buildings: A Vocabulary of Modern Architecture* (New York: Thames & Hudson, 2000), p. 206. Here Forty offers a good summation and astute summary of the several ways in which architecture and memory have been related in architectural discourse in the modern period, offering both a broader context for it and a cogent critique of current assumptions.
5.   For example, Paul Connerton, *How Societies Remember* (Cambridge and New York: Cambridge University Press, 1989).

6. Forty, 'Memory', p. 219.
7. Letter from David Brock to President MacKenize, 13 Feb. 1946, President's Office Fonds, Special Collection, UBC, Roll No. 435.
8. Ibid.
9. Letter from President MacKenzie to David Brock, 15 Feb. 1946, President's Office Fonds,. Special Collections UBC, Roll No. 435.
10. Hillel Schwartz, 'Torque: The New Kinaesthetic of the Twentieth Century', in Jonathan Crary and Sanford Kwinter (eds), *Incorporations (Zone 6)* (New York: Urzone, 1992), 106, n. 75.
11. Macginnis, 'Living Memorials,' pp. 106–10.
12. Ibid., p. 107.
13. Ibid., p. 166.
14. H.M. Willmot, 'Living War Memorials Honour the Fallen', *Saturday Night*, 64 (6 Nov. 1948), pp. 24–5.
15. Forty, 'Memory', p. 206.
16. Although Adolf Loos asserted that only the monument and the tomb were really architecture, all else should strive to be building, his own 'buildings' were and are recognized as 'architecture'. He designed one monument; it was never built – it was also historicist in its language.
17. On memory, Benjamin, Proust and Freud, see Sigrid Weigel, *Body – and Image – Space: Rereading Walter Benjamin* (London and New York: Routledge, 1996). See especially ch. 6 'From topography to writing: Benjamin's concept of memory' and 'Readability: Benjamin's place in contemporary theoretical approaches to pictorial and corporeal memory'. There are four articles about Freud in the journal which Le Corbuiser edited along with Amédée Ozenfant and, for a while, the 'dadaist' Paul Dermé. They are written by Dr Allendy and Dr Laforgue. Le Corbusier appears to have been rather cynical about André Breton and the surrealists who took inspiration from Freud and his notions of memory. Lasserre was interested in the pedagogy of Gropius at Harvard, Wurster at MIT and Chermayeff at Chicago, and while his enthusiasm for Le Corbusier may have lessened somewhat after his exposure to Lubetkin's office in England – Tecton – he generally supported the modernism canonized by Giedion; the latter was the key text chosen by Lasserre for the new School of Architecture in 1946.
18. Ormonde J.Hall, 'Speaking Editorially', *The Graduate Chronicle*, 2, 3 (Oct. 1948), p. 17.
19. Ibid., p. 36.
20. Ibid., p. 17.
21. The model university cited by Hall is Illinois Institute of Technology, just then being redesigned and built by Mies van der Rohe. The exemplary spokesperson of modernism referred to is Harvard's Dean Hudnut, who was responsible for bringing Gropius to the Harvard School of Design. Interestingly, his 'modern university designer' is also male, as is obvious from the space of his imaginary modernism.
22. Hall, 'Speaking Editorially', p. 36.
23. Lynda H. Schneekloth and Karen A. Frank, 'Type: Prison or Promise?', *Ordering Space: Types in Architecture and Design* (New York: Van Nostrand Reinhold, 1994), p. 15.
24. For an historical account of the development of the sports environment and its increasing immuration, see Henning Eichberg, 'The Enclosure of the Body: The Historical Relativity of "Health", "Nature" and the Environment of Sport', in John Bale and Chris Philo (eds), *Body Cultures: Essays on Sport, Space and Identity* (London and New York: Routledge, 1998), pp. 47–67.
25. Stow, founder of a model Infant School in Drygate, Glasgow, 1828. Quoted in Thomas Markus, *Buildings and Power: Freedom and Control in the Origins of Modern Building Types* (London and New York: Routledge, 1993), p. 78.
26. Markus, *Buildings and Power*, p. 92.
27. For example, Markus comments that in seventeenth century classrooms boys learned to read, girls did not.
28. Eichberg, 'The Enclosure of the Body', p. 55.
29. Ibid.
30. Ibid., pp. 47–8.
31. For example, Marcel Breuer designed a gym as a complement to a bedroom in his house for Piscator in 1927, and Siegfried Giedion's *Liberated Dwelling* (1929) dedicated more than half of its illustrations to hospitals and sports – in a book on dwellings. See Beatriz Colomina, 'The

Medical Body in Modern Architecture', in Cynthia C. Davidson (ed.), *Anybody* (New York: Anyone Corporation, 1997), p. 230.

32. Anon., 'Competitive design for a gymnasium for Brown University, Providence, R.I.', *The American and Building News*, XXVI, 728 (7 Dec. 1989), p. 256. It was replaced in 1928. See 'Brown University Gymnasium', *American Architect*, 134 (5 Dec. 1928), pp. 761–5. The new gymnasium has lost the billiard tables, bowling alleys, piano and Professor's private rooms, rowing machines, sponge bath areas and the cage for baseball. It did have differentiated offices (general, main, Director's), a ticket office, a lecture room, four differentiated locker and shower areas and rooms for boxing, wrestling and fencing. It had three basketball courts on the main floor with a running track above. Its exterior form was still in the Georgian style.

33. E. F. Guilbert, 'Public School Gymnasiums: Practical Suggestions for the Design and Construction of Apparatus Rooms, Dressing Rooms, Lockers, Showers, etc.', *The American City*, 12 (1915), p. 104. The author comments that his firm had built some 20 gymnasiums in the previous five years and had learned from these experiments.

34. Robert L. Davidson, 'Gymnasium Planning', *Architectural Record*, 69 (Jan. 1931), pp. 63–90.

35. Ibid., p. 66.

36. Ibid., p. 67. Swimming and diving were ranked 8 out of 10, Marching 2 out of 10. Basketball was given a 7.4 out of 10. A total of 30 activities were ranked.

37. Authors were either educators on building committees and hence clients who wrote the commission briefs, architects in the employ of school districts for whom they spoke, or educators involved in physical education. This is evident in the listings found in the Avery Architectural Periodical Index for the period.

38. Harry R. Allen, 'Gymnasiums in Public Schools: Physical Education a Great Factor in Promoting Health, Order, Discipline and Stability of Character', *The American City*, 7, 4 (Oct. 1912), pp. 335–8.

39. Frank G. Lopez, 'Building For Athletics and Recreation', *Architectural Record*, 5 (July 1949), p. 116.

40. Ibid.

41. The 'Guide' was a product of a National Facilities Conference 1946 and published by *The Athletic Institute*, Chicago, 1947. See Lopez, 'Building', p. 121.

42. Letter from G. Kelso of Sharp, Thompson, Berwick & Pratt to the National Recreation Association, 8 Sept. 1947. It mentions letters sent to the Association by Kelso, 15 Aug. 1947 and C.E. Pratt, 19 Aug. 1947. A Letter from Portland Cement Association to C.E. Pratt, 19 Aug. 1947, Box 17, File 9, Special Collections, UBC.

43. Anne Fromer, 'Canada Plans a National Recreation Program', *Saturday Night* (14 Nov. 1942), p. 7.

44. Major Ian Esenhardt quoted in Janet R. Keith, 'How Shall We Honour Them', *Canadian Business*, 18 (Aug. 1945), p. 30.

45. Keith, 'How Shall We Honour Them', p. 32.

46. Ibid.

47. See the photographic archive of Special Collections, UBC.

48. *UBC Calendar* (1924/25).

49. Ibid., (1936/37).

50. Ibid., (1947/48), p. 125.

51. A design or building concept for a War Memorial Gymnasium was first unveiled some time in 1946. In January 1945 when the campaign for a memorial building was first announced, there were three possibilities – a hall of residence, a student union building or a gymnasium. A scale model of the new gymnasium was published as part of Homecoming Week news by the *Vancouver News Herald*, 26 Oct. 1946. A drawing of the model was circulated during the campaign. The building was decidedly more monumental than its 1929 predecessor, although still recalling the collegiate neo-gothic of the campus. It had a regularized arrangement of standardized windows and a more complex façade elevation replete with projecting frontispiece, sculptural flourishes, entry along its long, rather than gable side, and projecting end pavilions; it is much more impressive than its predecessor (Vancouver City Archives). Adorning UBC Homecoming publicity, the image was annotated with a text which enthused 'from here will come the physical education instructors who will help build stronger, healthier citizens'.

52. Pierre Winter, 'Le Corps nouveau', *L'Esprit Nouveau* (15 Feb. 1922). This being published in Le Corbusier's Paris journal makes it especially pertinent to this study.

53. The history of the medical profession's participation in architecture and especially urban production dates at least to the early nineteenth century when doctors began to survey major cities such as London and Paris and began to prescribe sunlight and air. A close alliance between medical opinion and architectural practice had been forged by 1900. Although this took place especially in philanthropic and social housing circles initially, the medical framing of architecture was to be prevalent in the avant-garde as well, as will be discussed later. See Marie-Jeanne Dumont, *Le Logement social à Paris, 1850–1930: Les Habitations à bon marché* (Liège: Mardaga, 1991). Fred Lasserre was similarly involved with urban slum clearance and social housing at Strathcona in the late 1940s and early 1950s and a similar discourse can be found there.

54. Sigfried Giedion, *Mechanization Takes Command: a Contribution to an Anonymous History* (New York: Oxford University Press, 1948), p. v.

55. Ibid., pp. 46, 77.

56. Ibid., pp. 100–2. Giedion speaks about Freud, noting that he 'opened up new access to the structure of the psyche. Inside processes were revealed by sharp analysis' (p. 100). He identifies movement as the source of subconscious pictorial art (p. 109), and that line in movement gives 'insight into the inner most processes of the psyche' (p. 102).

57. Diane Agrest, 'Architecture from Without: Body, Logic and Sex', *Gender Space Architecture: An Interdisciplinary Introduction* (London and New York: Routledge, 2000), p. 359.

58. There are multiple ways in which industry infiltrated the discourse of modern architecture, from Taylorization in general to the Werkbund in particular. On Taylorization see Mary McLeod, 'Architecture or Revolution: Taylorism, Technology, and Social Change', *Art Journal*, 43, 2 (Summer 1983), pp. 132–47.

59. Giedion, *Mechanization*, pp. 653–60.

60. Gary Cross, *A Social History of Leisure Since 1600* (State College, PA: Venture Publishing, 1990). See especially pp. 116, 145.

61. Giedion, *Mechanization*, p. 503.

62. Colomina, 'The Medical Body', pp. 234–5.

63. Ibid., p. 230.

64. See K. Michael Hays, *Modernism and the Posthumanist Subject: The Architecture of Hannes Meyer and Ludwig Hilberseimer* (Cambridge, MA: MIT Press, 1992), p. 17. In *Space, Time and Architecture* (Cambridge MA: Harvard UP, 1974, [Original lectures 1938–39, first publication, 1943], Giedion juxtaposes a photomontage of Rockefeller Center with a speed photograph of a golf stroke. In the caption to the Rockefeller Center he states: 'To obtain a feeling for their interrelations the eye must function as in the high-speed photographs of Edgerton.' In the text he elaborates that the eye 'has to pick up each individual view singly and relate it to all others, combining them into a time sequence' (5th edn, 1967), pp. 852–3.

65. Schwartz, 'Torque', p. 88.

66. Ibid.

67. Giedion, *Space, Time and Architecture*, pp. 13–4.

68. Alberto Perez-Gomez, 'Chora: The Space of Architectural Representation', in Perez-Gomez and Stephen Parcell (eds), *Chora 1: Intervals in the Philosophy of Architecture* (Montreal, PQ: McGill University Press, 1994), p. 26.

69. Ruth Morrow, 'Architectural Assumptions and Environmental Discrimination: The Case for more Inclusive Design in Schools of Architecture', in David Nicol and Simon Pilling (eds), *Changing Architectural Education: Towards a New Professionalism* (London and New York: E. & F.N. Spon, 2000), p. 43.

70. Fred Lasserre joined Tecton's firm in 1936. He is described in a recent history of Berthold Lubetkin as 'draftsman', and as 'a student friend of Peter Moro [a Tecton member] who subsequently moved to Canada'. The author also states that 'all Tecton members, including Lubetkin were enamoured of Le Corbusier and other modernists in Europe. May, Karl Moser, Mart Stam but not Gropius, the Bauhaus – or Mies'. Lasserre is not mentioned as one of the six colleagues in Tecton. In John Allan, *Berthold Lubetkin. Architecture and the Tradition of Progress* (London: RIBA Publications Ltd., 1992), pp. 108–9.

71. Lubetkin built several houses with this combination in the early to mid 1930s when Lasserre was present in the firm. In addition, Priory Green Housing, Finsbury, of 1937–51, included a landscaped area for recreation. See Malcom Reading and Peter Coe, *Lubetkin and Tecton* (London: Triangle Architectural Publishing, 1992), pp. 45–6, 102.

72. C.E. Pratt, 'Contemporary Domestic Architecture in British Columbia', *Journal of the Royal Architectural Institute of Canada*, 24, 6 (June 1947), p. 179.

73. Robin Ward, 'Ned Pratt: An Architect Ahead of His Time', *Vancouver Sun*, 9 March 1996, D7; Miro Cernetig, 'Lives Lived: Ned Pratt, *Globe and Mail*, 4 April 1996, A2; Sean Rossiter, 'Our Most Important Architect', *Vancouver Sun*, 29 Feb. 1996.

74. Rossiter, 'Our Most Important Architect'.

75. The photo of Pratt illustrated Pierre Berton', 'A Native's Return to B.C.', *Maclean's National Magazine*, 7, 10 (10 May 1958), p. 15.

76. Robert Galstar, 'Master of Building Design Dies', *North Shore News*, 8 March 1996, p. 8; Catherine Chard Wisnicki, *Canadian Encyclopedia Online*.

77. C.E. Pratt, 'Architects with Aspirations', *Vancouver Sun*, 1 March 1990.

78. Pratt, 'Contemporary Domestic Architecture', p. 179.

79. Rossiter, 'Our Most Important Architect'.

80. Letter from Lasserre to Findlayson (n.d., July 1946), President's Office Fonds, Special Collections, UBC, Roll No. 242.

81. Unidentified newspaper clipping, 4 Dec. 1947, President's Office Fonds. Special Collections, UBC, Roll No. 242.

82. 'Architecture', Faculty of Applied Science, *UBC Calendar* (1947–48).

83. When Lasserre sought an architectural education in the mid 1930s there were, with the exception of the Bauhaus (founded in 1918), two general options – academies of fine arts or technical schools. Lasserre chose the latter; he received his Bachelor of Architecture from the Technical School, Toronto (1934), and a diploma from the Federal Polytechnic School, Zurich (1936). Letter from Lasserre to MacKenzie, 3 May 1949, President's Office Fonds, Special Collections, UBC, Roll No. 242. He then joined the English firm Tecton, headed by Lubetkin, which was considered 'leftist', to use the terminology of the day. As with most European modernists of the inter-war years, Lasserre's interests ranged from industrial design to community planning. These interests formed the basis of his new curriculum for UBC. He informs us, in his curriculum vitae, that he was the co-author of 'the best-selling book' on *Planned Air Raid Protection*, and that he was co-designer of the 'history-making' MARS Exhibition in London (1938). From this we learned, at least, that he knew the value of publicity!

84. Lasserre requested travel funds to visit Gropius and Hudnut at Harvard, Wurster at MIT and Chermayett at Chicago. Chermayett Chicago Institute of Design was considered 'to a large extent the spiritual parent of our courses here.' He also wished to visit Bland at McGill and Russell at Manitoba.

85. Letter from Lasserre to MacKenzie, 4 April 1952, President's Office Fonds. Special Collections, UBC, Roll No. 242.

86. Letter from H.A. Young (CMHC) to Lasserre (14 March 1947) is in response to Lasserre's request for assistance of CMHC in this. Lasserre's letter is not extant. President's Office Fonds, Special Collections, UBC, Roll No. 242. His models seem to have been ACSA reports and McGill. Lasserre report on Staff Requirements for the Department of Architecture, Sept. 1947, President's Office Fonds. Roll No. 242, Special Collections, UBC.

87. See Kenneth Frampton, *Modern Architecture: A Critical History* (London and New York: Thames & Hudson, 1985), p. 249.

Chapter 7

1. Robin Evans, 'Figures, Doors, Passages', *Translations from Drawing to Building* (Cambridge, MA: MIT Press, 1997), p. 56.

2. Fred Lasserre, 'University of British Columbia Department of Architecture', *Journal of the*

Royal Architectural Institute of Canada (May 1949), p. 150.

3. Siefried Giedion, *Space, Time and Architecture*, quoted in K. Michael Hays, *Modernism and the Posthumanist Subject: The Architecture of Hannes Meyer and Ludwig Hilberseimmer* (Cambridge, MA: MIT Press, 1992), p. 18.

4. There are similarities of course. Both buildings have a large single volume encircled with bleachers that accommodate ancillary services beneath them. Both use clerestory lighting for the main gymnasium and both derive their scale from the dictates of game rules and sport etiquette.

5. *UBC Calendar* (1931–32), p. 38, Special Collections, UBC.

6. Letter from Lasserre to MacKenzie, 22 March 1951, President's Office Fonds, Special Collections, UBC, Roll No. 242.

7. J. Delisse Parker, 'B.C. Builds 'em Better', *The Vancouver Province B.C. Magazine* (3 Jan. 1953), p. 6. See also letter from Sharp, Thompson, Berwick and Pratt to N.A.M. MacKenzie, 15 Sept. 1949, President's Office Fonds, Special Collections, UBC, Roll No. 242.

8. Le Corbusier's superimposition of a scale determined by the golden section and a human figure is seen as a revisiting of the anthropomorphic principles developed by Matila Ghyka in the 1920s. In 1931 Ghyka published a comparison of a golden section-derived scale and the figure of a nude male athlete in *Le Nombre d'Or*. See Dario Matteoni, 'Modulor', in Jacques Lacan (ed.), *Le Corbusier: une encyclopédie* (Paris: Centre Georges Pompidou, 1987), pp. 259–61. Le Corbusier mentions the substitution of the dimensions of a French male body (1.75 m) with that of the body found in 'English detective novels, the good-looking men, such as the policemen, [who] are always six feet tall'. Le Corbusier, *The Modulor: A Harmonious Measure for the Human Scale Universally Applicable to Archtecture and Mechanics* (London: Faber & Faber, 1954), p. 56.

9. AFNOR, the Association Française pour une Normalisation du Bâtiment, was engaged in systematizing construction measures via the imposition of a single modular system. Its metric measurements also meant it was incompatible with products manufactured outside France. See also Matteoni, 'Modulor', p. 260.

10. For a discussion of contemporary sports see Varda Burstyn, 'Spectacle, Commerce, and Bodies: Three Facets of Hypergender in the Sport Nexus', *The Rites of Men: Manhood, Politics, and the Culture of Sport* (Toronto, ON: University of Toronto Press, 1999), pp. 132–62.

11. Luisa Matina Colli, 'Musique', in Lacan (ed.) *Le Corbusier: une encyclopédie*, p. 268. Translation by the author. 'Dalcroze avait été frappé par la découverte que l'essence de toute composition musicale – le rythme – est aussi l'essence du mouvement naturel, depuis le battement du coeur et la respiration jusqu'à la mécanique musculaire du geste; ce dernier est aussi à l'origine de toute création d'espace par les tracés d'orientation qui transforment le chaos en un lieu.'

12. For an enlightening discussion of the demise of the humanist subject and the rise of the post-humanist subject, see Hays, *Modernism*, pp. 4–21.

13. Ibid., pp. 12–13.

14. Ibid., p. 6. Also see Hays' discussion of the conceptualization of subjectivity, pp. 7–8 and 290, n. 3.

15. The Department of National Defence was still in possession of property, some 3.06 acres along Marine Drive, in 1948. See 'Report of Interview between Major A.D. Dare and President MacKenzie' (1948), President's Office Fonds, Special Collections, UBC, Roll No. 432. There was much discussion of this fact throughout 1948. Dean Clement and President MacKenzie were in lengthy negotiations with Major Dare. The phrase 'by way of trespass' is President Klinck's understanding of the military presence; it is used in his 1941 Report and referred to again after the war. Letter from F.E. Brick to President MacKenzie, 1 April 1946, President's Office Fonds, Special Collections, UBC Roll No. 432.

16. Documents relating to the military occupation of the campus can be found in the President's Office Fonds, Special Collections, UBC, Roll Nos 435, 436, 369, 381. The Jericho Station military headquarters continued to influence decisions about the use of University space after the war. This was especially the case with the locating of the President's Residence, which was along this northern militarized zone. Board of Governors Meeting, 29 Nov. 1948. President's Office Fonds, Special Collections, UBC, Roll No. 342.

17. 'Plans for a New Traffic Artery resulting from the Diversion of Marine Drive', n.d. (*c*.1946)

President's Office Fonds, Special Collections, UBC, Roll No. 432. The proposal for the road amendment 'to skirt the gun emplacement' seems to date from about January 1941.

18.   *UBC Calendar* (1941/42), p. 103; (1947–49), pp. 125–7; (1950/51), pp. 116–17; (1952/53), p. 208–13.

19.   In addition to Isadora Duncan and Josphine Baker, there were Martha Graham and Loie Fuller. Most of the images documenting the modern dance movement also show women usually in flowing Grecian-style dresses. Schwartz also lists, in addition to Duncan and Graham, Gertrude Colby, Helen Moller, Ruth St Denis, Mary Wigman, Annie Beck, Clara Brooke, Suzanne Perottet and Jeanne Alleman. Hillel Schwartz, 'Torque: The New Kinaesthetic of the Twentieth Century', in Jonathan Crary and Sanford Kwinter (eds), *Incorporation (Zone 6)* (New York: Urzone, 1992), pp. 72–5.

20.   Albert Jeanneret, 'La Rythmique', *L'Esprit Nouveau*, 2 (Nov. 1920), p. 230, reprinted in Stanilaus von Moos (ed.), *L'Esprit Nouveau: Le Corbusier und die Industrie 1920–1925* (Zurich and Berlin: Museum für Gestaltung and Wilhelm Ernst, 1987), p. 10. Translation by the author. '... le rythme est à la base des arts comme de la vie ... Les problèmes résolus de la mécanique font désire pour cette machine rhythmée qu'est le corps humain, ou plutôt pour cette harmonisation à établir entre le corps et l'esprit, la même possibilité de précision.'

21.   Jeanneret wrote an article about Jaques-Dalcroze for *L'Esprit Nouveau* (7 April 1921). See Colli, 'Musique', p. 270.

22.   Le Corbusier published *L'Esprit Nouveau* jointly with Amédée Ozenfant and briefly with André Dermée between 1920 and 1925. Le Corbusier appeared under several names, including Jeanneret-Gris and Jeanneret-Saugnier.

23.   Caroline Constant, 'E.1027: The Non-heoric Modernism of Eileen Gray', *Journal of the Society of Architectural Historians*, 53, 3 (Sept. 1994), pp. 265–79, and *Eileen Gray: An Architecture for all the Senses* (Tübingen: Ernst J. Wasmuth, 1996).

24.   'Idea Building' is a notion taken from Leoni Battista Alberti, the 'father' of the modern architectural profession with his treatise, *de re aedificatoria* (*c.*1485). His aim had been to elevate the architect above the mechanical arts and to associate him with rhetoric, mathematics and the other liberal arts. He also wrote a text on the family, which assigned (ideally) women to sequestered interior spaces and men to the streets.

25.   Mark Wigley, 'Untitled: The Housing of Gender', *Sexuality and Space* (New York: Princeton University Press, 1992), pp. 327–89.

26.   The term 'masculine territory' comes from Leonore Davidoff, 'Old Husbands' Tales: Public and Private in Feminist History', *Worlds Between: Historical Perspectives on Gender and Class* (Cambridge: Polity Press, 1995).

27.   Katerina Reudi Ray, 'Bauhaus Hausfrau: Gender Formation in Design Education', *Journal of Architectural Education* (Nov. 2001), pp. 73–80.

28.   Ibid., pp. 73–80.

29.   Ibid., p. 78.

30.   Catherine M. Chard, 'What is an Architect?' *Journal of the Royal Architectural Institute of Canada*, 19, 2 (Feb. 1942), p. 33.

31.   Curriculum Vitae of Catherine Chard Wisnicki, The University of British Columbia, dated 18 October 1977, President's Office, University of British Columbia.

32.   She began her career at UBC as a part-time lecture in 1963, became a full-time lecturer in 1966 and Assistant Professor in 1969 she was granted tenure in 1973. Curriculum Vitae of Catherine Chard Wisnicki, 1977.

33.   Curriculum Vitae of Catherine Chard Wisnicki, 1977.

34.   In the publication of the W.S. Brooks House, Sharp, Thompson, Berwick & Pratt were listed as the Architects, Mrs P. Wisnicki was listed as a Consulting Engineer. Anon., 'Cliff house whose interlocked elements exploit a magnificent site is Canadian contribution to organic architecture', *Architectural Forum*, 89 (1948), pp. 96–100.

35.   Women in Architecture, *Constructing Careers, Profiles of Five Early Women Architects in British Columbia* (Vancouver, BC: Women Architecture Exhibits Committee, 1996), pp. 43–9. The Women in Architecture Exhibition notes her as having 'assisted in the design of the War Memorial Gymnasium', while Annmarie Adams, in her albeit necessarily short biography in *The Canadian Encyclopaedia Online*, highlights only her residential design with Porter and Pratt.

36. Brian Hemmingway, 'Symposium: The Changing Nature of Architectural Practice in Post-War Vancouver', *Trace, 5* (Fall 2001), p. 7.
37. Telephone conversation, author (Vancouver) with Catherine Chard Wisnicki (Naramata) 14 Nov. 2001. The term 'employee' was Wisnicki's.
38. Curriculum Vitae of Catherine Chard Wisnicki, 1977.
39. Telephone conversation between author and Wisnicki (14 Nov. 2001).
40. Chard, 'What is an Architect?' p. 33.

Chapter 8

1. Elliott Gorn, 'Professing History: Distinguishing Between Memory and the Past', *Chronicle of Higher Education*, 46, 34 (28 april, 2000).
2. Walter Benjamin, 'Theses on the Philosophy of History [1940]', in Hannah Arendt (ed.), *Illuminations* (New York: Schoken Books, 1968), p. 257.
3. Thomas A. Markus, *Buildings and Power* (London and New York: Routledge, 1993), p. 5. We can make a useful analogy with the design of health care spaces. They can best be understood, says Prior, 'in relation to the discursive practices which are disclosed in their interiors. The architecture of the hospital is therefore inextricably bound up with the forms of medical theorizing and medical practice which was operant at the hour of their construction … all subsequent modifications to hospital design can be seen as a product of alterations in medical discourse'. L. Prior, 'The Architecture of the Hospital', *British Journal of Sociology*, 39 (1988), p. 110.
4. Spaces may thus offer cues to actors as to how they might engage with the environment and with others. Nick J. Fox, 'Space, Sterility and Surgery: Circuits of Hygiene in the Operating Theatre', *Social Science Medicine*, 45, 5 (1997), pp. 649–57. See also, Edward Relph, *Place and Placelessness* (London: Pion, 1976), p. 6.
5. The staff lounge was completed in 1984.
6. Megan Thomas, 'UBC's Outdoor Pool Flushed. Commercial Development Considered on University Boulevard', *The Ubyssey*, 26 Nov. 2002, p. 1.
7. In 1991, funding was finally provided by the administration to renovate and upgrade the original short-changed women's changing rooms in the War Memorial Gym. Memorandum from Michael Kelly to Vice-President of Student and Academic Services re project No.6768, 4 Dec. 1991.
8. The Department of Athletics and Sport Services was formed in 1993 with Bob Philip as Director.
9. The Recreation programme begun by Bob Osborne was closed down during a budget crisis in the early 1980s by the Provost, who felt that it was not central to the University's academic mission.
10. This despite the fact that students contributed $5 million toward the facility in their athletic fees.
11. The Director, Bob Osborne, retired in 1978 and was replaced by Dr Bob Morford, who held the position until 1995.
12. Some of the older physical education faculty saw this as the death knell of a broad-based physical education programme and left or took early retirement in protest.
13. Pressures for change have also hit faculties of Education and those teaching teacher education courses fight for survival in the press to focus upon social issues, technological advances and organizational rearrangements.
14. Interview of Bob Osborne by Edmund Arthur Hunt, 'A History of Physical Education in the Public Schools of British Columbia from 1918 to 1967' (MA thesis, University of Washington, 1967), p. 186. Certainly things had changed for the better from the days of Chant's Royal Commission on Education in 1958, when local groups such as the Duncan Dogwoods Chapter of the Imperial Order of the Daughters of the Empire recommended the abolition of physical education and its teachers and a return to daily drill focused on posture-forming and conditioning exercises. Brief 261 to Chant Commission. See Hunt, 'A History of Physical Education', p. 150.

15. Robert F. Osborne, 'Principles and Objectives', in Maurice Van Vliet (ed.), *Physical Education in Canada* (Scarborough, ON: Prentice-Hall of Canada, 1965), p. 46.

16. During the late 1950s, the Kraus Weber tests of youth physical fitness caused a public uproar in the United States by drawing attention to the lack of fitness of American youth. The same anxieties were felt in Canada and brought to public attention by a speech from the Duke of Edinburgh to the Canadian Medical Association in 1959. His rebuke to Canadians for their complacency about lack of fitness among youth was one of a series of concerns leading to the passage of Bill C-131, An Act to Encourage Fitness and Amateur Sport. William A.R. Orban, 'The Fitness Movement', in Van Vliet (ed.), *Physical Education in Canada*, pp. 244–5.

17. Luther Halsey Gulick, 'Physical Education, A New Profession', Proceedings of the 5th Annual Meeting of the American Association for the Advancement of Physical Education (Ithaca, NY: Andrus and Church, 1990), pp. 59–66.

18. Franklin M. Henry, 'Physical Education: An Academic Discipline', *Journal of Health, Physical Education and Recreation*, 35, 7 (1964), pp. 32–3, 69. Henry, and subsequently other physical educators, were responding to an attack on the very existence of physical education in higher education levelled by James Conant.

19. James B. Conant, *The American High School Today* (New York: McGraw Hill, 1959), p. 201.

20. Astute commentators pointed out that school physical education had failed in both its hygienic and its educational goals by virtue of its sustained emphasis on broad social goals of games and play. In his book, *Beyond the Boundaries of Physical Education* (London: Falmer Press, 2000), Anthony Laker puts the cause of the crisis of school physical education down to the fact that 'physical educators have for too long clung to a now outmoded traditional role as expert teachers of sports skills, while the emerging need in troubled times is for physical education to contribute to the complete development of the individual. In fact, the jury remains out on whether physical education has at any point in the last 150 years actually managed to assist the social and moral development of young people.'

21. Hal A. Lawson, 'Specialization and Fragmentation among Faculty as Endemic Features of Academic Life', *Quest*, 43, 2 (1991), pp. 280–93, 282.

22. This was because the profession of physical education tried to establish its legitimacy by placing its discourse under the sign of science. Many departments of physical education thus failed to maintain a common enterprise in which both the scientific study of physical activity and its logical professional connections would stay together. At the University of Queensland, for example, the Department of Movement Science voted to move away from the Faculty of Education to the Faculty of Science in 1988 in order to emphasize applied sport science. Many other departments in North America and Australia, now dominated by the natural sciences, found their homes in colleges of Education to be unworkable. At the same time, those who moved to faculties or colleges of Applied Science rarely prospered as a group in competition with more established scientific disciplines and sub-disciplines. Jim McKay, Jennifer M. Gore and David Kirk, 'Beyond the Limits of Technocratic Physical Education', *Quest*, 42, 1 (1990), pp. 52–76.

23. Andrew Abbott in *Chaos of Disciplines* (Chicago, IL: University of Chicago Press, 2001), underscores the strength of disciplinary practice, but points out how easily the system of disciplines at North American universities survive the destruction of one or several of its elements. This is precisely the case with many kinesiology departments which have disappeared from the disciplinary scene in the past two decades.

24. Abbott, *Chaos of Disciplines*, p. 130.

25. Physical education, like medicine, has been pressed by society's needs to give birth to a scientific discipline, and both professions have flourished or floundered based in large part on their ability to satisfy market forces derived from changing conceptions of health and the body. Patricia Vertinsky, 'Science, Social Science and the Hunger for Wonders in Physical Education', *The Academy Papers, New Possibilities, New Paradigms*, American Academy of Physical Education Papers, No. 24 (Champaign, IL: Human Kinetics, 1990), pp. 70–88. See also Roberta J. Park, 'On Tilting at Windmills while Facing Armageddon', *Quest*, 43 (1991), pp. 247–59.

26. Quarrels raged over discipline versus profession, basic versus applied, quantitative versus qualitative, theory versus practice, reductionism versus chaos, physical education versus

kinesiology. James E. Lidstone and Ronald S Feingold, 'The Case for Integration and Collaboration, Reprise', *Quest*, 43, 3 (1991), pp. 241–56. S.J. Hoffman, 'Specialization +Fragmentation = Extermination', *Journal of Physical Education, Recreation and Dance*, 56, 6 (1985), pp. 19–22.

27. The body, as an axis of cohesion, never became the central principle of the discipline which slowly lost legitimate authority over its various clientele as their knowledge became commodified by other professions and the marketplace.

28. Donald T. Campbell, 'Ethnocentrism of Disciplines and the Fish Scale Model of Omniscience', in M. Sherif and C. Sherif (eds), *Interdisciplinary Relationships in the Social Sciences* (Chicago, IL: Aldine, 1969), pp. 323–48.

29. Burton R. Clark, *The Academic Life: Small Worlds, Different Worlds* (Princeton, NJ: Carnegie Foundation for the Advancement of Teaching and Princeton University Press, 1987).

30. Where the highest status was accorded to those faculties in the 'hard sciences'.

31. Hal A. Lawson, 'Occupational Socialization, Cultural Studies and the Physical Education Curriculum', *Journal of Teaching in Physical Education*, 7, 4 (1988), pp. 265–88. The dangers of this sport science approach have been described by John Hoberman: 'This sports science approach does not physically hybridize humans and machines ... instead sports science treats the human organism as though it were a machine, or as though it ought to be a machine. This technologized human organism comprises both mind and body, for which there are distinct sets of strategies. The implicit demand of these strategies ... is a streamlined and decomplexified image of the human being.' John J. Hoberman, 'Sport and the Technological View of Man', in W. Morgan and K. Meier (eds), *Philosophic Inquiry in Sport* (Champaign, IL: Human Kinetics, 1988), p. 325 .

32. Linda L Bain, 'Further Reactions to Newell: Knowledge as Contested Domain', *Quest*, 43, 2 (1991), pp. 214–17.

33. David J. Whitson and Donald Macintosh, 'The Scientization of Physical Education Discourses of Performance', *Quest*, 42, 1 (1990), p. 42.

34. Ibid., p. 45.

35. R. Rorty, *Philosophy and the Mirror of Nature* (Princeton, NJ: Princeton University Press, 1979), p. 10.

36. Franklin M. Henry, 'The Academic Discipline of Physical Education', *Quest*, 29, 2 (1978), p. 2.

37. Hoffman, 'Specialization', p. 20.

38. Richard A. Swanson and John D. Massengale, 'Exercise and Sport Science in 20th Century America', in J.D. Massengale and R.A. Swanson (eds), *The History of Exercise and Sport Science* (Champaign, IL: Human Kinetics, 1997), p. 11.

39. At the last count, out of 17 faculty members only two women occupied the gym's office space.

40. Interview with female faculty member in Human Kinetics (Vancouver, Jan. 2001).

41. According to a letter from Choukalos, Woodburn, Mckenzie, Maranda Ltd, to Plant Operations in UBC, 9 Sept. 1987, 'the spring on the floor is due to the resilience of the permacushion sleepers and pads that are located under the floor system and on top of the timber joists'.

42. Varda Burstyn, *The Rites of Men: Manhood, Politics and the Culture of Sport* (Toronto: University of Toronto Press, 1999), p. 266.

43. Jack Drover, 'Big Athletic Awards are Inconsistent with University Goals', *University Affairs* (March 2002), p. 41.

44. Canadian Intercollegiate Athletic Union Men's Basketball rules are a combination of International FIBA rules and NCAA rules.

45. In the 'Tree of Architecture', which served as the frontispiece to the 1901 edition of Fletcher's book, *A History of Architecture and the Comparative Method*, the western tradition, from the Parthenon to the classicized skyscraper forms the upright trunk of the tree; other traditions such as Japanese, 'Saracenic' and Indian are considered lesser branches. This hierarchy is elaborated in the text which, for example, indicates that there is little of interest in Chinese, Indian or Japanese architecture because they were primarily concerned with decoration rather than structure and the innovation of forms based on the logic of new materials.

46. This paradigm, which denigrated ornament, began to shift by the late 1950s. It is in a small way evident in campus buildings such as the Koerner Graduate Building and the Freddy Wood Theatre where wood detailing or screens were added as a reference to the importance of wood

in the local economy and to local architectural practice.

47. Lefebvre, *The Production of Space* (Oxford: Oxford University Press, 1991), p. 221.

48. Neil Leach (ed.), 'Henri Lefebvre', *Rethinking Architecture: A Reader in Cultural Theory* (London: Routledge, 1977), p. 138.

49. Lefebvre, *The Production of Space*, p. 223.

50. Greg Lynn, 'From Body to Blob', in Cynthia Davidson (ed.), *Anybody* (New York: Anyone Corporation, 1977), pp. 161–73.

51. Lynn, 'From Body to Blob', p. 163. It should be noted that architectural theorists, such as Lynn, also argue that this new body can only be tracked via advanced technologies of organization and more complex systems of relation, and hence the ever greater mediation and abstraction of representations of space that Lefebvre might abhor.

52. Donna Haraway, *Simians, Cyborgs and Women: The Reinvention of Nature* (New York: Routledge, 1991).

53. In 1977, Kent Bloomer and Charles Moore could still assert that most architects continued to privilege the visual – seeing – as the primary experiential relationship with architecture. *Body, Memory, and Architecture* (New Haven, CT: Yale University Press, 1977).

54. Maire Eithne O'Neill, 'Corporeal Experience: A Haptic Way of Knowing', *Journal of Architecture Education*, 55, 1 (Sept. 2001), p. 4.

55. The UBC Student Recreation Centre was built by Henriques & Partners with IBI Group and opened in 1995. See a discussion of the building in 'Recreation Centre: Decorated Shed', *The Canadian Architecture*, 42, 4 (April 1996), p. 21.

56. Richard Henriques (of Henriques and Partners, architect of the Osbourne Centre) has lectured and written about the issues of architecture and memory.

57. 'Canadian Campus', *The Ubyssey*, 4 Dec. 1945, p. 1.

58. A.M. Peers, 'Dear Sir', *The Ubyssey*, 12 Nov. 1946, p. 2; Effie Smallwood, 'Luxury Drive', *The Ubyssey*, 21 Nov. 1946, p. 2; John Randall, 'Noisy Memorial', *The Ubyssey*, 26 Nov. 1946, p. 5; Livingstone to Haar, 13 June 1950, p. 3, Box 66, Folder 16, Alma Mater Society (AMS) Fonds, UBC Archives.

59. James E. Young, *At Memory's Edge* (New Haven, CT, and London: Yale University Press, 2000), p. 94.

60. Svetlana Bohn, *The Future of Nostalgia* (New York: Basic Books, 2000).

Select Bibliography

Abramson, D., 'Make History, Not Memory', *Harvard Design Magazine* (Fall, 1999), pp. 78–83.

Adams, M.L., *The Trouble With Normal: Postwar Youth and the Making of Heterosexuality* (Toronto, ON: University of Toronto Press, 1997).

Ainsley, R. (ed.), *New Frontiers of Space, Bodies and Gender* (London and New York: Routledge, 1998).

Alexander, J.M. and Mohanty, C., 'Introduction: Genealogies, Legacies, Movements', in J.M. Alexander and C. Mohanty (eds), *Feminist Genealogies, Colonial Legacies, Democratic Futures* (New York: Routledge, 1997).

Allen, M.R., 'The Development of Beauty in College Women through Healthy Physical Education', archived in M.R. Allen Papers, Box 160–4, Folder 4 (Maryland-Sprinarm Research Center, Howard University, Washington, DC, 1938) .

Argyle, M., *The Social Psychology of Leisure* (New York: Penguin, 1996).

Armstrong, P., 'The Welfare State As History', in R. Blake et al. (eds), *The Welfare State in Canada: Past, Present, and Future* (Toronto, ON: Irwin Publishing, 1997), pp. 52–73.

Armstrong, T. (ed.), *American Bodies: Cultural Histories of the Physique* (New York: New York University Press, 1996).

Baerwald, T.J., 'Basketball', in K. Raitz (ed.), *The Theatre of Sport* (Baltimore, MD: Johns Hopkins University Press, 1995), pp. 168–207.

Bailey, B., *From Front Porch to Back Seat: Courtship in Twentieth Century America* (Baltimore, MD, and London: Johns Hopkins University Press, 1988).

Bale, J., *Landscapes of Modern Sport* (Leicester: Leicester University Press, 1994).

Bale, J. and Philo, C. (eds), *Body Cultures: Essays on Sport, Space and Identity – Henning Eichberg* (London and New York: Routledge, 1997).

Banet-Weiser, S., 'Hoop Dreams: Professional Basketball and the Politics of Race and Gender', *Journal of Sport and Social Issues*, 23, 4 (Nov. 1999), pp. 403–20.

Banet-Weiser, S., *The Most Beautiful Girl in the World: Beauty Pageants and National Identity* (Berkeley, CA: University of California Press, 1999).

Becker, J., 'Culture Note: Ten-Pins Anybody?' *MacLean's Magazine*, 74 (1961), p. 74.

Bell, F., 'What's Behind this Bowling Business', *Canadian Business*, 25 (Feb. 1952), pp. 24–6, 102–3.

Berenson, A.S. (ed.), *Spalding's Official Basketball Guide for Women* (New York: American Sports Publishing Company, 1912).

Bernard, E., 'A University at War: Japanese Canadians at UBC during WW2', *B.C. Studies*, 35 (Aug. 1977), pp. 36–55.

Betsky, A., *Building Sex. Men, Women, Architecture and the Construction of Sexuality* (New York: William Morrow, 1995).

Beyer, C., 'A Break for Pinboys', *Children* (Sept. 1954), pp. 185–8.

Birney, E., *Record of Service in the Second World War* (The University of British Columbia, 1955.)

Blake, A., *The Body Language: The Meaning of Modern Sport* (London: Lawrence and Wishart, 1996).

Blake, C.N., 'The Usable Past, the Comfortable Past, and the Civic Past: Memory in Contemporary America', *Cultural Anthropology*, 14, 3 (1999), pp. 423–35.

Bloomer, K.C. and Moore, C.W., *Body, Memory and Architecture* (New Haven, CT, and London: Yale University Press, 1977).

Booth, D. and Tatz, C., 'Reply to the Reviewers of One-Eyed', *Sporting Traditions*, 17, 11 (Nov. 2000), pp. 125–8.

Borg, A., *War Memorials from Antiquity to the Present* (London: Leo Cooper, 1991).

Boys, J., 'Beyond Maps and Metaphors: Rethinking the Relationships between Architecture and Gender', in R. Ainsley (ed.), *New Frontiers of Space, Bodies and Gender (London and New York: Routledge, 1998)*, pp. 203–17.

Boys, J., 'Women and Public Space', in Matrix Books Group (eds), *Making Space: Women and the Man-Made Environment* (London: Pluto, 1984), pp. 37–55.

Brand, D., '"We Weren't Allowed to Go into Factory Work Until Hitler Started the War": The 1920s to the 1940s', in P. Bristow et al. (eds), *We're Rooted Here and They Can't Pull Us Up: African Canadian Women's History* (Toronto, ON: University of Toronto Press, 1994), pp. 171–92.

Brightbill, C.K. and Meyer, H., *Recreation: Texts and Readings* (New York: Prentice-Hall, 1953).

Broom, E., *Leisure Services in British Columbia* (Victoria, BC: Ministry of Travel Industry, 1974).

Browne, L., *Girls of Summer: In Their Own League* (Toronto, ON: Harper Collins, 1992).

Burstyn, V., *The Rites of Men: Manhood, Politics, and the Culture of Sport* (Toronto, ON: University of Toronto Press, 1999).

Butler, J., *Bodies That Matter: On the Discursive Limits of 'Sex'* (New York: Routledge, 1993).

Cahn, S., *Coming On Strong: Gender and Sexuality in Twentieth Century Women's Sport* (New York: The Free Press, 1994).

Callahan, C., 'Down the Alley', *Journal of Health and Physical Education*, 11 (Feb. 1940), pp. 90–2.

Carranza, L.E., 'Le Corbusier and the Problems of Representation', *Journal of Architectural Education*, 48, 2 (1994), pp. 70–81.

Caudwell, J., 'Women's Football in the United Kingdom: Theorizing Gender and Unpacking the Butch Lesbian Image', *Journal of Sport and Social Issues*, 23, 4 (Nov. 1999), pp. 390–402.

Charlesworth, J. (ed.), *Leisure in America: Blessing or Curse?* (Philadelphia, PA: American Academy of Political and Social Science, 1964).

Chepko, S., 'The Domestication of Basketball', in Hult and Trekell, *A Century of Women's Basketball: From Frailty to Final Fair* (Reston, VA: National Association for Girls and Women in Sport, AAPHERD, 1991) pp. 109–24.

Clugston, K., 'When Pin-Setters are Children', *Survey*, 81 (1945), pp. 9–10.

Coalter, F. (ed.), *Freedom and Constraint: The Paradoxes of Leisure* (New York: Routledge, 1989).

Colomina, B. (ed.), *Sexuality and Space* (Princeton, NJ: Princeton University Press, 1992).

Colomina, B., 'The Split Wall: Domestic Voyeurism', in B. Colomina (ed.), *Sexuality and Space* (Princeton, N.J: Princeton University Press, 1992), pp. 73–130.

Colomina, B., *Privacy and Publicity: Modern Architecture as Mass Media* (Cambridge, MA: MIT Press, 1994).

Colomina, B., 'Battle Line E1027', in J. Borden, J. Kerr, A. Pivaro and J. Readell (eds), *Strangely Familiar: Narratives of Architecture in the City* (London: Routledge,1996).

Connor, R., *The Sky Pilot in No Man's Land* (New York: George H. Doran, 1919).

Cosco, V., '"Obviously Then I'm Not Homosexual": Lesbian Identities, Discretion, and Communities' (unpublished MA Thesis, Department of History, University of British Columbia, 1996).

Crafter, J., 'Varsity Girls Off to PNW Grass Hockey Tourney', *The Ubyssey*, 34, 18 (Nov. 1951), pp. 2, 4.

Crafter, J., 'Women's Sport', *The Ubyssey*, 34, 12 (19 Oct. 1951), p. 4.

Crafter, J., 'Girls' Hoop Team Plays Roamers in Gym Today', *The Ubyssey*, 34, 54 (29 Feb. 1952), p. 4.

Crosby, T., *The Necessary Monument* (London: Studio Vista, 1970).

Curtis, W., *Le Corbusier: Ideas and Forms* (London: Phaidon Press, 1986).

Davis, L., 'A Postmodern Paradox? Cheerleaders at Women's Sporting

Events', in S. Birrell and C. Cole (eds), *Women, Sport and Culture* (Champaign, IL: Human Kinetics, 1994), pp. 149–58.

Davis, L., *The Swimsuit Issue and Sport: Hegemonic Masculinity in Sports Illustrated* (Albany, NY: State University of New York Press, 1997).

De Certeau, M., *The Practices of Everyday Life* (trans. S. Randall), (Berkeley, CA: University of California Press, 1984).

Dean, P., '"Dear Sisters" and "Hated Rivals": Athletics and Gender at Two New South Women's Colleges, 1893–1920', *Journal of Sport History*, 24, 3 (Fall 1997), pp. 341–57.

Dewar, J., 'The Edmonton Grads: The Team and its Social Significance from 1915–1940', in R. Howell (ed.), *Her Story in Sport: A Historical Anthology of Women in Sports* (New York Leisure Press, 1982), pp. 541–47.

Dovey, K., 'Putting Geometry in its Place: Toward a Phenomonology of the Design Process', in D. Seaman (ed.), *Dwelling, Seeing and Designing* (New York: Suny Press, 1993), pp. 247–70.

Dulles, F.R., *America Learns to Play* (New York: Appleton-Century, 1940).

Dunn, K.T., 'Why the Ladies Love to Bowl', *Today's Health*, 39 (March 1961), pp. 36–9, 72–3.

Durning, L. and Wrigley, R. (eds), *Gender and Architecture* (Chichester: Wiley, 2000).

Dutton, K.R., *The Perfectible Body: The Western Ideal of Physical Development* (London: Cassell, 1995).

Eaton, J.D., 'Dr A.S. Lamb: His Influence on Canadian Sport', *Proceedings of the 1st Canadian Symposium on the History of Sport and Physical Education* (Edmonton: University of Edmonton, Alberta, May 1970), pp. 417–30.

Eckert, H., 'Women and Competitive Basketball', *Journal of CAHPER*, 26, 6 (1960), pp. 5–8.

Eichberg, H., 'The Enclosure of the Body – On the Historical Relativity of "Health", "Nature" and the Environment of Sport', *Journal of Contemporary History*, 21 (1986), pp. 99–121.

Eichberg, H., 'Race-track and Labyrinth: The Space of Physical Culture in Berlin', *Journal of Sport History*, 17, 2 (1990), pp. 245–60.

Eichberg, H., 'New Spatial Configurations of Sport? Experiences from Danish Alternative Planning', *International Revue for Sociology of Sport*, 28, 2/3 (1993), pp. 245–63.

Eichberg, H., 'New Spatial Configurations of Sport', in J. Bale and C. Philo (eds), *Body Cultures: Essays on Sport, Space and Identity – Henning Eichberg* (London and New York: Routledge, 1997), pp. 68–83

Falcaro, J. and Goodman, M., *Bowling for All* (New York: Ronald Press, 1957).

Ferguson, B., *Who's Who in Canadian Sport*, 2nd edn (Toronto, ON: Summerhill Press, 1985).

Fidler, V., 'Something on Bowling', *The Canadian Banker*, 69 (Autumn 1962), pp. 103–10.

Filey, M., *Toronto Sketches: 'The Way We Were'* (Toronto, ON: Dundurn Press, 1992).

Florio, A.E., 'Bowling as Part of the Curriculum', *Journal of Health and Physical Education*, 11 (April 1940), pp. 232–4.

Fosburg, C., 'Hints on Bowling Organization', *Journal of Health and Physical Education*, 18 (Feb. 1947), pp. 96–7.

Fotheringham, A., 'Freshettes, Femmes, and Rhododendrons', *The Ubyssey*, 36, 35 (2 Feb. 1954), p. 2.

Foucault, M., *Discipline and Punish* (New York: Vintage Press, 1979).

Foucault, M., *The History of Sexuality*, Vol. 1, (New York: Vintage Books, 1980).

Foucault, M., 'Of Other Spaces' (trans. J. Miskowiee), *Diacritus*, 16 (1986), pp. 22–7.

Frymer, A.W., *Basketball for Women* (New York: A.S. Barnes, 1930).

Furlong, W.B., 'Big Strike – From "Alley" to "Supermarket"', *The New York Times Magazine* (29 Nov. 1959), pp. 42, 47–8, 50.

Geertz, C., *The Interpretation of Cultures* (New York: Basic Books, 1973).

Gendel, E., 'Women and the Medical Aspects of Sport', *Journal of School Health*, 37 (1967), pp. 422–31.

Gillis, J.R., 'Memory and Identity: The History of a Relationship', Introduction to J.R Gillis (ed.), *Commemorations: The Politics of National Identity* (Princeton, NJ: Princeton University Press, 1995), pp. 1–24.

Grant, R., 'The Cold War and the Feminine Mystique', in P.R. Beckman and F. D'Amico (eds), *Women, Gender, and World Politics: Perspectives, Policies, and Prospects* (London: Bergin and Garvey, 1994), pp. 119–29.

Griffin, P., *Strong Women, Deep Closets: Lesbians and Homophobia in Sport* (Champaign, IL: Human Kinetics, 1998).

Grosz, E., *Space, Time and Perversion* (London and New York: Routledge, 1995.)

Grover, K. (ed.), *Hard at Play: Leisure in America, 1840–1940* (Amherst, MA: University of Massachusetts Press, 1992).

Gurney, H., *Girls' Sports. A Century of Progress in Ontario High Schools* (Don Mills, ON: OFSAA Publication, 1979).

Hall, M.A., 'Creators of the Lost and Perfect Game? Gender, History and Canadian Sport', in P. White and K. Young (eds), *Sport and Gender in Canada* (Oxford: Oxford University Press, 1999), pp. 5–23.

Hall, M.A., *The Girl and the Game. A History of Women's Sport in Canada* (Peterborough, ON: The Broadview Press, 2002).

Hammonds, E., 'Towards a Genealogy of Black Female Sexuality: The Problematic of Silence', in M.J. Alexander and C. Mohanty (eds), *Feminist Genealogies, Colonial Legacies, and Democratic Futures*

(New York: Routledge, 1997), pp. 170–82.

Hartwig, M.D. (ed.), *Official Basketball and Officials Rating Guide for Women and Girls* (New York: A.S. Barnes, 1947).

Harvey, D., *The Condition of Postmodernity* (Oxford: Blackwell, 1990).

Harvey, D., 'Cosmopolitanism and the Banality of Geographical Evils', *Public Culture*, 12, 2 (2000), pp. 529–64.

Harvey, D., *Spaces of Hope* (Berkeley, CA: University of California Press, 2000).

Hayden, D., *The Power of Place. Urban Landscapes as Public History* (Cambridge, MA: MIT Press, 1995).

Hayden, J.A. (ed.), *William Wordsworth, Selected Prose* (Harmondsworth: Penguin, 1988).

Healey, J.F., 'An Exploration of the Relationships between Memory and Sport', *Sociology of Sport Journal*, 8, 3 (1991), pp. 213–27.

Higdon, H., 'Five-Pin Bowling: The Canadian Version', *Popular Mechanics* (May, 1960), pp. 106–7.

Horsman, N., 'The Good Sports. Do They Have a Sporting Chance?' *UBC Reports*, (5 Nov. 1975), p. 129.

How, D., 'Blonde on Blades', *MacLean's* (15 Feb. 1947), pp.45–6.

Howell, R. (ed.), *Her Story in Sport: A Historical Anthology of Women in Sports* (New York: Leisure Press, 1982).

Hult, J. S. and Trekell, M., *A Century of Women's Basketball. From Frailty to Final Four* (Reston, VA: National Association for Girls and Women in Sport, AAPHERD, 1991).

Hunt, E.A., 'A History of Physical Education in the Public Schools of B.C.' (MA thesis, University of Washington, 1967).

Hurley, A., *Diners, Bowling Alleys and Trailer Parks: Chasing the American Dream in Postwar Consumer Culture* (New York: Basic Books, 2001).

Iacovetta, F., 'Recipes for Democracy? Gender, Family, and Making Female Citizens in Cold War Canada', *Canadian Woman Studies Journal*, 20, 2 (Summer 2000), pp. 12–21.

Imrie, R., 'The Body, Disability and Le Corbusier's Conception of the Radiant Environment', in R. Butler and H. Parr (eds), *Mind and Body Spaces: Geographies of Illness, Impairment and Disability* (New York: Routledge, 1999), pp. 25–45.

Jacobs, J., *The Death and Life of Great American Cities* (New York: Vintage Books, 1992).

Jencks, C., *Le Corbusier and the Tragic View of Architecture* (London: Penguin, 1987).

Jenger, J., *Le Corbusier: Architect, Painter, Poet* (New York: Harry N. Abrams, 1996).

Johannes, T. and Bull, C.N. (eds), *Sociology of Leisure* (Beverly Hills, CA: Sage, 1971).

Jordanova, L., *History in Practice* (New York: Oxford University Press, 2000).

Kane, M.J. and Lenskyj, H., 'Media Treatment of Female Athletes: Issues of Gender and Sexualities', in L.A. Wenner (ed.), *Media Sport* (New York: Routledge, 1998), pp. 186–201.

Kaplan, M., *Leisure in America: A Social Inquiry* (New York: Wiley, 1960).

Kearns, S., 'Female Hockey Players Seek 200 Blind Dates – Pacific Northwest Grass Hockey Finals Hosts Thirteen Entrants', *The Ubyssey*, 33, 17 (2 Nov. 1950), p. 4.

Kearns, S., 'Women's Sport', *The Ubyssey*, 33, 65 (29 March 1951), p. 8.

Keyes, M., 'Women and Sport', in D. Morrow, M. Keyes, W. Simpson, F. Cosentino and R. Lappage (eds), *A Concise History of Sport in Canada* (Toronto: Oxford University Press, 1989), pp. 230–55.

Keyes, M.E., 'The Administration of the Canadian Women's Intercollegiate Athletics Union', *CAHPER Journal*, 40, 6 (1974), pp. 21–3, 32–3.

Kidd, B., *The Struggle for Canadian Sport* (Toronto, ON: University of Toronto Press, 1996).

King, A., *Memorials of the Great War in Britain. The Symbolism and Politics of Remembrance* (Berg: Oxford, 1998).

King, S., 'Consuming Compassion: AIDS, Figure Skating, and Canadian Identity', *Journal of Sport and Social Issues*, 24, 2 (2000), pp.148–75.

Kinsman, G., 'Constructing Gay Men and Lesbians as National Security Risks', in G. Kinsman et al. (eds), *Whose National Security? Canadian State Surveillance and the Creation of Enemies* (Toronto, ON: Between the Lines, 2000), pp. 143–53.

Kleindienst, V. and Weston, A., *Intramural and Recreation Programs for Schools and Colleges* (New York: Appleton-Century-Crofts, 1964).

Kukla, E., 'Suburban Parties: The Real History of Lesbian Butch and Femme', *Xtra! West* (21 Sept. 2000), p. 12.

Kwint, M., Breward, C. and Aynsley, J. (eds), *Material Memories* (New York: Berg, 1999).

Lamb, A.S., 'Physical Education for Girls', *Proceedings of the 62nd Annual Conference of the Ontario Educational Association* (Toronto, ON: Clarkson W. James, 1923), p. 288.

Laqueur, T.W., 'Names, Bodies and the Anxiety of Erasure', in T.R. Shatzki and W. Natter, *The Social and Political Body* (London: The Guilford Press, 1996).

Lathrop, A.H., 'Portrait of A Physical: A Case Study of Elizabeth Pitt Baron (1904–98)', *Historical Studies in Education*, 11, 2 (Fall 1999), pp. 131–46.

Le Corbusier, *The City of Tomorrow and its Planning* (trans. from *Urbanisme* 1925) by F. Etchells) (New York: Dover Publications, 1987).

Le Corbusier, *The Decorative Arts of Today* (London: Architectural Press, 1925).

Le Corbusier, *Vers une Architecture* (trans. F. Etchells) (New York: Dover Publications Inc., [1927] 1986).

Le Corbusier, *When the Cathedrals Were White: A Journey to the Country of Timid People* (London: Routledge, 1925).

Lefebvre, Henri, *The Production of Space* (Oxford: Oxford University Press, 1991).

Leiper, J., 'Women's Sport', *The Ubyssey*, 34, 4 (2 Oct. 1951), p. 4.

Lenskyj, H., *Out of Bounds: Women, Sport and Sexuality* (Toronto, ON: Women's Press, 1986).

Lenskyj, H., 'No Fear? Lesbians in Sport and Physical Education', *Women in Sport and Physical Activity Journal*, 6, 2 (1997), pp. 7–22.

Leverenz, D., *Manhood and the American Renaissance* (Ithaca, NY: Cornell University Press, 1989).

Liberti, R., '"We Were Ladies, We Just Played Basketball Like Boys": African American Womanhood and Competitive Basketball at Bennett College, 1928–1942', *Journal of Sport History*, 26, 3 (Fall 1999), pp. 567–84.

Logan, H.T., *Tuum Est: A History of the University of British Columbia* (Vancouver, BC: Mitchell Press, 1958).

Lombardi, G., 'How to Teach Bowling', *Athletic Journal*, 43 (Oct. 1962), pp. 34–5, 72–8.

Lumpkin, A. and Williams, L., 'An Analysis of Sports Illustrated Feature Articles, 1954–1987', *Sociology of Sport Journal*, 8 (1991), pp. 16–32.

Lynes, R., 'Bowling Goes Bourgeois', *Horizon*, 5 (March 1963), pp. 89–95.

Mackey, E., 'Postmodernism and Cultural Politics in a Multicultural Nation: Contests over Truth in the Heart of Africa Controversy', *Public Culture*, 7 (1995), pp. 403–31.

Madow, P., *Recreation in America* (New York: H.W. Wilson, 1960).

Maier, C.S., 'A Surfeit of Memory? Reflections on History, Melancholy and Denial', *History and Memory*, 5, 2 (Fall/Winter 1993), p. 141.

Manfredi, J., 'Peptalk: The History of Cheerleading', *Seventeen*, 42 (1983), p. 94.

Markels, R.B., 'Bloomer Basketball and its Suspender Suppression: Women's Intercollegiate Competition at Ohio State, 1904–1907', *Journal of Sport History*, 27, 1 (Spring 2000), pp. 31–49.

Massey, D., *Space, Place and Gender* (Minneapolis, MN: University of Minnesota Press, 1994).

McClintock, A., *Imperial Leather: Race, Gender, and Sexuality in the Colonial Conquest* (New York and London: Routledge, 1995).

McDowell, L., *Gender, Identity and Place: Understanding Feminist Geographies* (Minneapolis, MN: University of Minneapolis Press, 1999).

McLeod, J.D., 'Facts and Figures for Organizers, Speakers and Canvassers for the U.B.C. War Memorial Gymnasium Campaign', Facts and Figures for Organizers, Speakers and Canvassers for the UBC War Memorial

Gymnasium Campaign (Vancouver, BC: 1946), pp. 1–33.

McLeod, M., '"Other" Spaces and "Other", in D. Agrest, P. Conway and L.K. Weisman, *The Sex of Architecture* (New York: Harry Abrams, 1996).

McNeil, F., 'Negligee, Swim Suit Capture Men's Eyes', *The Ubyssey*, 35, 54 (27 Feb. 1953), p. 1.

Melman, B., 'Gender, History and Memory: The Invention of Women's Past in the Nineteenth and Early Twentieth Centuries', *History and Memory*, 5, 1 (Spring/Summer 1993), p. 9.

Metheny, E., 'The Design Conference', *Journal of Health, Physical Education and Recreation*, 37, 5 (1966), p. 6.

Metheny, E., *Vital Issues* (Reston, VA: American Alliance for Health, Physical Education and Recreation, 1977).

Michelson, E.B., 'The YMCA Brings Basketball to Canada, 1892–1914', in *Proceedings of the 1st Canadian Symposium on the History of Sport and Physical Education* (Edmonton, AB: University of Alberta, May 1970), pp. 267–78.

Milton, B.G., *Social Status and Leisure Time Activities: National Survey Finding for Adult Canadians* (Montreal, PQ: Canadian Sociology and Anthropology Association, 1975).

Mitchell, D., *Cultural Geography. A Critical Introduction* (Oxford: Blackwell , 2000).

Molloy, P., 'Lest We Remember – War, History and the Commemorative Practice as a Form of Forgetting', *Krieg/War* (Vienna: Wilhelm Fink Verlag, 1999), pp. 361–74.

Moore, R.B. 'An Analytic Study of Sex Differences as they Affect the Program of Physical Education', *Research Quarterly*, 12 (Oct. 1941), pp. 595–601.

Mosse, G.L., *The Nationalization of the Masses* (New York: Howard Fertig, 1975).

Mumford, L., 'The Case Against Modern Architecture', *Architectural Record*, 131 (April 1962), pp. 155–62.

Naegele, D., 'Review of Le Corbusier, the Noble Savage', *Harvard Design Magazine* (Fall, 1999), pp. 100–01.

Nast, H. and Pile, S. (eds), *Places Through the Body* (London and New York: Routledge, 1998).

National Council on Physical Fitness, *National Survey of Recreation in Canadian Communities* (Ottawa: Author, 1951).

Neumann, K., 'Cropped Images', *Humanities Research*, 1 (1998), pp. 23–46.

Nicholas, A.B., 'Citizenship Education and Aboriginal People: The Humanitarian Art of Cultural Genocide', *Canadian and International Education*, 25, 2 (1996), pp. 59–107.

Nora, P., 'Between Memory and History: Les Lieux de mémoire' (trans. M. Rousebush), *Representations*, 26 (Spring 1989), pp. 7–25.

Oglesby, C.A., 'Bowling and Women', in *Encyclopedia of Women and Sport in America* (Phoenix, AZ: Oryx Press, 1998), pp. 34–6.

Ormsby, M., *B.C: A History* (Toronto, ON: Macmillan, 1958).

Osborne, R.F., 'Origins of Physical Education in British Columbia', in *Proceedings of the First Canadian Symposium on the History of Sport and Physical Education* (Ottawa: Department of National Health and Welfare, 1970), pp. 363–93.

Osborne, R.F., 'Principles and Objectives', in Maurice Van Vliet (ed.), *Physical Education in Canada* (Scarborough, ON: Prentice-Hall of Canada, 1965), pp. 32–49.

Owens, L., 'Pure and Sound Government: Laboratories, Playing Fields, and Gymnasia in the 19th Century Search for Order', *ISIS*, 76 (1985), pp. 182–94.

Owens, L.F., *So You Want to Bowl: Techniques of 5 pin Bowling* (Vancouver, BC: Copp Clark Publishing, 1959).

Park, R.J., 'The Second 100 Years: Or, Can Physical Education become the Renaissance Field of the 21st Century', *Quest*, 41 (1988), pp. 1–27.

Penn, D., 'The Sexualized Woman: The Lesbian, the Prostitute, and the Containment of Female Sexuality in Postwar America', in J. Meyerowitz (ed.), *Not June Cleaver: Women and Gender in Postwar America, 1945–1960* (Philadelphia, PA: Temple University Press, 1994), pp. 358–81.

Phillips, M. and Summers, D., 'Bowling Norms and Learning Curves for College Women', *The Research Quarterly*, 21 (1950), pp. 377–85.

Phillips, M., Fox, K. and Young, O., 'Sports Activities for Girls', *Journal of Health, Physical Education and Recreation* (30 Dec. 1959), pp. 25–54.

Probyn, E., *Sexing the Self: Gendered Positions in Cultural Studies* (London, Routledge, 1993).

Pronger, B., *The Arena of Masculinity: Sports, Homosexuality, and the Meaning of Sex* (New York: St Martin's Press, 1990).

Pronger, B., 'Outta My End Zone: Sport and the Territorial Anus', *Journal of Sport and Social Issues*, 23, 4 (1999).

Putnam, R., *Bowling Alone: The Collapse and Revival of American Community* (New York: Simon & Schuster, 2000).

Rail, G., 'Physical Contest in Women's Basketball: A First Interpretation', *International Review for the Sociology of Sport*, 25 (1992), pp. 269–85.

Raitz, K. (ed.), *The Theatre of Sport* (Baltimore, MD: Johns Hopkins University Press, 1995).

Raitz, K., 'Place, Space and Environment in America's Leisure Landscapes', *Journal of Cultural Geography*, 8, 1 (1988), pp. 5–16.

Raymer, M., 'Bowling, A Recreation of Youth', *Journal of Health and Physical Education*, 22 (Sept. 1951), pp. 11–12.

Raymer, M., *Curriculum for the Teaching of Class Room Bowling for Junior and Senior High Schools and Colleges and Universities* (Chicago, IL:

American Junior Bowling Congress, 1958).

Raymond, F., 'Bowling in Canada is Now Big Business', *Saturday Night*, 77 (Nov. 1962), pp. 27–8.

Rehill, A.C., 'Where Women Played', *The Penn Stater*, 85, 6 (July/Aug 1998), pp. 36, 53–5.

Relph, E., 'Modernity and the Reclamation of Place', in D. Seaman (ed.), *Dwelling, Seeing and Designing* (New York: Suny Press, 1993), pp. 25–40.

Relph, E., *Place and Placelessness* (London: Pion, 1976).

Royal Commission Report on the Status of Women in Canada (Ottawa: Information Canada, 1970.)

Robinson, L., *She Shoots, She Scores: Canadian Perspectives on Women and Sport* (Toronto, ON: Thompson Educational, 1997).

Rojek, C., *Leisure and Culture* (London: MacMillan Press, 2000).

Roman, L., Opening Remarks, The University as/in Contested Space, UBC Conference, Vancouver, 1 May 1998.

Rose, G., *Feminism and Geography: The Limits of Geographical Knowledge* (Minneapolis, MN: University of Minnesota Press, 1993).

Roth, M.S., *The Ironist's Cage: Memory, Trauma and the Construction of History* (New York: Columbia University Press, 1995), p. 9.

Rothschild, J. (ed.), *Design and Feminism: Re-visioning Spaces, Places and Every Day Things* (Rutgers: University of New Brunswick Press, 1999).

Roy, R., *Sherwood Lett. His Life and Times* (Vancouver, BC: UBC Alumni Association, 1991).

Ruedi, K., Wigglesworth, S. and McCorquadale, D., *Desiring Practices: Architecture, Gender and the Interdisciplinary* (New York: Black Dog, 1996).

Rybcznski, W., 'Le Corbusier', *Time*, 51, 22 (8 June 1988), pp. 56–7.

Said, E.W., 'Invention, Memory and Place', *Critical Inquiry*, 26 (Winter 2000), pp. 175–92.

Samuel, R., *Theatres of Memory in Past and Present Contemporary Culture*, Vol. 1 (London: Verso, 1994).

Savage, C., *Beauty Queens: A Playful History* (Vancouver, BC: Greystone Books, 1999).

Savage, K., 'The Past in the Present', *Harvard Design Magazine* (Fall 1999), pp. 14–19.

Schwarz, B., 'The Social Context of Commemoration: A Study in Collective Memory', *Social Forces: An International Journal of Social Research*, 61, 2 (Dec. 1982), pp. 374–402.

Schwartz, H., 'Torque: The New Kinesthetic and the Twentieth Century', Jonathan Crary and Sanford Kwinter (New York: Zone Books, 1992), pp. 76–126.

Scott, S. and Morgan, D. (eds), *Body Matters: Essays on the Sociology of the Body* (London: Falmer Press, 1993).

Sears, A., 'Something Different to Everyone: Conceptions of Citizenship and Citizenship Education', *Canadian and International Education*, 25, 2 (1996), pp. 1–16.

Sennett, R.D., *Flesh and Stone: The Body and the City in Western Civilization* (New York: W.W. Norton and Co., 1994).

Shatz, A., 'Inside Publishing. How Nations Think', *Lingua Franca* (Feb. 1997), pp. 21–2.

Shearman, J., 'Letter', *The Ubyssey*, 29, 50 (20 Feb. 1947), p. 4.

Shebby, P., 'Strikes and Spares in Physical Education Class', *Journal of Health and Physical Education*, 34 (March 1959), pp. 34–5.

Shipley, R., *To Mark Our Place. A History of Canadian War Memorials* (Toronto, ON: NC Press, 1987).

Simon, R.A., Rosenberg, S. and Eppert, C. (eds), *Between Hope and Despair: Pedagogy and the Remembrance of Historical Trauma* (New York: Rowman and Littlefield, 2000).

Smith, N. and Katz, C., 'Grounding Metaphor. Towards a Spatialized Politics', in M. Keith and S. Pile (eds), *Place and the Politics of Identity* (New York: Routledge, 1993), pp. 67–83.

Somers, F., *Principles of Women's Athletics* (New York: A.S. Barnes, 1930).

Somers, F., 'Ideals for Girl's Athletics', *NAC*, 47, 16 (March 1936), pp. 9–10.

Stanley, G.K., *The Rise and Fall of the Sportswoman: Women's Health, Fitness and Athletics, 1860–1940* (New York: Peter Lang, 1996).

Statistics Canada, *Culture Statistics: Recreational Activities* (Ottawa: Author, 1976).

Stewart, L., *It's up to You: Women at UBC in the early years* (Vancouver, BC: University of British Columbia Press, 1990).

Stuart, B., 'Chalk Talk', *The Ubyssey*, 29, 18 (5 Nov. 1946), p. 4.

Sykes, H., 'Lesbian and Heterosexual P.E. Teachers' (unpublished Doctoral thesis, Department of Educational Studies, University of British Columbia, 1998).

Terry, J., *An American Obsession: Science, Medicine, and Homosexuality in Modern Society* (Chicago, IL, and London: University of Chicago Press, 1999).

Tillotson, S., *The Public at Play: Gender and the Politics of Recreation in Postwar Ontario* (Toronto, ON: University of Toronto Press, 2000).

Tschumi, B., *Architecture and Disjunction* (Cambridge, MA: MIT Press).

Turner, B., *The Body and Society* (New York: Basil Blackwell, 1996).

Turner, C., 'Chalk Talk', *The Ubyssey*, 29, 50 (20 Feb. 1947), p. 4.

Turner, C., 'Report of the Investigating Commission on the Position of the Women's Athletic Directorate' (28 Feb. 1949).

'400 Mums and Orchids Bribe Gals to Come', *The Ubyssey*, 31, 14 (14 Oct. 1948), p. 3.

'Beauty Queens and Cheer-leaders for Game Sunday', *The Ubyssey*, 31, 18 (21 Oct. 1948), p. 4.

'Budget Outline for AMS, 1951/52', *The Ubyssey*, 34, 3 (28 Sept. 1951), p. 3.

'Democracy Wins: Plebs Elect Seven Queens', *The Ubyssey*, 32, 42 (31 Jan. 1950), p. 1.

'Fashion Briefing', *The Ubyssey*, 32, 41 (27 Jan. 1950), p. 3.

'Games to be Televised', *The Ubyssey*, 37, 8 (5 Oct. 1954), p. 4.

'Hoops, Dear, in Iowa', *Life*, 42 (4 March 1957), pp. 95–6.

'Kinsey Called Defense Threat Sending Mom to Pub for Sex', *The Ubyssey*, 36, 25 (8 Jan. 1954), pp. 1, 3.

'Lethargic Football Fans will be Drawn to Games by New Lure', *The Ubyssey*, 32, 13 (20 Oct. 1949), p. 1.

'Let's Not Quit Now', *The Ubyssey*, 33, 53 (27 Feb. 1951), p. 2.

'Marshall Announces Plan to Increase Enthusiasm', *The Ubyssey*, 33, 13 (24 Oct. 1950), p. 1.

'Minister's Son Does his Part to Crush Kinseyism', *The Ubyssey*, 36, 29 (19 Jan. 1954), pp. 1, 3.

'Powell River Gives Varsity a Loss', *The Ubyssey*, 33, 38 (19 Jan. 1951) p. 4.

'Revived Drum Majorettes Show First at Homecoming', *The Ubyssey*, 33, 16 (31 Oct. 1950), p. 1.

'Sex to Spark Lunch Time Basketball Fixture', *The Ubyssey*, 31, 56 (28 Jan. 1949), p. 4.

'Students Show Apathy at MAD, WAA Elections', *The Ubyssey*, 31, 67 (16 Feb. 1949), p. 4.

'Thunderbird Cage Gals Face Choc Co-Eds Tuesday', *The Ubyssey*, 32, 53 (24 Feb. 1950), p. 4.

'Totem Queen, Jan Olsen, Editorial', *The Ubyssey*, 31, 51 (20 Jan. 1949), p. 4.

'Understanding Wives Help Veterans on Campus', *The Ubyssey*, 31, 37 (25 Nov. 1948), p. 1.

'War Memorial Gym Bonds Show Large Profit in Sales and Interest – Profits go to Gymnasium Fund', *The Ubyssey*, 32, 33 (6 Jan. 1950), p. 1.

US Department of Labor, *The Boy Behind the Pins, US Department of Labor Bulletin, 170* (Washington, DC: Author, 1953).

Van Vliet, M.L. (ed.), *Physical Education in Canada* (Scarborough, ON: Prentice Hall, 1965).

Vance, J.F., *Death So Noble. Memory, Meaning and the First World War* (Vancouver, BC: University of British Columbia Press, 1997).

Vancouver Sun, 'Gyms Favoured as Memorials', (11 Jan. 1945).

Vancouver Sun, 'Kitsilano Plans Centre as Memorial', (31 Jan. 1945), p. 2.

Vancouver Sun, 'War Memorial Gym for All UBC Sport', (2 Feb. 1946), p. 13.

Verbrugge, M.H., 'Recreating the Body: Women's Physical Education and the Science of Sex Differences in America 1900–1940', *Bulletin of the History of Medicine*, 71, 2 (1997), pp. 273–304.

Vertinsky, P., 'Reclaiming Space, Revisioning the Body: The Quest for Gender-Sensitive Physical Education', *Quest*, 44 (1992), pp. 373–96.

Vertinsky, P., *The Eternally Wounded Woman: Women, Doctors and Exercise in the Late 19th Century* (Urbana and Chicago, IL: University of Illinois Press, 1994).

Vertinsky, P. 'Aging Bodies, Aging Sport Historians, and the Choreographing of Sport History', *Sport History Review*, 29 (1998), pp. 18–29.

Vertinsky, P. and Captain, G., 'More Myth than History: American Culture and Representations of the Black Female's Athletic Ability', *Journal of Sport History*, 25, 3 (Fall 1998), pp. 532–61.

Vogt, A.M., *Le Corbusier, the Noble Savage* (Cambridge: MIT Press, 1998).

Von Krafft-Ebing, R., *Psychopathia Sexualis with Especial Reference to the Antipathic Sexual Instincts*, (trans. F.J. Rebman) (Brooklyn: Physicians and Surgeons Book Co., 1908).

Warren, C., 'Letter', UBC Special Collections, Box 9-13, Athletics, Women, Misc. 1949–1960, (9 Feb. 1956), p. 1.

Wearing, B., *Leisure and Feminist Theory* (London: Sage, 1998).

Welky, D.B., 'Viking Girls, Mermaids, and Little Brown Men: U.S. Journalism and the 1932 Olympics', *Journal of Sport History*, 24, 1 (1997), pp. 24–49.

Wilman, J., *Better Bowling* (New York: A.S. Barnes, 1953).

Windsor-Liscombe, R., 'The Modernist Surburbanization of Vancouver', *Intersects* (2000), pp. 1–7.

Windsor-Liscombe, R., *The New Spirit: Modern Architecture in Vancouver, 1938–1963* (Douglas and McIntyre, Vancouver: Canadian Centre for Architecture, 1997).

Winter, J., 'The Generation of Memory: Reflections on the 'Memory Boom' in Contemporary Historical Studies', *GHI Bulletin*, 27 (Fall 2000), pp. 69–92.

Wood, N., 'Memory's Remains/Les Lieux de Mémoire', *History and Memory* 6, 1 (Spring/Summer, 1994), pp. 31–2.

Wynne, D., *Leisure, Lifestyle and the New Middle Class* (New York: Routledge, 1998).

Young, J.E., *The Texture of Memory. Holocaust, Memorials and Meaning* (New Haven, CT, and London: Yale University Press, 1997), p. 93.

Young, J.E., 'Memory and Counter Memory', *Harvard Design Magazine* (Fall 1999), pp. 5–13.

Zacnic, I., *Le Corbusier. The Final Testament of Père Corbu* (New Haven, CT, and London: Yale University Press, 1997).

Zerbe, L., 'The 1930 UBC Women's Basketball Team: Those Other World

Champions', in Howell, *Her Story in Sport*, pp. 549–51.

Zimet, J., *Strange Sisters: The Art of Lesbian Pulp Fiction 1949–1969* (New York: Penguin Books, 1999).

Index